The Arabs

The Arabs

Myth and Reality

Gerald Butt

I.B.Tauris Publishers
LONDON • NEW YORK

Published by arrangement with Harper Collins Publishers Ltd, London.
The original English edition of this book is entitled "A Rock and a Hard Place"

Published in 1997 by I. B. Tauris & Co. Ltd.
Victoria House, Bloomsbury Square, London WC1B 4DZ
175 Fifth Avenue, New York, NY 10010

In the United States of America and Canada distributed by
St Martin's Press, 175 Fifth Avenue, New York, NY 10010

A full CIP record for this book is available
from the British Library

ISBN 1 86064 157 1

Printed and bound in Great Britain by WBC Book Manufacturers Ltd,
Bridgend, Mid Glamorgan

For Amelia, Miranda and Marcus

Contents

Acknowledgements

I want to thank all the people around the Arab world who gave me their time and shared their knowledge and views with me. Many kindly allowed themselves to be quoted by name. Others preferred to keep their identities hidden, and I have respected their wishes.

My special thanks go to Walid Khadduri, who not only encouraged me, but went out of his way to give the kind of sensitive help and guidance without which such a project would have been difficult, if not impossible.

List of Illustrations

Introduction

The twentieth century began with Western powers seeking to impose a new order on the Middle East. It is ending in similar fashion.

At the start of the century, Egypt was under British occupation. Colonial officials in Cairo plotted against and connived with Arab dignitaries around the Middle East as well as with other foreign powers as they attempted to put a European stamp on the region. In the closing years of the century, it is the turn of the Americans to seek to impose a new order, with the Europeans in their shadow. Egypt is, once again, an important centre for the dominant outside power. In the view of an eminent social scientist in Cairo, 'American influence in Egypt is supreme. This is an undeclared colony. If we were in the age of colonialism there would be a high commissioner in the embassy. It's a mirror of the 1920s with the American flag instead of the British flag.'[1]

Britain and France — the two dominant colonial powers in the first half of the century — joined with the United States in the aftermath of the 1991 Gulf war in establishing no-fly zones in large areas of northern and southern Iraq. There was no United Nations mandate for such zones; they were regarded as illegal, not only by Iraq but also by the overwhelming majority of Arabs in other countries. When, in January 1993, the USA, Britain and France together took military action against the Iraqis to try to enforce Baghdad's compliance with their demands, a spokesman for President Bush described the operation as 'just a spanking for Saddam [President Saddam

Hussein], not a real beating'. In a popular British newspaper the banner headline the next day read: 'Spanks and Goodnight'. In Arab eyes, this action against Iraq was a continuation of Western colonialism. Not even the tone of the language used by Western officials had changed. 'When Saddam Hussein accuses the West of launching a new crusade, and of using colonial tactics with help from their agents in the region,' an Arab diplomat in Cairo said, 'it is difficult now for anyone in the region to argue with him – much as we detest him as a person.'

Government officials in America and Europe made little effort to disguise the fact that the real aims of both the economic embargo, which was imposed on Iraq after its invasion of Kuwait in 1990, and the military pressure, kept up by the West after the Gulf war, were to topple Saddam Hussein's regime. The establishment of a no-fly zone in southern Iraq was part of the same process. The declared aim was to protect the Muslim Shiite community there from attacks by the Iraqi army. 'In reality,' one prominent figure in the Iraqi opposition movement said, 'we all knew you could never protect the Shiites from the air. It could only be done on the ground.' The real purpose of the zone, according to Iraqi exiles, was to encourage a revolt in the ranks of the Iraqi army deployed there. Military strategists argued that the troops would not be inclined to rebel knowing that the regime in Baghdad would send in the air force against them at the first sign of organized revolt. If the Western allies kept Iraqi aircraft out of the area, the soldiers on the ground would feel more confident in challenging the Baghdad authorities.

While the legality of the zones was widely challenged in the Middle East and beyond, many Arabs also accused the United States and its allies of using the United Nations Security Council as an instrument to serve Western interests in the region. Why else – the question could be heard from one end of the Middle East to the other – was the West using force to implement UN resolutions relating to Arab countries, while appearing to ignore those concerning Israel and other nations with pro-Western inclinations? Even as Western planes and missiles were striking targets in Iraq in January 1993, 413 Palestinian deportees were stuck on a cold hillside in no-man's-land near the Lebanese–Israeli border. They had been deported one month earlier, and Israel had refused to comply with UN Security Council Resolution 799 ordering it to take them back. 'There seems to be a feeling in the West,' an Arab academic commented, 'that the Arabs are fair game for anything. We are just fed up with Western double standards.'

The incidents in Iraq in January 1993 revealed in microcosm Arab–Western attitudes which had built up over the earlier years of the century. The motives of the West in this post-Cold War era are similar to those which drove the colonialists in the shadow of the Victorian age: to secure strategic and commercial interests in the region and to encourage – by whatever means necessary – the creation of regimes which will safeguard and promote Western interests.

'The West' is an imprecise geographical term in the same way that the single word 'Arabs' is inadequate to convey the variety of outlook and experience of a people numbering more than 200 million and inhabiting territory stretching from the Atlantic Ocean to the doorstep of the Indian sub-continent. In the decades up to the end of the Second World War, Britain and France were the main players; after the war, the United States began to take over the leading role. The collapse of the Soviet Union strengthened American influence and leverage still further.

The West pursued its goal in the opening decade of this century with self-assurance and confidence bred from a colonial and imperial tradition. Most countries in the Arab world were, to some degree, living under foreign domination and its elites were easily moulded by Western statesmen. Some pockets of Arab intellectual life – notably in Egypt and among the Christian communities of Lebanon and Syria – were attuned to developments in the outside world, but most Arabs had severely limited access to education and other sources of knowledge. Algeria and Tunisia were under French control; and Aden and the Gulf region, as well as Egypt, came under Britain's umbrella. More important than this, the heartland of the Arab world and of Islam – modern-day Iraq, Syria, Lebanon, Jordan, Israel/Palestine and western Saudi Arabia – was part of the four-hundred-year-old Ottoman empire.

The degree of control which the Sultan in Constantinople exercised over the outer reaches of the empire varied considerably. In general, though, Arabs in this central region of the Middle East found their gaze directed more at Constantinople than at other centres of the world, mesmerized by an imperial authority long in decline and which, by the opening years of the twentieth century, was close to collapse. Despite the frailty of the empire's health in its latter years, it continued to represent a cohesive force for the Arab/Islamic world from caliphate-centred Constantinople. In simple terms, the Arabs were not properly prepared for the arrival of the Western world.

The twentieth century brought many changes and by its closing decades the Arab world had established itself as a patchwork of independent nations exuding self-confidence. Most Arab states, through their membership of global organizations and on the basis of their respect for the international rule of law, are accepted as responsible and unexceptional members of the world community. Most of the states, too, have acquired many of the material benefits of the twentieth century. The rich oil-exporting countries have led the way in the purchase of the latest technology from the West; and all the Arab states have spent huge sums on the acquisition of armaments – to the extent that the Middle East has become the most heavily armed region of the world. The international arms industry, not surprisingly, has been happy to satisfy the Arabs' hunger for weaponry without questioning whether or not the purchases were justified, or whether (as some Western military strategists suggest) there was a danger of the arms being misused.

The aggressive self-confidence which seems to characterize some Arab regimes is not shared by the people of the region. As part of the process of modernization throughout this century, Arab governments have established schools, universities and other centres of learning. But the education provided by Arab states has not encouraged their people to analyse or criticize the circumstances of their lives. More often than not Arabs have had no choice but to accept the bombast of their leaders, with little prospect of being able to assert their views or to acquire the accompanying self-respect. Still less have they been able to alter their countries' destinies.

The frustration felt by the majority of Arabs has been camouflaged by the apparent integration of the region within the international community and with the West in particular. The impression of Middle Eastern and Western worlds coming together has been enhanced by the latter's dependence on Arab oil and the subsequent web of mutual economic and political interests which has been woven between the two regions. Aside from this pragmatic relationship, Arabs have occupied important positions in international bodies, and have achieved distinction in a number of fields. An Egyptian writer, Naguib Mahfouz, has won the Nobel Prize for Literature; Dr Boutrous Boutrous Ghali, another Egyptian, was elected Secretary General of the United Nations in 1991. The name of the Maktoum family from Dubai in the United Arab Emirates has become familiar on the racecourses of Europe; Omar Sharif is a star of the film screen; Dr Megdi Yacoub is one of Europe's leading heart surgeons.

Despite the superficial appearance of the two worlds merging, intellectuals in the Middle East point to severe limitations in the collective achievements of the Arab world this century, setting material gains made by oil-rich states against a sense of moral failure, inadequacy and defeat. A book on the region written by an Arab intellectual in the late 1980s opens with the following sentence which reflects a widespread feeling in the region: 'All is not well in the Arab world.'[2]

The perception that the West and the Arab world have moved closer together this century has been boosted by the increasing ease of travel and the subsequent increase in population movement between the two regions. Hundreds of thousands of Europeans and Americans have lived and worked in the Middle East – in Egypt, in Lebanon, in the oil-rich states of the Gulf, and elsewhere; equally, hundreds of thousands of Arabs have come to the West for study. Intermarriage between

Arabs and Westerners is not uncommon. Contact and the cross-fertilization have increased throughout the century. Plenty of time and opportunity, surely, for a deep basis of trust and understanding to be established.

There are occasions when, from a Western standpoint, there seems to be a comfortable (and comforting) mesh of style and attitudes. Cultures merge in the somewhat artificial atmosphere of international air travel. In October 1991, for example, I was on a Gulf Air flight soon to leave Larnaca in Cyprus for Bahrain. Only a handful of the one hundred or so passengers were dressed in the *thaub*, the full-length white garment worn by men in the Gulf; none of the other passengers was immediately and obviously identifiable as Arab, distinct from any other race with dark complexions. About half those on board appeared to be Europeans or Americans. A man in a brightly striped shirt took the vacant seat across the aisle from mine. He was clutching a Lebanese passport and wore a Rolex watch on his right wrist. A stewardess, who was British, approached. My neighbour asked in English if she had any newspapers.

'Sorry, sir, we didn't take on any in Bahrain.'

A moment later a young Arab steward came by. The Lebanese man asked, in Arabic, if he had any Arab papers. Or anything in French or German.

The English stewardess was not expected to speak Arabic or any other language but her own. Yet here was the international Arab, widely travelled, multilingual, and at ease in any environment. An Arab with whom a Westerner would feel comfortable.

Within a few minutes the Boeing 737 was on its way, with a muzak version of 'I'd rather be a hammer than a nail' competing with the roar of the engines; the serene ambience in the cabin was scarcely tinged by the atmosphere of the Arab world which we were about to cross. Viewed through Western eyes, here was evidence of the Middle East acquiring the pattern of life in Europe, the United States and other developed countries in the world.

In Bahrain, as in Kuwait and in other major cities in the region, there are many symbols of converging worlds: the

Hilton, the Sheraton, the Intercontinental; Kentucky Fried Chicken and Wimpy; Mercedes and BMW; and more. By being careful not to step out of these sanitized islands and by living in a world created by imported technology, a foreigner might be able to convince himself that Arabs and Westerners are in greater harmony than ever before.

The same foreigner might cite the Gulf war of 1991 as evidence to support his argument. That conflict has left images in the West of the Western allied forces arriving in the desert, preparing for battle, and finally fighting a war alongside troops from the Middle East on behalf of a joint Arab–Western cause. Victory for the allied coalition was swift and decisive. Western leaders made it clear when Iraq had been defeated that those Arabs who backed President Saddam Hussein had been mistaken in their judgement and would be made to pay dearly for their error. The message was that the 'good' Arabs and the West triumphed; the new world order would see to it that the rest of those in the Middle East either changed their attitude or faced being left out in the cold. By 'good' Arabs, Western leaders meant, in essence, those in the Gulf states where the major oil reserves are to be found. However, the West frequently overlooks the fact that the populations of the Gulf countries, while possessing the overwhelming proportion of the region's wealth, account for only about 10 per cent of all Arabs. The lifestyle, attitudes and concerns of the Gulf Arabs are not necessarily in harmony with those of the rest of the people in the region, the overwhelming majority of whom live in much humbler circumstances, if not in conditions of poverty and squalor.

Other Arab destinations can be reached from Larnaca. One evening in November 1991, I sat in the dimly lit cabin of a Syrian Air Tupolev 134 waiting for the plane to leave for Damascus. The ventilation ducts above our heads were puffing out streams of condensation like dragons' breath which crisscrossed the aisle. There was a strong smell of cigarette smoke. One of the male cabin attendants was sitting down chatting to a passenger. Both were smoking. There were cigarette burns on the faded, yellowy, leopard-spotted carpet. The seat pocket offered nothing to tempt the passenger but a folded sick-bag.

Our flight left two hours late. No explanation was given, nor was an apology offered. The smoking continued during take-off, climb, cruise, descent and landing. Service could be described as having been, at best, brusque. Yet none of the passengers, most of whom were Arabic speakers – probably Syrians – seemed perturbed.

This flight to Damascus gives a hint of the wide cultural gap that exists between the Arab world and the West. The attitude of haughty indifference on the part of those in uniform, and the resigned submissiveness and apathy of the rest of the population, combined with the shabbiness of goods and property because of neglect through lack of funds, are features of many Arab societies. Above all, the tendency to be submissive and apathetic in the face of authority sets Middle Eastern people apart from Westerners. Authority in Syria, as elsewhere in the region, demands unquestioning acquiescence. Syria was one of the Arab states to send troops to the Gulf during the war with Iraq. But the gesture, largely a political expedient, was not all it seemed. 'All ordinary Syrians, every one of them, supported Saddam Hussein,' a young Syrian friend said shortly after my arrival in Damascus. Within a few days it was clear that his assessment was accurate. Yet the history books will record the fact that Syria supported the West in the Gulf war. It will also be noted that President Hafez al-Assad, who despatched the Syrian force to the Gulf, received 99.9 per cent support from his people in a referendum at the close of 1991 to renew his term of office. The official outcome of the vote, which stretches credibility beyond breaking point, was designed to prove that Syria's Gulf war policy – an abrupt change in direction – had enjoyed overwhelming popular support. Historians will point out that at the time of the Gulf war, despite such contradictions, the West valued its friendship with Syria and was prepared suddenly to drop its criticism of the Damascus government for its failings on human rights and other issues.

This is nothing new. All governments deal with each other on the basis of political, economic or strategic expediency.

International relations are fraught with contradictions and inconsistencies. But one theme threads its way through Arab–Western relations in the decades of the twentieth century. No matter how much the Arabs have acquired by way of economic wealth, military might, or academic and technological prowess, most of them feel still that as a people they have never been anything other than pawns in the hands of the West. Because of this, many more ordinary Arabs than the Middle Eastern regimes in the region would care to admit felt instinctive admiration for President Saddam Hussein of Iraq, no matter how damaging his invasion of Kuwait turned out to be.

'For most Arabs, Saddam is the very personification of oppression,' according to the Egyptian writer and political commentator Muhammed Sid Ahmed. 'But Saddam dared to challenge the West, and that took precedence over everything else. The reason is frustration. There is a feeling throughout the region that Arabs are not masters of their fate, that other forces are able to manipulate them successfully and that Arab regimes contribute to the success of the others in manipulating them. So whoever dares, wrongly or rightly, whatever the price, wins popular support – even if in fact the results of what Saddam did brought his people more frustration rather than the opposite. It's the very logic of frustration to stand with whoever stands up, even if he does so in the wrong way. It's more an emotive reaction than a logical one.'[3]

Commentators in the Middle East become gloomy when they try to analyse why the Arabs should be so dispirited at the end of the twentieth century. 'Somehow,' one writer speculated, 'we Arabs have over the years managed to make ourselves prisoners of our own political stands, captives of our slogans and captives of our relations with the West and of our subservience to it. In an unending cycle, we have been transformed into an arena where outside powers play. Since the demise of the great Arab state hundreds of years ago, we – of our own volition, or through outside inspiration – have been attracting one power in order to supplant another.'[4]

Suppression by the ruling regime and manipulation from outside, plus a perpetual feeling of being frustrated, these

sentiments are voiced time and again, whether in connection
with high matters of state or the very lowest affairs of the
street.

Egyptians were deeply shocked early in 1992 by reports of an
unpleasant incident on the streets of Cairo. A twenty-three-
year-old woman was grabbed by young men as she was struggling to board a crowded bus late at night in a busy square. Then,
in front of everyone, she was molested and allegedly raped. The
case caused a national uproar and provoked discussion about a
number of social, moral and practical issues. One question was:
why did nobody on the bus rush to save the girl? The answer, in
the view of a leading Egyptian psychiatrist, was that 'a segment
of the people is suffering extreme frustration, which cannot find
a healthy outlet. Consequently, the people are listless and indifferent to what is happening around them.'5

This feeling of hopelessness was captured by the Iraqi poet
Nazik al-Mala'ika in the late 1950s in her poem 'New Year':

> New Year, don't come to our homes,
> We are echoes from a ghost world.
> People have dropped us,
> Night and the past have slipped from us,
> Fate has forgotten us.
> Drained of longing, drained of hope,
> We have no memory, no dream:
> Our calm faces have lost their colour,
> Lost their spark.6

Much popular frustration in the Arab world is directed at the
ruling regimes. While the outward appearances of governments, from Morocco in the west to the Gulf states in the
east, vary considerably, an underlying streak of single-minded
ruthlessness can be found in every one. The way in which
power and authority are exercised in the Arab world represents
one of the features which has kept wide the gulf between the
Middle East and the West throughout the century. Such an
observation would not be remarkable were it not for the fact
that Western powers continue, for the sake of expediency, to

support some of the more repressive regimes in the region, while continuing to emphasize the need to uphold human rights and democracy in others.

Institutionalized corruption in high places combined with blatant disparity of wealth are among other causes of popular frustration in the Arab world. One winter morning I set off by taxi from Zamalek, an affluent and leafy residential district near the centre of Cairo, inhabited by diplomats, other foreigners and wealthy Egyptians. Bright sunshine was throwing shadows from the maze of tall buildings on to the streets below, some-times catching a corner of one of the ornate colonial-style villas which still cling on in Zamalek. My taxi passed smart Western-style clothes shops – NafNaf, Mixnmatch – and antique furni-ture stores, before heading for an address in the south-eastern corner of the city. The taxi was old and in serious need of maintenance inside and out. The driver operated the horn by taking a piece of wire poking out from beneath the steering wheel and causing it to spark with the metal rim of the speed-ometer. As is often the case in Cairo, the journey took us through several apparently unrelated worlds. We passed soon from boulevards in sunlight, through commercial areas clogged with traffic, to a darker world with narrow streets of medieval gloom where petrol and diesel fumes had combined with the smoke of cooking fires to produce a lethal smog. This polluted air has coated the buildings in a corrosive grime which is gradu-ally eroding the fabric of the poor areas of Cairo. Little wonder that hopelessness and lethargy have taken root in the people consigned by fate to live there.

Millions of Arabs exist in poverty and amid squalor. The knowledge that a new world order is being shaped by the United States (or anyone else) is unlikely to bring them much comfort and for many Arab intellectuals the prospect is alarm-ing. Ghazi Ghoseibi, before he became Saudi Arabia's ambassa-dor to Britain in 1992, tried to take a balanced look at Arab misgivings about the new world order: 'Those who are troubled by the international situation see it not as an "order" but as hegemony, not as "world" but American, and not "new" but rather as a return to the era of gun-boat diplomacy. The truth, as is often the case in matters of a political nature like this, is a bit of both. There is no brand new world order, nor is it completely like the old one.'[7]

The United States and the West in general dismiss, of course, the suggestion that they are trying to reshape the Middle East simply to suit their purposes there. At the opening of the Middle East Peace Conference in Madrid on 30 October 1991 President Bush said that 'peace cannot be imposed from the outside by the United States or anyone else'.

Such assurances do not satisfy the sceptics in the region. The Egyptian author and political commentator Mohamed Heikal believes 'the United States wants to see the whole of the Arab world arranged according to its convenience. The US wants the region to be a land open before it, without obstacles and without even the slightest wrinkle in the way.'[8]

Western states, for their part, regard certain Arab countries as a danger both to world peace and to their own interests in the Middle East, accusing them of accumulating piles of dangerous weapons and of funding and promoting terrorism. Iraq was one such country. Libya, too, was singled out in 1992 for its alleged involvement in the bombing of a PanAm airliner over Lockerbie in Scotland in December 1988. The controversy surrounding the fate of the two Libyans accused of planting the bomb showed clearly the gulf in thinking between the West and the Arabs, with the former adamant that the Libyans should hand over the suspects for trial, while the latter believed that the demands being made of Tripoli were unreasonable. The West rejected the Libyan suggestion that the suspects be investigated and tried in Tripoli on the grounds that the trial would not be impartial. The Libyan authorities, on the other hand, argued that the suspects had already been adjudged guilty by governments and public opinion in the West and that, as a result, they would not receive a fair trial there.

This controversy increased the level of mutual distrust between the two regions. The fact, too, that Libya was being pursued with such vigour revived feelings, which have never been far below the surface this century, that the West – from its self-appointed position of moral and cultural superiority –

was intent on humiliating the Arabs as a whole. A newspaper cartoon in 1992 showed three helmeted and cruel-faced thugs with boxing-gloves lining up to punch a small figure dangling on a rope with his hands tied behind his back. The attackers were depicted to represent the United States, Britain and France. The victim, one eye bruised black but with a calm and resigned expression, was labelled 'The Arab Nation'.[9]

A columnist in an Egyptian newspaper made a list of other incidents in which passenger planes had been blown out of the sky by the armed forces of various governments around the world – the Libyan airliner brought down by the Israelis in 1972, the Korean jumbo jet attacked by fighters of the former Soviet Union in 1983, and the Iranian airliner shot down by the Americans over the Gulf in 1988. 'Why,' the writer wondered, 'in all these cases were there no armies threatening to invade the countries responsible? Why specifically Libya? . . . Because Libya is an Arab country, and the Arabs are those to be bullied in the new world order.'[10] Whether or not one wishes to take issue with statements of this kind, the fact that they are being made after a century of close and continuous contact between the Arab world and the West is clear evidence in itself of the gulf of mistrust which still exists.

Part of the problem, perhaps, is that the shadow of former Western colonialism has not yet disappeared; decades of enforced inferiority can not be erased overnight. Algeria, of all the Arab states, was most scarred by its experiences of more than a century of foreign domination, having been incorporated into France. The memories are fresh – the last French soldier left Algerian soil as recently as February 1968. Since then, aside from watching the emergence of a powerful Islamic movement, Algerians have been engaged in a painful debate about their identity and culture – even about which language they should speak, Arabic or French. As one Arab academic said bluntly: 'The observer of the past Western domination of Arab states can easily understand the reasons behind Arab alienation from the West.'[11]

A huge gulf exists between the Middle East and the West in matters of language, culture, social customs and temperament,

and these characteristics are focused in Western eyes by the
religion which has come to represent the Arab world: Islam.
Here lies the most profound source of mutual alienation. As
much as the Arabs may be blamed, say, for failing to throw off
feelings of inferiority, so the West must answer the charge that
during a century of contact with the Middle East it has made little
effort to understand Islam. The hysterical outbursts in Britain,
the United States and other countries in the heat of the controversy over Salman Rushdie's *The Satanic Verses* – condemned by
many Muslims as blasphemous and for which Ayatollah
Khomeini of Iran issued a *fatwa* condemning Rushdie to death
– harmed attempts to achieve a better understanding between
Islam and the West. The sight of Muslims in Britain and elsewhere angrily burning books damaged the cause of Islam in the
West by strengthening popular prejudices which perceive the
religion as harsh and intolerant. Muslims, on the other hand
(and in particular those who condemned the issuing of the *fatwa*)
were shocked and disheartened both by the abuse directed at
them in the Western media and by the ignorance displayed by
some of the people who were denouncing Islam.

The Rushdie affair opened up the gap that divides Western
and Middle Eastern cultures. The view in the West was that
the issue at stake was one of freedom of speech; for Muslims
in the Middle East, this was a difficult concept to grasp. Firstly,
freedom of speech is unknown in the region; secondly, it is
inconceivable to most Muslims that any book that was even
in danger of appearing blasphemous should be published in
the first place.

From whichever angle one views the Rushdie argument, it
is clear that damage was done. Arabs viewed the affair as a
further affront from the anti-Islamic West. Action sparked
reaction: denunciation in the West of anti-Rushdie protests
by Muslims added to the deep-seated suspicion that a plot was
being hatched to denigrate and subjugate Islam. In the chapters
which follow, the word 'Crusade' is used by Arabs in its original, literal sense, but, in the context of events in the closing
decade of the twentieth century, many times. As people in the
Middle East start talking in terms of facing a new Crusade from

the West, more and more of them are grouping behind the defences of Islam. Fighting talk is in the air.

A senior professor at Damascus University, a man who has spent several years living and teaching in the United States, believes the West would be making a serious mistake if it tried to suppress the Islamic movement in the Middle East as part of an attempt to impose a new order on the region. 'If I were the American president, whoever the man is, I wouldn't be thrilled about what is going on. They can impose their dictates on us now, and maybe for one more century. But let them bear in mind that what they are afraid of – Islamic fundamentalism in its true meaning – is going to be their enemy.'

Is the West bent on a new Crusade against Islam? Once again, the important point is that such assumptions are being aired in the first place. Events which seem, in the West, to be unrelated are linked easily in Arab minds. The prevailing view among Arabs of the persecution of Muslims in former Yugoslavia in 1992 and 1993 was that it too was part of a new Western offensive against Islam. Such feelings do not shape themselves overnight. Rather, they are the product of experience and of evolving attitudes. 'The fact that the Arabs do not seem to be able to let bygones be bygones,' one Arab academic wrote, 'is not because of a dogged and unforgiving memory but because the misdeeds of the past live into the present.'[12] The misdeeds, as perceived by the Arabs, were perpetrated by the West and by Western allies within the region. The Arabs' closeness to history and their refusal to shake off the shackles of the past are part of their problem. Another part is the sense of negativeness and despair within their society. 'We want to reject Westernism,' one academic said, 'but we cannot come up with an alternative that bridges our cultural past with modernity.' The Arabs see no clear road ahead on which to travel into the twenty-first century.

It is possible that the Arabs would have a vision for the future if there were fewer political differences among them. The West knows that the Arab world is beset with rivalries and disputes but it seldom addresses the question: why did the era of liberation from colonial rule in the Middle East fail to produce a united Arab nation – or at least an Arab nation with greater cohesion than that witnessed at the end of the century? The Arabs are quick to blame the ex-colonial countries for having divided up the Middle East when they handed over their power to regional governments, but this cannot be the whole story. Much of the fault lies with the Arabs who have taken over power in the post-independence period. This is not a history book; but it draws on history in order to show the origins of conflict among the Arabs themselves, as well as between the Arabs and the West. It looks at past and current events in an attempt to understand and explain why tension seems destined to persist.

CHAPTER ONE

Seeds of Betrayal

The pages of the History book are coarse and grainy. The text is printed in bold characters and accompanied by crudely drawn maps and occasional pen-sketched portraits of important people. The book is entitled *Modern History of the Arabs*. It is a standard work in the national syllabus for thirteen-to-fourteen-year-old students in Syria.

As much as the lay-out is bold and lacking in refinement, so the information in the text lacks detail and colour:

French and English ambitions in the Middle East, 1914–20

French and British designs on the Arab east emerged clearly during the First World War, 1914–18. At the same time as Britain was discussing with the Arabs the announcement of their revolution against the Ottomans and promising them both the independence of their country and the unity of their lands, it was also plotting with France for the division of this country between them – scorning the rights of the Arabs and breaching the promises and pacts to which they were bound . . .

1. The Sykes–Picot Agreement 16 January 1916

The agreement is named after the English representative Mark Sykes and the French representative Georges Picot who laid the basis for the division of Greater Syria and Iraq between their two countries . . . The Arabs got to know of this secret agreement by way of Ahmed Jemal Pasha who

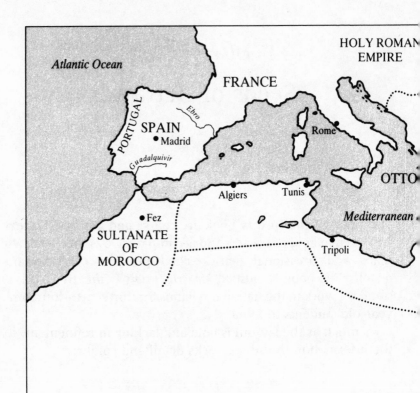

Atlantic Ocean

HOLY ROMAN
EMPIRE

FRANCE

PORTUGAL

SPAIN
•Madrid

Ebro

Guadalquivir

Rome

OTTO

Algiers   Tunis

Mediterranean

•Fez

SULTANATE
OF
MOROCCO

Tripoli

•••••••••••••••••••••••• Approximate frontiers of the Ottoman Empire

0   500 miles

0   800 kilometres

The Ottoman Empire at its height

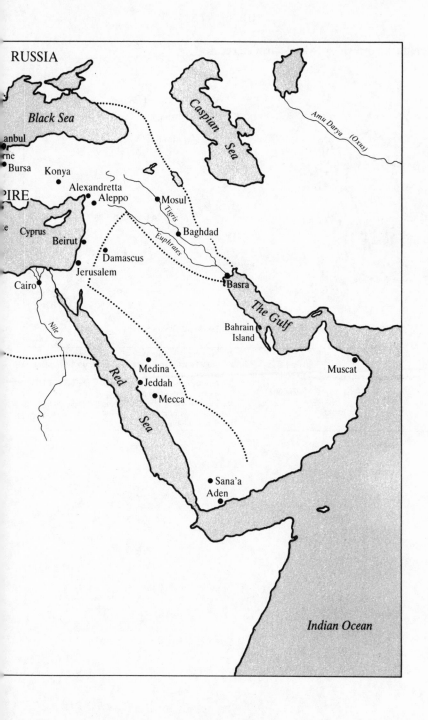

RUSSIA

Black Sea

Caspian
Sea

anbul

rne

Bursa

Konya

PIRE

Alexandretta

Aleppo

Mosul

Tigris

Baghdad

Euphrates

Cyprus

Beirut

Damascus

Jerusalem

Cairo

Basra

Amu Darya (Oxus)

The Gulf

Bahrain
Island

Muscat

Nile

Red
Sea

Medina

Jeddah

Mecca

Sana'a

Aden

Indian Ocean

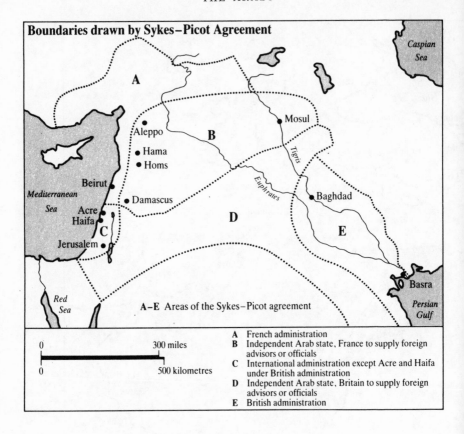

Boundaries drawn by Sykes–Picot Agreement

A–E Areas of the Sykes–Picot agreement

| 0 | 300 miles |
| 0 | 500 kilometres |

A French administration
B Independent Arab state, France to supply foreign advisors or officials
C International administration except Acre and Haifa under British administration
D Independent Arab state, Britain to supply foreign advisors or officials
E British administration

came upon it when the Soviet revolution occurred in Russia
and the Kaiser's papers were made public.
  But Britain made Sherif Hussein believe that its promises
to him formed the basis of the agreement . . .

There are phrases within that text which would benefit from
a little background explanation; and the accuracy of some of
the assertions has been challenged and disputed by a number
of historians. But what the Syrian schoolboy and schoolgirl are
reading today, and the stories they will hear from their elders
at home about the arrangement between Britain and France
during the First World War which came to be known as the
Sykes–Picot agreement, will have two basic themes: plot and
betrayal. This one event in history – or, more precisely, the
way it continues to be perceived in large areas of the Arab
world – has been a major factor in shaping attitudes towards
the West.
  As one of the maps in the Syrian History book shows, the
Sykes–Picot agreement envisaged the division of large areas
of the Ottoman empire at the eastern end of the Mediterranean
Sea into British and French zones of influence. Once the Ottomans had been defeated, Britain would have direct control of
Baghdad and Basra in Iraq, and Haifa and Acre on the Mediterranean coast. The rest of the coast would be under direct French
control. Britain would also have an area of indirect influence
covering Iraq and Jordan, while Lebanon and Syria were to
come under the wing of France. The agreement also said that
Britain and France were prepared to recognize and protect an
independent Arab state or confederation of Arab states in the
areas not under direct control from London or Paris.
  The British representative, Sir Mark Sykes, believed that he
had done a good job – that the deal with France not only
met the demands of the colonial powers but also met Arab
aspirations for self-government, as stated by Sherif Hussein bin
Ali, the head of the Hashemite clan and local ruler of the Ottoman province of Hejaz (modern-day western Saudi Arabia,
encompassing the sacred Islamic cities of Mecca and Medina).
Some academics have subsequently shared his view. Elie

Kedourie was one historian who believed that the British believed the claims of the Arabs had been recognized in the accord with France. Kedourie calls the Sykes–Picot agreement 'a workman-like device of reconciliation.'[1]

Unfortunately, Sykes and the Europeans on the one side, and the Arabs on the other, had very different ideas about the definition of the word 'independence'. In the minds of the colonial powers at this time, independence in the Middle East could only have meant limited autonomy under British or French rule. The Arabs took the word 'independence' literally – rather in the way that the British or French would were it applied to themselves. The collective grievance of the Arabs is that the Sykes–Picot accord, kept secret by Britain and France, deliberately undermined the Arabs' aspirations for independence and broke a clear promise which had been made to them. From their point of view, the accord was, in short, a blatant betrayal.

The Sykes–Picot agreement and its implications have become part of the collective consciousness of the Arabs. Evidence of this can be found in the pages of contemporary Arab writing, where the agreement is often cited without the need for accompanying explanations of its contents or significance. The same is true on the streets of Arab towns and cities. Sykes–Picot is a phrase which triggers an immediate response.

Sitting in a cafe in Damascus in 1991 with two Syrians in their early twenties, I asked what thoughts were evoked by the mention of the accord. 'Sykes–Picot was the first and biggest betrayal,' Adnan said. 'The Arabs put their trust totally in the British and the French to free them from the Ottomans, and got nothing.' His friend Nabil agreed: 'Sykes–Picot shaped Arab thinking towards the West even more than the mandates which followed.'

I approached a Syrian writer, Said al-Afghani, a short, dignified and grey-haired man in his eighties, as he was coming out of a library in Damascus and posed the same question. He said it was 'a common feeling among the population that this [the Sykes–Picot accord] was a betrayal. And this betrayal has continued ever since. The people know this. But we Arabs are still continuing down the same road. Arab leaders are a dim, gullible lot. That is a common feeling too.'

Said al-Afghani's assessment of popular reaction to Sykes–Picot was borne out in a series of conversations with shopkeepers and passers-by in the narrow and darkened streets of the old quarter of Damascus. The reaction of Samir, the doorman at the tomb of Salah al-Din (Saladin) al Ayubi, was typical. After a pause, he described the Sykes–Picot accord as 'the one which tore up the Arab world. Its effects are still felt today. Arabs used to feel powerful. Even under the Ottomans there was some kind of integration – even then.'

Has the West changed since those days? A further pause. 'There is no indication that the West's attitude has changed.'

In the Jordanian capital, Amman, Mustafa Hamarneh, a professor of Modern History, said that while Arabs did not discuss Sykes–Picot over dinner, the impact of the accord was deeprooted in the minds of the people. 'We do feel that a tremendous injustice has been inflicted on us. And the most tangible evidence of that is the division of Greater Syria into four states. Whenever you have, for example, a Saddam Hussein, immediately it is linked to a thought: finally someone is going to rectify injustices, finally someone is coming here, standing up to the West and saying ''No. We will take matters into our own hands, we want to unify our states and so on.'' People feel that our national aspirations can not really be fulfilled because we are not left alone. The foreign factor is omnipresent.'

Hazem Nuseibeh – an historian who held the posts of Foreign Minister of Jordan and Ambassador of the Hashemite Kingdom to the United Nations – said that Arabs still regarded Sykes–Picot as the first betrayal. 'I think that what brought about the hostility towards the West was the aftermath of World War One. We had been asked by the British to rally to their side, and our reward should have been a unified Arab state. If you read our press, very frequently they say that everything is the result of Sykes–Picot – the betrayal and the division of the Arab world.'

A car ride of about half an hour separates the comfort of the Nuseibeh apartment, with its dizzy view across the rolling hills

of Amman, from the shanty-town squalor of the Baqa'a Palestinian refugee camp north of the city. Izzamat, a teacher in his
forties with nine children, said that for him Sykes–Picot meant
'the domination of the region by France and Britain behind
our backs. I think the West wanted to set up a base here to
look after and serve its interests. Nothing has changed.'

In a tiny shop, its walls lined with video-cassettes for hire,
Ibrahim – again a young man, not directly affected by Sykes–
Picot – said the accord meant 'the destruction of the Arab
homeland. It was a colonial plan constructed by the West.'

In an even smaller shop – little more than a hole in the wall
– Hussein, who was born in 1950 in the Gaza Strip, and is now
the father of eight children, is a repairer of video-recorders. He
held a cigarette in his hand and flicked the ash to his right
as we spoke. When asked about the Sykes–Picot agreement,
Hussein scratched his head and said, 'I don't remember exactly
what was in it because there have been so many Sykes–Picots
since then.'

The Sykes–Picot agreement did not emerge from thin air,
nor was it the earliest example of the West trying to influence
the course of events in the Middle East. The Crusades represented the first major attempt by Europe to influence events
in the region, prompted by Western fears about the expansion
of Islam and the threat to Christians' access to the Holy Land.
The Arabs consider the Crusades unambiguously as the first
Western colonial footprint on the soil of the Middle East. The
next tentative entry of European powers was recorded just
before the end of the eighteenth century. In 1798, Napoleon
Bonaparte led a force of 40,000 French troops into Egypt in a
daring military strike against British interests, the aim being
'to cut Britain off from India, perhaps establish a French
imperium in the East – the prospects were limitless and, as
events proved, fanciful.'[2]

Britain responded to this challenge to its own economic and
political interests and to the authority of the Ottoman empire
(of which Egypt was a part) with a display of military force.
Less than a month after landing at Alexandria and defeating
the Mameluke army, Napoleon suffered a severe setback; his

fleet was sunk by Lord Nelson in Abuqir Bay. The following year the French leader returned home, while most of his force stayed on, harassed by British and Turkish troops for another two years. By 1805, British forces had also left Egypt. Britain was content to see Egypt back under the Ottoman umbrella. British statesmen (unlike the French) had not fully grasped the strategic importance of Egypt within the region and saw no reason to keep a military presence there.

The foreign troops had departed, but the West had placed a foot in the door leading to the Arab world. 'After Napoleon's military venture to the Eastern Mediterranean, British statesmen never ceased worrying about the lifeline to India.'[3] Therefore, Britain could never again be indifferent to events in the region.

There was another and equally important factor: Napoleon was accompanied to Egypt not just by a large force of troops but also by scientists and academics. The French set up an Institut d'Egypte to study antiquities and languages, made studies of the Egyptian economy and carried out a survey for a Suez Canal of the future.[4]

Such a brief brushstroke on the canvas of the Arab world made little immediate difference to the appearance of the region; and only a handful of Egyptians were touched by the French presence there. Nevertheless, the appearance of Napoleon formed the first connection in a chain to which links continue to be added in the closing decade of the twentieth century.

The seeds of Western intellectual stimulus fell on ground which had lain barren for centuries. Gradually the seeds developed roots. One can look back and say that Napoleon's brief venture into Egypt was important for 'the general Arab awakening which it kindled: national consciousness in its modern form cannot thrive in a stationary community. A second result – a concomitant of the first – was the introduction of the printing press, which gave impetus to the revival of Arabic classics and culture and hence to national consciousness. A third result was the introduction of the European idea of nationality. To the dislike of Turkish rule and the awakened sense of pride in their [the Arabs'] past heritage was added resentment against the encroachments of the West.'[5]

The introduction of the concept of nationality coincided with the appearance of new lines across the map of the Middle East drawn by Britain and France. Up to this point the Arabs were proud (as they are today) of being part of a large community stretching from the Atlantic to the Indian Ocean, bound by a common language, culture and heritage. Aside from their emotional attachment to their shared inheritance, Arabs' loyalties were, first and foremost, to their clan or tribe and to their extended family within the clan. Nationality, in the European sense, was slow to be adopted.

The appearance of new lines on the map and the gradual acceptance of national boundaries and loyalties were part of a slow and haphazard process. Within the joint British–Turkish force which in 1801 had driven the French out of Egypt was a unit of Albanians. Their leader was Muhammed Ali. He remained in Egypt, building up his power base, until a point came when the Ottoman authorities had no choice but to accept him as the governor of Egypt. Muhammed Ali went even further, turning Egypt into a strong and confident state in its own right. The Egyptian leader (who never learned to speak Arabic) realized the value of Western ideas and technology, not least in the creation of a strong army. Muhammed Ali set up schools in Egypt, and sent hundreds of young Egyptians to study and to attend military academies in France. He also organized land reform and the development of industries within Egypt.

In 1832, Muhammed Ali sent a force of his modernized and reorganized army, with his eldest son Ibrahim in command, to conquer Greater Syria (made up of the present-day state plus Lebanon, Jordan, Israel and Israeli-occupied Arab lands). Turkish forces were beaten and had to retreat. Suddenly, Cairo was the capital of a new Arab empire which stretched from the Libyan desert in the west, up through the eastern coast of the Mediterranean almost as far as Constantinople. The Ottoman empire looked to be under threat.

Although Muhammed Ali had fought on the same side as

Britain against the French 'he retained a permanent suspicion of British intentions towards Egypt'.[6] He might have surmised, therefore, that the British government would view with suspicion and possibly alarm the appearance of a burgeoning new power at the eastern end of the Mediterranean. Britain, with its heightened awareness of the vulnerability of the trade routes to India following Napoleon's escapade in Egypt, decided that Muhammed Ali had gone too far. British interests, it was agreed in London, were better served by the continuation of the Ottoman empire. The British Prime Minister, Lord Palmerston, recorded his views of the Egyptian leader in a letter to his country's ambassador in Paris. 'I hate Mehemet Ali, whom I consider as nothing better than an ignorant barbarian who by cunning and boldness and mother wit has been successful in rebellion . . . I look upon his boasted civilization of Egypt as the arrantest humbug, and I believe that he is as great a tyrant and oppressor as ever made a people wretched.'[7] (Over the subsequent century and a half, Western statesmen and foreign service officials have, on occasions, made assessments of other Middle Eastern leaders in language which bears a remarkable resemblance, in tone if not in substance, to that used by Lord Palmerston.)

Britain exerted all its diplomatic leverage to muster the support of France and other European powers. Then, through a combination of military pressure and the instigation of a revolt among the disaffected population of Syria, Britain was able to effect the withdrawal of Muhammed Ali's army to Egypt. The Syrian people had welcomed the arrival of the Egyptian force, until Ibrahim Pasha tried to introduce a centralized form of government which demanded high taxation and which cut across the interests of powerful semi-autonomous sects and clans in the area. As a result, rebellions broke out against the occupiers but were ruthlessly suppressed – until the British fleet appeared off the Syrian coast. Messages sent from the fleet to the local population urging them to revolt led to a widespread insurrection. The city of Beirut was bombarded by the British, after which the fleet headed for Alexandria. Egypt's grip on Syria was broken.

To this day there is a debate in the Arab world about what
Muhammed Ali might have achieved had Western powers not
intervened. Some historians have argued that a new Arab
empire – to match that which sprang up after the birth of
Islam in the seventh century – might have come into being.
On balance, this possibility seems unlikely. Islam and Arabism
gave the early empire both energy and cohesiveness. In the
middle of the eighteenth century most Arabs were content
to owe allegiance to the caliphate in Constantinople; and the
concept of Arab nationalism had not been born.

Having said that, the military defeat suffered by Muhammed
Ali's army at the hands of the West has not been forgotten by
the Arabs, who see it a precursor of later events. From this
moment, the West is seen as a predator in the region, seeking
either to devour or threaten Arab communities in any way
necessary to further its own interests. Hazem Nuseibeh, the
former Jordanian Foreign Minister, pointed out that 'when
Muhammed Ali tried to create a modern state, the Western
powers, Britain and France, ganged up on him. He was building
schools and colleges, and introducing technology. He had a
vision to modernize Egypt. The West said to themselves it's
obviously better to have a rotten Ottoman empire which will
fall by its own rotten weight than to have a rising young Arab
world.'⁸ This sense that the West is always trying to suppress
any potential power that might emerge in the Arab world is a
theme that recurs time and again, up to and beyond the defeat
of Iraq in the 1991 Gulf war.

Britain was able to impose physical restrictions on Egypt in
the 1830s, but was powerless to stop the emergence of new
generations of young people within the region who were
absorbing ideas from the modern world. While Syria was under
Egyptian control, Christian missionaries – mainly American
Protestants and French Catholics – began setting up schools
and colleges. It was natural, therefore, that Christian Arabs
living in the Ottoman empire should feature prominently
among the intellectuals of this period. Christian students of the
mission schools in Lebanon and Syria were unable to play as
direct a part as their Muslim colleagues in the government of

what was still an Islamic state, 'but they already had some indirect influence as interpreters in the local governments and foreign consulates, and in the 1860s were to acquire a new power as the first journalists of the Arab world. Among all these groups, all involved in some way in the process of change, the *idea* of reform had taken root, and in the 1860s it found expression in a movement of thought, directed in the first instance at the specific problems of the Near East, but raising once more by implication the general questions of political theory: what is the good society, the norm which should direct the work of reform? Can this norm be derived from the principles of Islamic law, or is it necessary to go to the teachings and practice of modern Europe? Is there in fact any contradiction between the two?'[9]

While, in the 1860s, the seepage of Western ideas into the region was well under way, before the end of the century a physical European presence had returned. Algeria was already under French control; Tunisia fell to France in 1881; and in 1882 British troops moved into Egypt.

By this time Egypt had both a railway and the Suez Canal – the latter designed and built, with opposition from Britain, by the French. The canal was completed in 1869, but the cost was crippling. Britain, seeing Egypt on the verge on bankruptcy, seized an opportunity to re-establish its footing in the country by buying the shares in the Suez Canal Company which the Egyptian government owned. The measure helped the country's chronic economic problems only a little, and served to heighten the Anglo-French rivalry for control of Egypt.

In 1875 the khedive (a title accorded to the Ottoman viceroy), Ismail, was forced by Britain and France to stand down. He was succeeded by his son Tewfik. In a move to stem the profligate expenditure of the ruling dynasty some of the khedive's power was transferred to government ministers. But the economic problems continued. Also an increasingly influential nationalist movement was making its voice heard among a population facing punishing tax demands to raise funds to meet Egypt's huge debts. A key figure in the nationalist movement was an army officer, Colonel Ahmed Arabi.

The government in London, reflecting the public mood in Britain, was reluctant to involve its armed forces on the ground in Egypt, hoping instead that the Ottoman authorities would make the necessary moves to restore stability there. But attitudes changed in July 1882. With a joint British and French naval force standing off the Egyptian shore a major riot broke out in the city of Alexandria on the Mediterranean coast, leaving several hundred people killed or injured, including some fifty Europeans.[10] Two months later, the British Prime Minister, William Gladstone, citing the need to maintain the security of the Suez Canal, denounced Colonel Arabi and his supporters as anti-Christian militarists before requesting and receiving parliamentary support for an expeditionary force to be sent to Egypt. [11]

The British occupation of Egypt opens up a new chapter – that of the decades of struggle for independence which dominated life in the country for the first half of the twentieth century. Egypt, in company with the states of north Africa and the Gulf, was not directly affected by the Sykes–Picot agreement, but Cairo was the base for British colonial experts who had the task of advising London in the opening decade of the twentieth century on what its policy in the Middle East should be. In other words, the chemistry of Anglo-Egyptian relations was bound to have a bearing on how British officials in Cairo were going to judge the behaviour (or possible behaviour) of Arabs further afield. Also, the results of that chemistry, revealed in British attitudes and mannerisms in their dealings in Egypt, coloured the way Arabs viewed the West then and in the decades which followed. The Sykes–Picot agreement was a product of these relationships.

The Arabi affair, and in particular the emotions it aroused, was the first of many bruising encounters between the British and the Arabs in the decades leading to the outbreak of the First World War. The affair also brought briefly on stage one of the handful of colourful, eccentric Englishmen associated with the Arab world in the nineteenth and twentieth century: Wilfrid Blunt, 'a good minor poet, an aristocrat of wayward and amorous temperament . . . a lover of strange places and Arab horses',[12] travelled extensively through the Middle East with his wife in the last quarter of the nineteenth century. At the time of the Arabi crisis, Blunt tried to mediate between the nationalist leader and the British government. But by his involvement in the affair he unwittingly helped to open up a gulf of mistrust between the Egyptians and the British. Blunt 'failed to make any impression on Gladstone' and 'perhaps misled the Egyptians about the extent of his influence and what England was likely to do'.[13] Egyptian nationalists later accused Blunt of having betrayed Arabi and the Egyptian people.

Blunt himself noted a marked change in Egyptian attitudes to Britain in the period after 1882. He quoted Muhammed Abduh, a leading Egyptian nationalist and Islamic thinker, as saying that 'the dominant feeling now is hatred for England'. While there was resentment before 1882 at British interference in Egypt's financial and political affairs, it was Britain's refusal to acknowledge the extent of support for Colonel Arabi and his movement – a stand which precipitated the British invasion – which angered the Egyptians. This was not the last time that British officials failed (whether deliberately or not) to recognize evidence of the strength of national movements in the Arab world.

By 1884, Egyptians were demanding independence from Britain. Muhammed Abduh, interviewed by Blunt that year, repeated the Egyptian demand, adding the poignant comment: 'Do not attempt to do us any more good. Your good has done us too much harm already.'[14]

Muhammed Abduh was one of an influential group of thinkers who, at the turn of the century, were grappling with the problems of how a society steeped in the traditions of Islam should bring about religious and political reforms. Abduh and others were disciples of Jamal al-Din al-Afghani whose thoughts acted as a catalyst for movements seeking change in the opening decades of the twentieth century. Afghani's origins are obscure; he is believed to have come, not from Afghanistan as his name suggested, but from Iran. He believed that Muslim society should return to the fundamental principles of Islam and, by doing so, should stand up to the encroachments of the West in the Middle East. In essence, the debate which he started continues today. Should the Arabs return totally to Islam and turn their backs on the West? Should they compromise, adhering to the principles of religion, but making necessary adjustments to accommodate the modern world? Or should they seek a purely secular way forward?

The debate at the start of this century was restricted to individual intellectuals who formed only a tiny fragment of the Arab population. Their task in putting across their message to a wider audience was made harder by the fact that the overwhelming majority of the population were unaware of the rapid developments on their doorstep. 'Not only was the Arab East almost untouched by the torrents of modern Western thought: it was also out of touch with its own great tradition. No wonder, then, the small vanguard of intermediaries had to move slowly and carefully in order to avoid shocking their countrymen, either into violent revulsion and recoil from menacing innovations or into suicidal disintegration, the latter being as serious in consequences as the first.' [15]

Abduh said his aim was '"to achieve the regeneration and the strengthening of one of the Islamic states so that it may reach the level of the great powers and thereby restore Islam to its past glory." This included the unification of the whole Islamic world under one caliphate. In his day the Ottoman Empire seemed the best-qualified candidate for the role.'[16]

In the early years of this century, while Egyptians were seeking ways of removing the British from their country, nationalist ideas in the Arab world were expressed in terms of changes and reforms being carried out within the existing empire. Little consideration was given to the possibility of the empire collapsing, even though Egypt had effectively fallen out of Constantinople's hands with the start of the British occupation. Arab nationalism, in its purest sense, still had not been born. 'The majority of Arabs, even with their sense of cultural identity, were not yet prepared to abandon the larger political identity of the Ottoman Empire or the religious identity of Islam as

represented by the sultan-caliph of that Empire for political
Arabism.' [17]

More ambitious Arab nationalist ideas began to be voiced as
a result of changes imposed on the empire by the Young Turks,
whose revolt began in 1908. They believed that Constantinople
could keep the empire together only by stressing its Turkish
roots. This caused a reaction among the Arab communities,
which resented the imposition of the Turkish language in place
of Arabic in schools and in public offices as much as they dis-
liked being administered by Turkish officials sent from Constantinople. Other grievances arose from the dispatching of
Arab troops to Yemen to fight other Arabs, and from what the
population felt was discrimination in election laws. As a result,
'Arab leaders began to assert their demands for reform and
autonomy more strongly than before, both in parliament and
through the formation of numerous clubs and societies.'[18]

Even though nationalist feelings were growing in the years
leading up to the outbreak of the First World War, Arabs still
did not imagine that European powers would have any long-
term interest in acquiring territory in the Middle East. Britain's
occupation of Egypt was seen in terms of London looking after
its trade connections with India; and British officials in Cairo
were constantly stressing, in the early days, that the occupation
would be brief.

The senior British official in Egypt from 1883 to 1906 was
Lord Cromer. The khedive was still the nominal ruler of Egypt,
but Cromer, as proconsul, took steps to repair the damage to
the economy caused in the years before the British invasion.
He did nothing, however, to stimulate the intellectual health
of the Egyptian people – in fact quite the contrary. The British
authorities abolished the provision, established by Muhammed
Ali, of free state education and showed no inclination to
encourage schooling beyond the elementary level. Lord
Cromer wanted to minimize the chances of institutes of higher
education becoming seed-beds of nationalism; and he thought
that there was no point in training an elite with the view that
one day they should take power for the simple reason that, in
his opinion, Egyptians would never be capable of doing so. He

argued that since Egypt could never become a self-governing nation ('The ideal of the Moslem patriot is, in my opinion,' he wrote, 'incapable of realization'), the best that its citizens could hope for would be some kind of autonomy. Reaching this stage 'may take years – possibly generations . . . but if the Egyptians of the rising generation will have the wisdom and foresight to work cordially and patiently, in co-operation with European sympathizers, to attain it, it may possibly in time be found capable of realization.'[19]

Despite Lord Cromer's views on Egyptian nationalism and the value of education, he allowed a free press to operate. With the Ottoman authorities cracking down on the other established centres of journalism and intellectual debate – Syria and Lebanon – many Arab writers and journalists came to Egypt. One of the newspapers which appeared in Cairo at this time was *Al-Liwa*. It was published by Mustafa Kamel, who is still revered today as a giant of Egyptian nationalism. His thoughts and writings also influenced nationalists far beyond Egypt's borders. Little wonder, given the universally populist appeal of his words. 'The "little man", for whom the great care not,' he wrote, 'is in reality the backbone of Egypt and the producer of its wealth. He forms its army, its police force, he produces its wealth, he provides the livelihood of the princes and the great. How then are his rights infringed, and how is he subjected to ill-treatment? Don't you see that the great are enjoying their present status because the peoples themselves carry them over their heads and obey their orders?' [20] These questions are as relevant for the greater part of the Arab population in the Middle East today as they were at the start of the century.

Mustafa Kamel died in 1908, aged thirty-four. Egyptians described his funeral in Cairo as 'the first great popular manifestation of the new national spirit'. [21] But a radically different assessment of that same event was made by the British Oriental Secretary, Sir Ronald Storrs. He called the funeral 'a slap-up affair', and dismissed Kamel as 'a charlatan of the first order', although he was forced to admit, 'it was evident that he had a great hold on the town effendis'.[22]

A similarly contemptuous and ill-judged assessment was

made by the British of another giant of the Egyptian nationalist movement, Sa'ad Zaghloul. An Egyptian Legislative Assembly was set up in 1914 and held one session before being suspended indefinitely (to the relief of British officials who were alarmed at the way it had become a forum for nationalist speeches) because of the outbreak of the First World War. The assessment of historians is that the assembly was the vehicle which brought Zaghloul to his position as the overall leader of the anti-British opposition movement in the years which followed. British officials in Cairo, in a report on the assembly, said curtly that Zaghloul 'has all the makings of a successful demagogue'.[23]

By the time the Legislative Assembly had been set up, Lord Cromer had been succeeded first by Sir Eldon Gorst and then by Lord Kitchener. The latter, in later years, played an important part in the formulation of the Sykes–Picot agreement. Kitchener, a national hero in Britain because of his military record in Sudan, found Egypt in 1911 in a state of near-rebellion, with nationalist sentiments growing. The anti-British feelings had been fuelled by an attempt by Gorst to extend the concession of the Suez Canal Company. Kitchener took immediate and firm measures to quell the trouble. The new proconsul was a no-nonsense man. 'Unlike Cromer,' Sir Ronald Storrs recalled, 'Kitchener was neither a scholar nor a writer, nor even a serious reader.' [24]

Kitchener, in common with other British officials in Cairo, was contemptuous of Egyptian intellectuals and had a romanticized vision of the integrity and dignity of the peasants, the fellahin. Much has been written about Kitchener's concern for their plight and the steps he took to improve their lot. He did this in imperious style, without getting his hands dirty, nor even breathing much of the country air. 'Kitchener did not confine his contacts to Agency callers,' Storrs wrote, 'but made a practice of returning provincial calls *en masse* and in the grand manner, by visiting the Provinces and seeing for himself the condition of the Fellahin. These semi-Royal visits in special trains (in which the *Wagons-Lits* provided lunch on an heroic scale) were, like his accessibility in Cairo, most popular all over the countryside though regarded without enthusiasm by the

Khedive . . . He was considered the real friend of the Fellah, and none that saw will ever forget his gazing from his railway coach in deep contentment upon the green illimitable wealth of the Delta.'²⁵

The Khedive's displeasure at Lord Kitchener's semi-royal excursions reflected the hostility between the two men. Sir Eldon Gorst's policy had been to 'restore the authority of the khedive which had been emasculated by Cromer'.²⁶ But Kitchener reversed that policy, ignoring the pretence that it was the Khedive, rather than the British, who were ruling Egypt. Kitchener had no respect for the Khedive, as is evident from a report of a meeting in November 1913 between the two men sent by the proconsul to the Foreign Secretary, Sir Edward Grey. 'After the usual compliments, I said, "I must inform your Highness that the recent attempt that was made during my absence in the month of Ramadan to resuscitate the Nationalist party in Egypt created a very bad impression in England."' The Khedive denied any knowledge of the matter. Kitchener dismissed this response as 'a clumsy untruth'.²⁷

British officials in Cairo led a sheltered, colonial life. (In November 1916, with the war raging and with the Arab Revolt under way, there was still time for a letter to be sent to Viscount Grey at the Foreign Office referring to a telegraphed despatch of 1910. 'I have the honour to inform you that the two bicycles then sanctioned for the use of the Residency messengers are now completely worn out; and I venture to suggest that the purchase may be allowed of two new bicycles.'²⁸) The relative isolation in which the officials lived meant that the British rulers and policy-makers in Cairo frequently failed to understand what was happening in the real world of Egypt. Still less did they understand the workings of the wider Arab region. In October 1914, Sir Ronald Graham, the Adviser to the Ministry of the Interior, sent to London a report on the 'General Situation in Egypt'. In this he made reference to rumours that Britain was deliberately sabotaging the Egyptian economy (by reducing the price of cotton) to leave it impoverished for the day when the Turks invaded. The possibility of an invasion at that time seemed real. Given both the tension associated with that prospect and the undercurrent of nationalist feelings in the country, it is not difficult to imagine alarmist rumours of this kind spreading fast. Particularly in a part of the world prone to rumours because of the absence – then and in the subsequent decades – of media providing free and reliable information. But Sir Ronald Graham commented that 'even to those who know Egypt well, it was surprising how easily these stories obtained credence among all classes of cultivators, and how quickly the sympathetic attitude of the population towards us changed to one of mistrust and hostility . . . It must be remembered that arguments, which would be easily refuted amongst educated people in Europe, carry great weight in a country where even the upper class have, for the most part, only a varnish of education.'[29] The fact is that the British were unwilling to confront the evidence before their noses: that the attitude of the population was far from sympathetic to the continuation of foreign domination. They did not understand either that denying education to Egyptians was doing nothing to stop the growth of popular support for the nationalist movement.

People holding views such as those expressed by Sir Ronald Graham could not have imagined that certain groups of Arabs (perhaps those lucky enough to have acquired 'a varnish of education') were beginning to discuss how the Middle East might look after the war and what opportunities the conflict might throw up for the inhabitants of the region. There was speculation that it 'might lead to the collapse of the empire, the grant of independence or the imposition of a new control. There was already a group of nationalists who looked to one or other of the Powers of Europe to help them improve their position, and some were already in touch with representatives of England and France.'[30]

One Arab leader had made contact with the British several months before the start of the war: Sherif Hussein bin Ali, the head of the Hashemite clan and local ruler of the Ottoman province of Hejaz. The Sherif had ambitions of establishing Hejaz as an independent state around which other Arab provinces freed from Ottoman rule would cluster. In February and April 1914, one of the Sherif's sons, Abdullah, had talks with

British officials in Cairo to see if Britain would be prepared to back a revolt against the Turks. Britain was not interested. British officials told Abdullah in the April meeting that 'the Arabs of the Hejaz could expect no encouragement from us and that our only interest in Arabia was the safety and comfort of Indian pilgrims [to Mecca].'[31]

The outbreak of war in August 1914 changed the picture dramatically. In September, Lord Kitchener (who had been appointed Minister of War in London) told Sir Ronald Storrs in Cairo to send 'a carefully chosen messenger from me to Sherif Abdullah' to ascertain whether 'he and his father and Arabs of the Hejaz would be with us or against us' in the event of the Ottomans being prevailed upon by Germany to carry out 'acts of aggression and war against Great Britain'.[32]

By the last day of October, with Turkey siding with Germany, Lord Kitchener had a concrete proposal to put to the Hashemite leaders in Mecca. 'If the Arab nation assist England in this war, England will guarantee that no intervention takes place in Arabia and will give Arabs every assistance against foreign aggression.'[33]

The path from here to the negotiations between Britain and France which led to the Sykes–Picot agreement and events beyond it is long and tortuous. In the view of one historian, 'the British moved toward a fully elaborated Arab policy in fits and starts'.[34] That is a neat summary of a convoluted process described in fascinating detail by David Fromkin in *A Peace to End all Peace – Creating the Modern Middle East 1914–1922*. British interests were pulled several ways, with the India Office resenting what it regarded as Cairo's meddling in its affairs in Arabia, with the British officials in the Egyptian capital (backed by Lord Kitchener in London) dreaming of a new Arab world flourishing under Britannia's guidance and protection, and with Whitehall – while keeping an eye on French moves in the Middle East – not wishing to become involved in the acquisition of territory in the region.

In Fromkin's words, 'Kitchener's proposal was that, after the war, Britain should arrange for her own nominee to become caliph. The Prophet Mohammed had been an Arabian;

Kitchener proposed to encourage the view that Mohammed's successors as caliph should be Arabian, too. The advantage of this was that the coastline of the Arabian peninsula could easily be controlled by the British navy; Britain would be able to insulate the caliph from the influence of Britain's European rivals. Once Britain could install the caliph within her sphere of influence in Arabia, Kitchener believed she could gain control of Islam. And even before the Ottoman Empire entered the war, Kitchener's lieutenants in Cairo reminded the War Minister that an obvious candidate to be the Arabian caliph – the ruler of Mecca – had already been in touch with him.'[35]

Fromkin pointed out that the most serious flaw of this argument rested in Kitchener's belief that Britain could 'gain control of Islam'. This assumption was based on the commonly held, but mistaken, belief in the West – then and now – that Islam can be viewed in isolation from politics or any other aspect of life. The spiritual role of caliph as religious leader could not be extracted from his political role as temporal leader, as Kitchener and his team wanted. Fromkin asserted, too, that much of the subsequent misunderstanding between the West and the Middle East could be traced to Lord Kitchener's initiatives at this time. 'The peculiarities of his character, the deficiencies of his understanding of the Moslem world, the misinformation regularly supplied to him by his lieutenants in Cairo and Khartoum, and his choice of Arab politicians with whom to deal have coloured the course of political events ever since.'[36]

That statement is true. But at least as much of the misunderstanding and distrust stems from accumulated Arab resentment at the attitude of British officials towards the people of the region; Lord Kitchener was only perhaps the most forthright and ambitious personality in a cast of characters (appearing up to and far beyond the First World War) steeped in a particular tradition in which the West automatically assumes an air of moral superiority, tinged, frequently, by racism.

An equally important source of misunderstanding is the Arab perception of what happened during and immediately after the First World War – the perception of betrayal. A considerable

amount of research has been conducted in the decades since
that period into what exactly Britain promised the Arabs, and
to what extent they were justified (if at all) in feeling betrayed.
Expositions of the various arguments have been published in
numerous historical books. What is important today is that the
commonly held perception in the Middle East of the events of
1915 and 1916 is identical to that which is summarized in the
entry on the subject in the Syrian schoolbook quoted at the
start of this chapter. Arabs point to a letter sent by the British
High Commissioner in Cairo, Sir Henry McMahon, to Sherif
Hussein in Mecca on 24 October 1915. The Sherif had proposed
the setting up of an independent Arab state incorporating all
Arab provinces in the Ottoman empire. McMahon's reply said
that the districts of Mersina and Alexandretta and 'portions of
Syria lying to the west of the districts of Damascus, Homs,
Hama and Aleppo cannot be said to be purely Arab, and should
be excluded from the limits demanded'. Two paragraphs later
this crucial sentence appears: 'Subject to the above modifications, Great Britain is prepared to recognize and support the
independence of the Arabs in all the regions within the limits
demanded by the Sherif of Mecca.' The letter goes on to say
that the vilayets of Baghdad and Basra would be subject to
special British arrangements; also McMahon speaks of the
Arabs agreeing to 'seek the advice and guidance of Great Britain
only, and that such European advisers and officials as may be
required for the formation of a sound form of administration
will be British'.[37]

The ambiguity is obvious, and was apparently deliberate. But
the standard Arab interpretation of the letter is that in spirit –
and at that point, it is argued, there were no grounds upon
which to doubt the sincerity of that spirit – the Arabs were
being promised independence in return for supporting the
Allies against the Turks.

With this promise in mind, the Arab interpretation of history
continues, the following summer the Sherif of Mecca proclaimed the Arab revolt against the Ottoman empire. Historians
have since suggested that the timing was motivated more by
fear of imminent attack by a joint Turkish–German force than

anything else. But once again, Arab perceptions are what count.

At the Martyrs' Memorial Museum in the Jordanian capital Amman, the story of the Arab revolt is told through the images of relics from that era – like the ivory-headed walking-stick of Sherif Hussein – and illustrated by models and maps. The accompanying text leaves no room for ambiguity. 'The Arab Revolt was proclaimed on Saturday morning 9th Shaaban (10th June) 1916. The Arabs undertook this for the purpose of setting up a greater Arab state and restoring to the Arab people their ancient glories, thereby achieving unity and independence.'

Yet, as the Syrian schoolbook pointed out, Britain had already entered into a private agreement with France for the division of Ottoman territory following the defeat of the Turks – the Sykes–Picot agreement.

Sir Mark Sykes, a Member of Parliament for the Conservative Party, became involved in British machinations in the Middle East when he began working with Lord Kitchener in 1915. But Sykes had acquired some knowledge of the region through extended travel, both as an adolescent with his father and later as an adult. Sykes considered himself an expert on the Middle East and was reckoned thus by most of his colleagues. But in essence he was a classic amateur – master of no particular trade or skill. In the view of Sir Ronald Storrs, 'Mark Sykes could have made a reputation in at least half a dozen careers.'[38]

The role for which he will be remembered (or, from an Arab perspective, perhaps, one should say the role for which he will never be forgotten or forgiven) was that of statesman negotiating with France the future shape of the Middle East after the collapse of the Ottoman empire. His credentials for this role were shaky, to say the least. Sykes's views on the Middle East and the people living there developed through his life in fits and starts, much as British policy did. In 1904, he published a book *Dar ul Islam*, based on his travels in the east. It was clear from what he wrote that he was as convinced as the British

officials in Cairo of the inability of the Arabs to govern their
own affairs. 'The inhabitants of Mosul are of the true, proud,
bigoted, conceited town Arab tribe, such as inhabit Hama,
Homs and Damascus. Eloquent, cunning, excitable and cowardly, they present to my mind one of the most deplorable
pictures one can see in the East: diseased from years of foul
living, contemptuous of villagers, with the loathsome contempt
of a stunted cockney for a burly yokel; able to quote poetry
in conversation; hating the Turks – their immeasurable
superiors – as barbarians; idle beyond all hope, vicious as far
as their feeble bodies will admit; ready to riot and slay for
the sake of fanaticism as long as there is no danger; detesting
Europeans with a bigoted, foolish, senseless hatred; insolent
yet despicable; ready to cry Kafir [infidel] to a stranger and fly
ere his head is turned; with the minds of mud larks and the
appearance of philosophers they depress and disgust the
observer.'[39] In the same book, he called the Armenians an
'abominable race'; yet when he died he was known as a sympa-
thizer with both Arab nationalism and Armenian independence.[40]

Given the paucity of published material about the Arabs at
the turn of the century one can surmise that *Dar ul Islam*, and
other publications of this kind, must have contributed to the
establishment of the gulf in Arab–Western relationships in the
twentieth century. A major problem, according to his biogra-
pher, was that Sykes's intellect was shallow. 'While he was
highly observant and described his reactions honestly, the only
basis for evaluation was what he had seen elsewhere or on an
earlier visit. This was sufficient for his and others' amusement
and to feed personal prejudices, but it did not go below the
surface. He had insights but lacked understanding. To have
understood the East, he would have had to learn Arabic,
Persian and Turkish, study Islamic religion and civilization,
and steep himself in history . . . To those people in England
who lacked such knowledge and training, however, Sykes
appeared to be an expert on the East.'[41]

Sporting these dubious qualifications Sykes was appointed
by Lord Kitchener in 1915 to the de Bunsen committee which

was charged with deciding on future British policy in the region. Britain and France had already reluctantly agreed to the demand of the Russians that, following the collapse of the Ottoman empire, Constantinople and the Dardanelles should go to them. Britain was keen to block French ambitions in the Middle East, but recognized towards the end of 1915 that the French claims to Lebanon and Syria would have to be addressed. Britain asked the Paris government to send a representative to London to discuss this issue. Talks began on 23 November while Sykes was on a visit to the Middle East. A month later, with the negotiations bogged down, Sykes was appointed to take over as Britain's negotiator.

The future shape of the Middle East was arranged in the centre of Sykes's London world – the world of Belgravia and Knightsbridge. Sykes went each morning from his house in Buckingham Gate the short distance to the French embassy at Albert Gate to meet Picot. The two men finally reached agreement on 3rd January 1916. Nearly two years passed before news of the existence of the accord leaked out.

The Sykes–Picot agreement, aside from the plans it contained for the division of territory, has been significant in shaping Arab attitudes to the West. In the words of Nabil, one of the young men in Damascus, 'ever since Sykes–Picot, people here have seen a conspiracy in everything that happens. Not just involving the West – but even in what other Arab countries are doing. So that, for example, people are wondering what was behind the Gulf war. Some are even saying that Saddam Hussein was in league with the Americans, that it was all part of a bigger plot. Not just one or two people, hundreds are saying it. Can you believe it? It all goes back to the experience of Sykes–Picot.' The conspiracy theory dominates Arab analysis of political developments. A Jordanian commentator, writing in a daily newspaper in April 1992, wondered why several dormant border disputes involving Arab Gulf states had suddenly and simultaneously reawakened. The writer asserted that the manner and timing of the flare-ups could not be a coincidence. Then, after denying that he was falling into the trap of assuming there to be 'a hidden foreign hand behind everything

that happens to us', went on to accuse the West of being
responsible. 'The aim', the commentator concluded, 'is to make
permanent the current state of Arab disintegration and increase
the fear which prompts some to adhere to America as their
supreme protector and guardian.'[42]

When seeking to find links between the malaise afflicting
the Middle East and Western designs on the region, Arab commentators always place modern events in a historical context.
This instinctive reference to history appears to be much more
a characteristic of Arabs than of Westerners. Rabee' Dejani is
a management consultant in Amman. He was born in Britain
and studied there, and later lived in the United States and in
France, as well as in the Gulf state of Kuwait. 'Awareness of
history in the West', he said, 'is limited to the elite. Outside
the elite, people may be able to tell you the date of the Battle
of Hastings or Waterloo or whatever. But they do not know
history and they do not perceive a mechanics in history in
the same sense that Hegel did. Here it is essentially different.
Understanding of history may be limited to the intellectual
elites. Awareness is not. Awareness is very general. Herein lies
the basic distinction, the basic difference between us.'[43] A Palestinian writer living in Amman, Rami Khouri, told me how
'historical memory and the role of the past are very powerful
in Arab minds. You walk around the Arab world and you are
in a kind of historical and cultural continuity that can take you
back thousands of years. You can find people using pottery
forms in the Jordan valley, or on the Mediterranean coast, or
in the Nile Delta that have not changed for about six thousand
years – it is extraordinary. Even the construction of housing.
So the historical power of this land and the political force of
history are very, very strong. People constantly see around
them tremendous, beautiful and powerful reminders of the
days of Arab glory. You see the Ommayad Mosque in Damascus; you walk around ancient Cairo; you go around the Haram
al-Sharif – the Noble Sanctuary – in Jerusalem, and you are
moved by this extraordinary memory of what the Arabs and
the Muslims once did in ancient history.'[44]

A common view among intellectuals in the Arab world is

that the preoccupation with history is directly linked to the malaise from which the region seems destined to go on suffering. Professor Hamarneh in Amman believes that many Arabs take refuge in history 'because we have nothing to look forward to. We keep looking back. It is like a messy case of divorce; you keep going back to the old story. You are unable to move forward precisely because of what has happened to you. We have no present and no foreseeable future, so we look back to the glories of the past.'

Hazem Nuseibeh was not afraid to admit that he too took refuge in history. 'We have a fixation with the past,' he said. 'It is amazing, even a person like myself who is forward-looking, and so on. I very much enjoy reading about our past history. For me it is medicinal. Sometimes when I feel that we are at such a level of inferiority, on matters of technology and civilization, and so on, I just go back and read old history. I read the pages which tell of when we (the Arabs) were still leading the world, when we were still active and dynamic. I find comfort in it.'

Arab intellectuals have suggested more than once that this obsession with the past rather than with the future is hindering both spiritual and material development in the Middle East. Part of the problem is that the reading of history tends to be selective. There is revelling in past glories, but little attention is given to the cruelty and bloodshed with which even the most glorious events of Arab history are associated. 'When we look at our history carefully,' an Iraqi intellectual said, 'we see that because of continuing despotism down the ages, much is the same; only the details have changed.' Kemal Shaer, a doctor in Amman, said that, while awareness of history was 'part of our nature as Arabs', the drawback was the inability of the people of the Middle East to prepare for the future. 'As a man of science myself, I cannot accept this idea that it is an inherent thing in us, part of our genes, to be always backward and to be thinking of the past. But I admit that whenever something fails for us we do cling even more to the past. The [Christian] twenty-first century is nearly here with new facts and realities. And yet we insist on the values of the seventh century, or the

values between the seventh and twentieth centuries. We refuse
to look ahead to the next one.'[45]

The importance which many Arabs attach to history is
matched by dismay at the way in which the West seems to be
able, whenever it is expedient, to turn its back on selected
events from the past. At the opening of the Middle East Peace
Conference in Madrid at the end of October 1991, the Syrian
Foreign Minister Farouq al-Sharaa caused a sensation when,
in the course of his address, he produced a 'Wanted' poster of
the Israeli Prime Minister Yitzhak Shamir. The poster had been
printed by the British mandate authorities in the late 1940s, at
a time when Shamir was a leading member of an underground
Jewish terrorist group. Mr Sharaa's action in brandishing the
poster and making reference to Mr Shamir's past caused outrage, not just in Israel but also in many Western countries. But
in the Arab world Mr Sharaa was applauded. This was in part,
no doubt, because he had derided the enemy in such a public
and dramatic way; but more than this, he had reminded the
world of the historical context in which Arabs continue to view
both the creation of Israel and the search for peace in the
Middle East. It is a context which, in the view of many Arabs,
people in the West choose to ignore. For similar reasons, the
argument goes, the words Sykes–Picot do not ring bells of
recognition in many minds in the West.

Arabs in the central part of the Middle East point to other
events in the decades after Sykes–Picot which they also regard
as betrayals. Some of these events have long since evaporated
from the pool of popular Western awareness of Middle Eastern
history. 'It was not just Sykes–Picot,' Adnan in Damascus said.
'People here still remember Alexandretta as a betrayal.'

The Alexandretta affair dates from the period just before the
outbreak of the Second World War. France, the colonial power,
was busy arranging the final shape of what became modern-
day Syria. Turkey was still pursuing a long-standing claim for
the district of Alexandretta (Iskenderun). With the world slid-
ing fast into war, France wanted to win the support of Turkey
– or to ensure, at least, that it remained neutral. Alexandretta
first became an autonomous region and then, in June 1939,

despite the high proportion of Arabs within the population, was handed over to Turkey by the French. The Syrians have never forgotten, and their claim on Alexandretta has never been dropped.

French concerns in the Middle East in the 1950s centred on the growing crisis in Algeria; Britain, in the meantime, was gradually cutting its ties with the region. Taking the place of these two former colonial nations as the dominant power-broker in the Middle East was the United States. Since that time, the Arabs, watchful for further betrayals, have concentrated their gaze more closely on Washington than on London or Paris.

Britain and France, the powers which had begun jostling for control of Egypt at the time of Napoleon Bonaparte, made one final flourish there before bowing out – although the United States played an important part in the build-up to the performance.

After coming to power in Egypt in the aftermath of the July 1952 military coup which toppled the monarchy, President Nasser cultivated good relations with the Americans, stressing his anti-communist credentials by cracking down hard on Moscow-sympathizers in his country. The honeymoon period did not last long. As the negotiations with Britain for the withdrawal of forces from Egypt dragged on, the Americans delayed the supply of military and economic aid. The two major Arab powers at the time were Egypt and Iraq; each hoped to exploit friendship with the West in order to boost their efforts to become the leading state in the region. When, in April 1954, the United States sold arms to Iraq, Nasser became convinced that 'the Americans were not much different from the British in their relations with the Arab world. The American policy-makers (like the British) had placed more weight and trust on Nuri al-Said [Prime Minister] of Iraq and the traditional elite, and less on the new nationalist leaders like Nasser.'[46]

In the following year the Baghdad Pact was formed – it was a Western-led grouping that joined Iraq, Iran, Turkey and Pakistan. This development was followed immediately by a major

Israeli raid on the Gaza Strip (at that time still part of Egypt) in retaliation for border incursions. As a result of these developments the Egyptian leader realized 'that his moderate policies towards the West and Israel would have to be terminated and a more aggressive strategy towards them initiated as soon as possible. He felt betrayed by the West, and realized that he had been used as a tool for accomplishing Western strategy, especially that of the United States.'[47]

To counter American moves, Nasser sought closer relations with the Soviet Union. Partly out of annoyance at this trend and partly out of anger at Egypt for recognizing the communist republic of China, in July 1956 the United States and Britain abruptly cancelled their support for a World Bank loan to fund the construction of a high dam at Aswan. One week later President Nasser, in a characteristically emotional speech to the Egyptian people, announced the nationalization of the Suez Canal Company, adding that revenue from this would replace the cancelled Western finance for the dam.

The details of the events which followed in what became known as the Suez Crisis are the subject of several recent books. The nub of the matter is that the British Prime Minister, Sir Anthony Eden, on hearing the news of the nationalization of the canal, stated that, 'Nasser must not be allowed to get away with it.'[48] In the weeks that followed, Britain and France connived with Israel in a plot against Egypt. Each country had its reasons for wanting to see the downfall of Nasser. Britain regarded the move against the canal as a slap in its face; it believed, furthermore, that Nasser was a dangerous tyrant and feared for the safety of its shipping. France was increasingly angered by the support voiced by the Egyptian president for the nationalist movement in Algeria; and Israel was concerned about the flames of pan-Arab nationalism which were being fanned by Cairo.

In October 1956, as part of the secret tripartite deal, Israeli forces crossed the Egyptian border and advanced towards the Suez canal. Without informing the United States, Britain and France issued an ultimatum to both the Israelis and the Egyptians to withdraw from the canal zone. President Nasser obliged by rejecting the ultimatum, thus giving Britain and France the pretext they had been seeking to launch a joint attack. However, under pressure from both Washington and Moscow the foreign forces soon withdrew. The two countries which had plotted together successfully to carve up the Middle East during the First World War had on this occasion been humiliated. Several years later, the humiliation was exacerbated by the fact that Britain and France were forced to admit that their denials of connivance with Israel in the attack on Egypt had been false.

As the former colonial powers lost their grip on developments in the Middle East, the way was cleared for the United States to play the major external role in shaping the region. Washington had hoped in the early 1950s that Nasser would lead Egypt into peace with Israel, and that this move would be the first in a process culminating eventually in the settlement of the whole Middle East conflict. Their hopes were unfulfilled. In 1979, President Sadat of Egypt signed a peace treaty with Israel; but in the decade which followed, no other Arab state followed suit.

At the start of the 1980s, the Americans switched their attention to Lebanon, believing it could be the cornerstone of a regional settlement. This episode ended with accusations of betrayal directed at Washington, not from radical anti-American groups in Lebanon but from those which had for years identified almost exclusively with the West.

American marines were sent to Beirut as part of a multinational peace-keeping force established in 1982 in the wake of the Israeli invasion. The idea was to help Lebanon rebuild itself after years of civil war and Israeli–Palestinian fighting. Lebanese Christians, who identified more with the West than the rest of the Arab world, welcomed the prospect of increasing American involvement in their country. But Syria and its Muslim allies in Lebanon opposed the way Washington was trying to bring the country into the Western orbit, and, by extension, into a peace treaty with Israel. The United States's plans were derailed. In April 1983, the American embassy in Beirut was destroyed by a car bomb. In October, suicide bombers destroyed both the US marine base at Beirut airport and the French military headquarters in another part of the city. Following the killing of 241 American servicemen in those attacks, President Reagan insisted that his country's commitment to Lebanon and to the region as a whole would not be shaken, because the United States had 'vital interests in Lebanon. Peace in Lebanon is key to the region's stability.' Despite this apparently solid commitment to Lebanon and Middle Eastern peace, in February 1984 US marines pulled out.

Arabs, in particular those who counted themselves friends of the West, were baffled by the way in which Westerners were able to exclude immediately the experience of Lebanon from their collective consciousness. William Quandt, a former member of the National Security Council in Washington and an adviser to President Carter, accepts that 'among the Lebanese Christians who were counting on overt and active American military involvement on their side, there was a sense of disappointment and betrayal when we packed up and left rather abruptly in 1984'.[49] When Lebanon recaptured the headlines in the months which followed, with the kidnappings of US citizens and other Westerners in Beirut, the public perception in the West of Arabs was blackened further.

With the United States military force withdrawn from Lebanon, Syria and its Muslim allies increased their hold on the country, eventually forcing the Lebanese Christian community to accept reforms which resulted in their traditional hold on power being weakened. In 1991, Syrian troops, which had been stationed in Lebanon since the mid-1970s, were deployed for the first time, with the blessing of the United States, in Christian areas. Intelligence officers mingled with the population, leaving most Christians with strong feelings against the turn of events in their country afraid to express their views in public. Nevertheless, by the side of a swimming pool at Jounieh, north of Beirut, one young man named Samir, a gold cross around his neck glinting in the sun, was prepared to speak out on behalf of those Christians suffering an acute sense of being betrayed by the West. 'In the eyes of the international community,' he said, 'Lebanon is just one more Arab country. And Arab means bedouins, camels and tents. This is not true.

I am not Arab, I am Lebanese, and there is a big difference. We loved the United States, I love English. But not the regimes any more, because we have been tricked.'[50]

Lebanon is one of the countries created out of the Sykes–Picot agreement. Not all of the later betrayals can be blamed on this First World War accord; nor indeed is a sense of grievance against the West felt in the same way by all Arabs. The Gulf states, for example, with their tiny indigenous populations, were left largely untouched by Anglo-French intrigues at the start of the century. 'Sykes–Picot does not mean anything to the ordinary person,' one Bahraini writer said. While the pan-Arab policies of President Nasser in the 1950s inspired some of the small circles of intellectuals in the Gulf, the lack of a mass population meant there was no chance of a nationalist movement arising in that corner of the Arab world. The British presence in the Gulf, which was well established before the start of this century, did not please the entire local population; Western policies were not always trusted. But, in the end, there was no alternative. In later decades, ruling families in the Gulf, while not wanting to see the foreigners integrate into their society, needed Western co-operation and help for the exploitation of oil and the development of modern amenities financed by petroleum revenues; the aftermath of the Western-led military and economic campaign launched against Iraq on behalf of Kuwait in 1991 cemented still further relations between the Gulf states and the West.

In the opening years of the century, while Britain had ties with the tiny sheikhdoms in the Gulf, Egypt was Britain's base in the Middle East and from there British officials reviewed their approach to the entire region. By contrast, the Egyptians' struggle to end British domination of their country was carried out in isolation from regional developments. Osama el-Ghazali Harb, the director of Al-Ahram Center for Political and Strategic Studies in Cairo, believes that Egypt's unique position has given the country's legacy of distrust of the West a different complexion from that of other Arab countries. 'We differ greatly from the Maghreb states, the colonies of the French,' he said, 'as well as from the countries of the Mashrek (the Arab east).

The feelings of antagonism and bitterness that you see in Algeria, Morocco and Tunisia relate mainly to the political legacy of these countries during more than a century of occupation. All these people suffered from French efforts to suppress their identity. The British did not try to abolish Egyptian national feelings in this way. We do not have a severe complex about Westerners, about Americans. This is not a problem for us. It was not difficult for the ordinary Egyptian to imagine that at some point he might cooperate with the Americans in the allied force against Iraq. But it was impossible for the ordinary Algerian, for example, as it was for most other Arabs, to consider this.'[51]

Such shades of opinion across the range of the Arab world existed, no doubt, in the days of the First World War as much as they do today. But the British and the French did not take such factors into consideration as they planned the division of the region between them 'by lines running east and west against natural boundaries and communications, but [which] tallied with the strategic and financial interests of the two European states involved'.[52]

By the spring of 1917, the Arab revolt was well under way. The extent of Arab involvement in the military campaign against the Turks is another matter of controversy. Some recent assessments have concluded that it was limited to 'a few thousand tribesmen, subsidized by British money'[53] and that the call to rise up against the Turks went unheeded elsewhere in Arab provinces of the Ottoman empire.

This is not the version of events presented, say, in the Syrian schoolbook or in the war museum in Amman. In the latter, the official commentary states that the revolt 'was proclaimed in the name of all Arabs. All Arabia answered the summons; the revolt extended to the north where thousands of Jordanians, Syrians and Palestinians carried arms in its ranks. The regular army was composed mainly of Iraqis and Syrians who volunteered from prison camps and who deserted from the Ottoman army to join the Arabs. It is estimated that 100,000 men took part in the revolt, and that 10,000 were killed.'

Whatever the exact details, the joint Arab–British effort was successful in capturing Aqaba in July 1917. By the end of that year, the Bolshevik revolution had led to the Sykes–Picot agreement being made public. The Bolsheviks found documents relating to the accord in the imperial archives and passed on the information to the Turks. They, in turn, informed the Arabs 'as proof of treachery against the Muslim peoples of the Ottoman Empire by the Christian powers'.[54] Sherif Hussein demanded an explanation; he was told, vaguely, that it was no more than a provisional exchange of views which had been invalidated by the removal of Russia from the equation. Battles against the Turks continued throughout the Arab parts of the Ottoman empire during 1918 and 1919. On 9 December 1919, British forces led by General Allenby captured Jerusalem.

This might have been a moment of great triumph for a colonial power which had dreams of a post-war Arab world guided and directed by Britain. A widely published photograph of General Allenby passing through the Jaffa gate into the Old City of Jerusalem might well have stirred up images among the British public of the Crusaders, of Christian forces taking rightful charge once more of the most sacred sites of Christianity. The colonial administrators appointed to Jerusalem might have looked forward to easy postings in one of the most exhilarating cities in the world, among a population liberated from the yoke of Ottoman rule.

These might have been the circumstances if Britain had not, thirty-seven days before the capture of Jerusalem, made a commitment which was to ensure that peace would elude this city – sacred to Christians, Jews and Muslims – for many decades thereafter.

CHAPTER TWO

A Festering Grievance

A short news item in the *Palestine Post* on Sunday 16 May 1948 was headlined: 'Sir Alan Sails From Palestine'. It reported that Sir Alan Cunningham, the British High Commissioner, had appeared on the steps of Government House in Jerusalem for the last time at eight o'clock in the morning wearing a full general's uniform. The only remaining batch of British troops, fifty men of the Highland Light Infantry, played a bagpipe salute and accorded Sir Alan a guard of honour. Then he drove to Kalandia airfield north of Jerusalem and boarded a plane to Haifa. From there, the last British High Commissioner to Palestine sailed home. The *Palestine Post* noted that Spitfires and Lancasters had covered Sir Alan's car for the short journey from Government House to the Kalandia airfield.

Sir Alan's muted but heavily-guarded departure from Palestine, coinciding with the birth of the new state of Israel, came twenty-nine years after General Allenby's triumphal appearance at the Jaffa Gate.

During those years, against a background of violence and disorder, British policy seesawed awkwardly as it tried to satisfy two sets of competing and ultimately irreconcilable demands. Up to and during the First World War, Britain was concerned with maintaining its influence in the Middle East and keeping French and other competing European powers in check. The interests and aspirations of the people of the region were of little consequence. The Balfour Declaration – a commitment by Britain to work for the establishment of a Jewish homeland in Palestine – opened up a new era, in which a growing number of people arriving in the Middle East suddenly had very clear ideas, not only of what they wanted but also of what they intended, regardless of the difficulties, to get. This new body of people, the Zionist Jews arriving in Palestine, had a formidable weapon in their arsenal: links through world Jewry with decision-makers in London and Washington.

The task of colonial administrators was complicated greatly by new assertions of their national rights from the Jews and the Arabs, and it was eventually rendered impossible. The days of ruling by means of curt edicts delivered to a submissive population were over. The administrators faced new moral demands: the Jews claimed a moral right to return to their Biblical homeland; the Arabs, while slow to muster their opposition to the Zionist presence, presented a moral argument to back their claim of attachment to Palestine.

The basic claims and counter-claims have changed little throughout the century. Arab grievances rest on the fact that whenever the West has been presented with arguments based on the two competing moral claims, it has often recognized the rights of both; but has always, finally, supported the Jews rather than the Arabs. In other words, Arabs believe, the West has learned to live with the moral dilemma thrown up by the Arab–Israeli dispute by applying double standards. This belief is expressed frequently at all levels of society throughout the region. The attitude of Isa, a Palestinian schoolteacher at the Baqa'a refugee camp in Jordan, is typical. 'Britain and the West,' he said, 'have two standards in the region.'[1] The casualness of the remark, made in the course of a conversation about the plight of the Arabs, implied that neither explanation nor discussion of it was required.

The West's tendency to view the Jewish communities more sympathetically than those of the Arabs can be traced back to the commitment made by the British government to the Jews in November 1917. 'Western hostility and cynicism are best illustrated by the Balfour Declaration,' Professor Hisham Sharabi of Georgetown University said in 1980, 'where a British government minister offers a land not his own, to a people who do not possess it, against the will of those who do

... My point is that what would seem quite inconceivable in a Western context, say, Mr Balfour giving away a bit of Germany or Belgium to the Zionists, appears normal and perfectly acceptable in an Arab or a non-Western setting.'[2]

By the time Israel was created in 1948, the idea of a Jewish state in the Middle East may have been 'perfectly acceptable' to most people in the West. But that point was reached only after years of doubt and indecision – and the persecution and massacre of the Jews by the Nazis was finally a major influence on public opinion. When Britain first made its official commitment to work for a homeland for the Jews in 1917, the publication of the new statement of policy 'created a mere ripple of public interest',[3] not least because it coincided with and was overshadowed by news of the fall of the tsar of Russia.

Naturally, Zionist Jews viewed, and continue to view, the Balfour Declaration as an important step towards their goal of establishing a Jewish state in Palestine. Conversely, for the Arabs, Balfour remains a figure of hate; the mention of his name evokes images of Western duplicity.

The entry about Balfour in the Syrian schoolbook quoted at the start of Chapter One begins by denouncing Zionism as 'a political, racist movement formed by European Jews during the second half of the nineteenth century, aimed at establishing a national homeland for the Jews. There were differences on determining the region in which it should be set up. In the end, they settled on Palestine.'

The textbook speaks of the First World War providing 'favourable conditions' for the Jews, who 'obtained from Britain a promise to establish a Jewish national home in Palestine. This came in the form of a letter which Balfour, who was Foreign Minister at the time, sent to Lord Rothschild, leader of the Zionist movement.'

The section concludes with the Arabs hearing about 'this sinister commitment'. Sherif Hussein of Mecca contacted the British, seeking an explanation. 'But, as usual,' the text continues, 'Britain was evasive and made out that the fleeing of a group of homeless Jews to Palestine did not mean at all their occupation or ownership of it.'

Occupation and ownership were exactly what the Zionists intended to achieve. Britain's role in helping to bring this about (no matter how reluctantly, at times, that role was played) and the subsequent close relationship which developed between Israel on one side and Europe and the United States on the other have played an important part in keeping open the gulf between the Arabs and the West. In the view of the Egyptian writer and commentator Mohamed Heikal, 'the strained quality of the West's relations with the Arab world was further aggravated by the Zionist movement, which paved the way for the rape of Palestine'.[4] Such language might sound unacceptably extremist and intemperate to Western ears, but it represents accurately the extent to which Arab emotions are still aroused by the issue of Israel and by the West's involvement in Israel's creation.

Zionist historians, among others, would, naturally, not agree with Heikal's assessment or with that of an historian from Britain with pro-Arab sympathies who wrote of the Balfour Declaration that, 'measured by British interests alone, it was one of the greatest mistakes in our imperial history'.[5] This assessment carries weight, however, in the context of an objective examination of why the Arab–Western gulf remains wide.

Whether or not one takes the view that the Balfour Declaration was a mistake, there is no escaping the fact that its origins lay in the muddled thinking of British policy-makers, out of which the Sykes–Picot agreement had emerged. Indeed, Sir Mark Sykes played an important part in supporting calls for the establishment of a Jewish homeland in Palestine. His role in determining the future of the Jews was as erratic as his involvement in attempts to work out how the Arab world should look after the collapse of the Ottoman empire.

In their blueprint for the post-war Middle East, Sykes and Picot had left vague the future of Palestine, saying only that it would come under 'an international administration, the form of which is to be decided upon after consultation with Russia, and subsequently in consultation with the other Allies, and the representatives of the Shereef of Mecca'.[6]

At the time, Sykes for one seemed totally unaware of the

growing Zionist movement. Some months after the agreement with France was reached, Sykes's attention was drawn to the omission of any reference to the future of the Jews in the Middle East. 'Sykes was struck by the mention of Jews. Until then they had not figured in his calculations. Before leaving for Russia, Sykes therefore contacted Herbert Samuel, the Home Secretary, who was Jewish, hoping to learn about Zionism.'[7]

Sykes's tardy realization of the existence of Zionism is surprising in a man who was regarded in British government circles as an expert on the Middle East. The development of Zionism was plain to see. In the closing decades of the nineteenth century, there had been a steady stream of Jews arriving in Palestine from eastern Europe, founding colonies and working the land.[8] In 1896, an Austrian journalist, Theodor Herzl, had published a book which set out a programme for political Zionism. It envisaged the creation of a Jewish state in Palestine.

Herzl, as Zionist leader, had gone so far as to put a solid proposal to the Ottoman authorities that Palestine should become a state for Jews; but his idea was rejected. Two other sites for the proposed state were explored: Cyprus and El-Arish in Sinai. Britain ruled out both options. In 1903, the British government 'made a lukewarm offer of territory in Uganda, which Herzl reluctantly agreed to consider, but this was rejected by the sixth Zionist Congress shortly before his death in 1904'.[9]

Little practical progress was made towards the goal defined by Herzl in the years leading to the outbreak of war. Yet by 1914 some 80,000 Jews had settled in Palestine, giving them 10 per cent of the population.

As a young man, Sykes had had a poor impression of Jews. In Dar ul Islam he ráted them only a little above Armenians, for whom he had total contempt. 'Even Jews have their good points,' he said, 'but Armenians have none.'[10] By 1917, he was a convert to the cause of Zionism, even if he retained characteristically eccentric reasons for supporting the Jewish cause in Palestine. Sykes had a vision of the Zionists being purer and more noble than Jews who had been assimilated into Western society. The Jews in Palestine would be 'regenerated, they were to become a nation of genuine peasants and squires, like everybody else, not financiers, cosmopolitans and radicals. That was why Sir Mark Sykes was a Zionist. Zionism, Sykes believed, would show "the capacity of the Jews to produce a virtuous and simple agrarian population".'[11]

Sykes envisaged the Jewish homeland being set up in a British-controlled Palestine – although he realized that this would run counter to what was agreed with Picot and would also conflict with French desires to control the same region. The more fundamental problem, of matching Jewish and Arab claims to nationhood on the same patch of land, did not appear to Sykes as an obstacle. At a meeting in London in February 1917 with the British Zionist leader, Dr Chaim Weizmann, he said that 'the Arabs could be managed'.[12] In October of that year, he rebuffed the argument that the area of cultivable land in Palestine could not sustain a large influx of immigrants with the assertion that the land was barren because the Arabs were a 'naturally idle and indolent race'.[13]

While Sykes was slow to grasp the importance of the Zionist movement, David Lloyd George, who became Prime Minister in December 1916, was not. As a lawyer, Lloyd George had been involved in Herzl's attempts in 1903 to secure Sinai as a site for the Jewish homeland. He and other senior members of his Cabinet, along with some key advisers (including, by this time, Sykes), wanted to see Jewish Palestine as part of the British empire. This desire was based partly on grounds of security and the continuing need to strengthen the empire, and partly on 'the romantic appeal of the return of Jews to Zion, which, founded on Old Testament Christianity, was part of their Victorian background'.[14]

The commitment contained in the Sykes–Picot agreement to leave Palestine under international control should, in theory, have been an obstacle to Lloyd George's plan for the area. But the Prime Minister was unconcerned, asserting confidently that 'Britain could take care of the Holy Places better than anyone else', and adding that a French-controlled Palestine 'was not to be thought of'.[15] In May 1917, the War Cabinet accepted a sub-committee report proposing that Britain should keep control of German East Africa, Palestine and Mesopotamia in the interests of imperial security. It was also argued that 'Zionist sympathies for the Allied cause could help the war effort; Zionists in Russia could stop that country's drift out of the war; and in the United States Zionists could speed up the American contributions following the declaration of war [by the United States] on 3 April.'[16] Supporters of Zionism also urged the British government to come out in support of the movement without delay, for fear that either Germany or France, the two other major powers in Europe competing for influence overseas, might do so before it. Lord Rothschild, the head of the Jewish community in Britain, along with Weizmann, met the Foreign Secretary Lord Balfour in June 1917. Balfour asked for a draft of Zionist aspirations.[17]

The following month a document was presented, calling for Palestine to become 'the National Home for the Jewish people'. These statements were watered down in the final text because of objections within the Cabinet. This done, the document was sent as a letter by Lord Balfour on 2 November and has been known thereafter as the Balfour Declaration. It contained the following commitment:

'His Majesty's Government views with favour the establishment in Palestine of a national home for the Jewish people, and will use its best endeavours to facilitate the achievement of this object, it being clearly understood that nothing shall be done which may prejudice the civil and religious rights of existing non-Jewish communities in Palestine, or the rights and political status enjoyed by Jews in any other country.'

This amendment of the commitment to read 'a national home . . . in Palestine' (rather than calling Palestine as a whole 'the national home') disappointed British Zionist leaders. The change also failed to appease those in the government who had opposed in principle the issuing of the declaration. The chief opponent was the only Jewish member of the cabinet, Sir Edward Montague. At that time, many members of the Jewish establishment in Britain were uneasy about the growth of Zionism, fearing both a threat to their own privileged status and pressure to settle in Palestine. Montague raised a practical objection, too. He argued that Palestine was small and could support only a limited population. The 700,000 native Muslims, he said, would not be content 'either to be expropriated for Jewish immigrants, or to act merely as hewers of wood and drawers of water'.[18]

Sir Edward Montague was right on both counts. The steady expropriation of Arab land has never stopped: from within Palestine before 1948, from within the borders of Israel since then, and from within the occupied West Bank, Gaza Strip, Golan Heights and south Lebanon since 1967, although the agreements signed by Israeli and Palestinian leaders in September 1993, granting limited autonomy in some areas, could eventually reverse this trend. Some Israelis cite strategic reasons for the need to acquire and keep territory. They point out that Israel is a tiny country in a huge and hostile Arab world, and that the pre-1967 borders enabled Arab guns to fire on Tel Aviv and other cities. Other Israelis believe that justification for at least some of the expansionist moves can be found in the Old Testament, arguing that the occupied West Bank (Biblical Judea and Samaria) has always been a part of the Jewish homeland. A third group of Israelis favour handing back the occupied land to the Arabs, in exchange for peace.

While the future of the occupied territories remains a subject of debate in Israel, tens of thousands of Palestinians – including almost the entire workforce living within the Gaza Strip – provide cheap manual labour (as the modern-day equivalent of 'hewers of wood and drawers of water') for the Israeli population. As Montague correctly predicted, too, the Palestinians are far from happy at their plight, and their grievance lies at the centre of the Arab–Israeli conflict. Even if the autonomy agreement covering the West Bank and Gaza Strip signed in September 1993 leads eventually to the creation of an independent state, hundreds of thousands of Palestinian refugees will remain stranded in exile.

The Balfour Declaration paved the way for the creation of Israel. But it has left many festering problems. There are constant reminders of these – in the blank looks on the faces of Palestinian workers piled into ageing Peugeot taxis at dawn every day in the Gaza Strip, heading off to what have appropriately been nicknamed 'slave markets' on the outskirts of Israeli cities, in the hope of getting a day's hire; in the crazed expressions of hate on the faces of the crowd of Palestinians whom I watched rioting in Nablus early in 1988 after troops had opened fire on youths throwing stones and petrol bombs at the army, killing a teenager and an old man and injuring several other people; in the crazed expressions of hate I saw on the faces of a crowd of angry Israelis on the Jaffa Road in Jerusalem calling for revenge after an Arab had stabbed to death two Jews in a flower shop.

Back in November 1917, the Lloyd George government believed that there were sound security and religious reasons for making the commitment to the Jews. It is highly unlikely that British ministers could have imagined the far-reaching consequences of their decision.

The Arabs in general and the Palestinians in particular have made progress during the last decade (and, in particular, in the latter half of 1993) in attracting international attention to their cause, but the results of their efforts look meagre when compared with the success of Zionist lobby groups which, in Arab minds, could not function without the connivance of the governments and institutions of the Western powers. The formulation of the Balfour Declaration was the first example of the Jewish lobby in action.

It would be hard to disagree with the assessment that in the weeks and months preceding the issuing of the Balfour Declaration 'the British Zionists excelled at tactics'.[19] For a start, they had an influential supporter in the person of C.P. Scott, the editor of the *Manchester Guardian*. While he was not a Jew, he was an ardent Zionist and happened to be a close friend of Lloyd George. He not only gave the Zionists access to the columns of a leading newspaper but also a direct line of contact to the Prime Minister. From this strong foothold the Zionist lobby in Britain 'converted newspapermen and Cabinet ministers. It worked on Foreign Office officials and military personnel. By October 1917 most of the key people concerned with Middle Eastern affairs in the War Cabinet and its secretariat, in the Foreign Office, and even in the military and intelligence services, were either convinced Zionists or Zionist sympathizers.'[20] The Arabs could never hope to compete at this level. Sir Ronald Storrs, in his autobiography, quotes a passage from the 'Survey of British Commonwealth Affairs 1918–36' which neatly summarizes the advantages that the Jewish lobby had then, and still has today, over the Arabs in winning influence in the West. The passage speaks of 'the inequality of access to the ear of British democracy. Jewry was represented in every layer of English society – in the Lords and the Commons, in powerful capitalistic organizations and in the Labour Party, in the press and in the Universities.' Storrs added his own comment: 'The Arab of Palestine therefore feels himself under an overwhelming inferiority in the presentation of his case to the world.'[21] The same is true today, substituting any major Western nation in place of Britain.

This inequality of access is a source of lingering Arab bitterness. In more than a decade of reporting in the Arab world, one of the allegations I have heard most frequently from government officials and from people in the streets is that the Arabs are victims of a conspiracy in a Western media dominated and controlled by Jews or Jewish money. So, according to the perceived view in the Arab world, the vast majority of written and broadcast material is biased in favour of Israel – thus reinforcing Western double standards when viewing developments in the Middle East. One can counter this argument with evidence of publications and news organizations which have no connection with the Jewish community and are not involved in conspiracies. But I have found the issue to be so emotive among Arabs that evidence of this kind is insufficient to bury the argument. The Arabs' perception of Western bias towards Israel in publishing and broadcasting is an exaggeration rather than a fabrication of the truth and illuminates a sharp and important difference in Arab and Western attitudes. In Arab society in general, widespread reference to Israel by name in the official media is a relatively new phenomenon. In the years after the creation of Israel the Jewish state was more often than not called the 'Zionist entity'. The word 'Israel' resounds in the ears of Arabs with associations of injustice which are foreign to Westerners. To Arabs, Israel is still not regarded as just another state in the Middle East, as it might seem to people in the West. To hear Israel referred to in, say, a news report with the unspoken assumption that it is like any other normal country is, therefore, anathema to Arab ears.

Another general belief in the Arab world is that even when there is equality of access to, for example, American network television, the Israeli spokesman has a better chance of being believed. This is in part because someone like Shimon Peres or Moshe Arens appears more comfortable in his use of the English language and more relaxed in the ambience of the Western television studio than PLO representatives like Yasser Arafat or Farouk Qaddoumi. The success achieved by Hanan Ashrawi, a frequent spokeswoman for the Palestinians on Western television in the early 1990s, with her impeccable English and urbane manner, appeared to confirm this theory. More important still, there is a belief that an inherent racism in the West will block out the message being put over by the Arab spokesman. Furthermore, it is argued, racism will thrive as long as the Arabs fail to promote their cause with the same vehemence as the Jews have been doing for the greater part of this century.

The power of the Jewish lobby in Britain in 1917 was clearly formidable; the Arabs, conversely, had no mechanism with which to counter the impact of the Balfour Declaration. That is not to say that Arabs had been unaware either of the development of political Zionism or of the possible threat to their interests in Palestine as the Jewish settlers, with their alien languages and cultural backgrounds, began acquiring land. Before the First World War one of the early Arab nationalist writers, Rashid Rida, 'was conscious of the danger of Zionist immigration to the Arabs of Palestine, and criticized the facilities given the Zionists, as he claimed, by the central government of the [Ottoman] empire'.[22] In 1914 *Al-Iqdam*, a weekly newspaper published in Cairo, carried an interview with Khalil Sakanini, who was trying to muster support to block Zionist ambitions in the area. 'The Zionists', he said, 'want to own Palestine, that is the heart of the Arab countries and the middle link between the Arab peninsula and Africa. Thus, it appears as if they want to break the chain and divide the Arab Nation into two sections to prevent its unification and solidarity.'[23]

When the Balfour Declaration was published Sherif Hussein of Mecca (by this time proclaimed King of Hejaz) expressed concern, recalling the promises which he believed had been made by the British for the establishment of an independent Arab state. The head of the Arab Bureau (the office in Cairo which advised on and directed British policies in the Middle East), Commander D.G. Hogarth, was sent to see Hussein and reassure him that Britain's promises for Arab independence had not been compromised by the Balfour Declaration, which would be implemented only as far as it was 'compatible with the freedom of the existing population'. Hogarth reported back to London that 'the King would not accept an independent Jewish State in Palestine, nor was I instructed to warn him that such a state was contemplated.'[24]

The convoluted vagueness of Hogarth's comment provides the opening to a period which saw Britain's grip on the Middle East begin to slip, and the emergence of the two mutually incompatible moral arguments. But among government officials in London in the early days after the publication of the Balfour Declaration, there seemed to be no reason to fear a collision of Arab and Jewish wills as a result of promises (or, at least, what were being interpreted as promises) made to both sides. Sir Mark Sykes, in a document circulated within the War Cabinet, assessed the likely impact on Arab opinion of the British capture of Jerusalem at a time when London was expressing support for a Jewish homeland in Palestine. Sykes used curious logic in asserting that while Jerusalem was a city sacred to all Muslims, 'the various Christian shrines of Calvary, the Holy Sepulchre, and Bethlehem are also regarded by the Moslems with great reverence. The effect of the fall of Jerusalem will therefore be considerable among Moslems as a whole, and have a tendency to produce Anglophile sentiments, and to lessen the malignant power of political Pan-Islamists.'

Sykes hinted at the possible difficulties ahead when he discussed the effect of the capture of Jerusalem on the Arab

Movement. In what must be one of the finest examples of understatement in the history of the Middle East, Sykes wrote: 'It is less satisfactory to consider that our adoption of Zionism and our capture of Jerusalem will tend to a certain extent to somewhat abate Arab enthusiasm.' Sykes pointed out that the Arabs might feel that the only definite result of their revolt thus far had been 'a declaration in favour of the Jews'. But with characteristic optimism, Sykes made light of this problem, predicting that the negative effect would be only transient if 'we take an early opportunity of showing that we are behind the Arabs, appreciate their assistance, and desire their liberation'.[25]

In the comfort of his office in London more than a year after this assessment had been circulated among Cabinet ministers, Lord Balfour was clearly confident that Britain still had full moral authority in the Middle East, having given support to the Zionist cause. Even though he admitted, in a letter to the Prime Minister, Lloyd George, that if the inhabitants of Palestine were consulted 'they would unquestionably give an anti-Jewish verdict. Our justification for our policy is that we regard Palestine as being absolutely exceptional, that we consider the question of the Jews outside Palestine as one of world importance.'[26] In other words, the Arabs of Palestine on the one hand and the Jews settling there on the other were being judged by different standards.

Balfour must have made his comment about the strength of anti-Jewish feeling in Palestine on the basis of despatches from Jerusalem. While Whitehall was still confident about the conduct of British policy, on the ground in Palestine the picture was very different. In fact, things were beginning to fall apart.

Sir Ronald Storrs, the Governor of Jerusalem and a supporter of Zionism, saw how the Arabs took fright even at the wording of the Balfour Declaration – to which the Middle East advisers to the government had apparently been insensitive. As Storrs recalled in his memoirs, 'the Declaration which, in addition to its main Jewish message, was at pains to reassure non-Palestinian Jews of their national status, took no account whatever of the feelings or desires of the actual inhabitants of

Palestine.' Other inhabitants of Palestine were not named 'either as Arabs, Moslems, or Christians, but were lumped together under the negative and humiliating definition of "Non-Jewish Communities".' Storrs also quoted Arabs who had noticed that the Declaration failed to mention their political rights. 'Clearly,' Storrs concluded, 'they had none.'

Storrs's task of trying to quell Arab fears was made even harder by the arrival in Palestine in January 1918 of a Zionist Commission (of which Weizmann was a member), sent by the British government to carry out the provisions of the Balfour Declaration. As the former British Governor of Jerusalem recalled, 'the Arabs felt that the Commission was the thin end of the wedge, the beginning of a Government within a Government.'[27]

The presence of the Commission in Palestine triggered the start of Arab resistance to Zionist activity in Palestine that continued up to the creation of the state of Israel and beyond. Despatches from Palestine to the Foreign Office in London indicate the extent to which the authorities were becoming alarmed by both Arab and Jewish militancy. One can sense from these reports, too, that British officials in the Middle East were increasingly frustrated, realizing that pronouncements from London were no longer sufficient to cool the passions or blunt the determination of either the Arab or Jewish community in Palestine.

A cable from Sir Reginald Wingate at the Arab Bureau in Cairo was quoted by Prime Minister Lloyd George at a War Cabinet meeting in January 1918. Wingate spoke of 'the present critical state of Arab feeling', adding that 'vague or general assurances about the future of the Arabs are not only ineffectual but harmful'.[28]

The conflicting pressures building up around Britain are well illustrated by sharply differing reactions to two military events of this period. In September 1918, Allied forces captured Damascus in their drive northwards through former Ottoman-controlled Syria. The editor of the *Jewish Chronicle* in London sent a telegram of congratulations to General Allenby. He said he rejoiced 'to feel that Battalions of Jews (the "Judeans") should have had the opportunity of contributing in so large a measure and with characteristic gallantry to the magnificent victory in our ancient land, which under the aegis of Great Britain and her allies is to become the "National Home" of the Jewish People . . .'

The *Jewish Chronicle*'s editor, it is worth noting, had chosen to use the original wording contained in the draft of the Balfour Declaration: the 'ancient land' (Palestine) would become 'the' national home for the Jews. The British government, whatever its protestations to the contrary, must have realized at this early stage that the Zionist movement would settle for nothing less than a Jewish state in Palestine.

One month after the fall of Damascus, Allied forces, continuing their advance against the Turkish army, captured the city of Aleppo. King Hussein of the Hejaz (the former Sherif) sent a telegram to King George V saying he wanted on behalf of himself 'and the Arab Nation to beg your Majesty and the Noble British nation to accept our thanks for the great and the precious help which we have received from you in the restoration of our independence. No Arab will ever forget such help for which we will remain grateful to the end of the world.'[29]

In the light of what happened to the dreams of post-war independence, Hussein's words make bitter and painful reading for Arabs today.

The standard Arab interpretation of events in Palestine in the period from 1918 to 1948 is that 'in order to force the implementation of that promise [the Balfour Declaration] on the Palestinian people, Palestine had to remain under British administration'.[30] Any attempt by the British since to plead for understanding and to urge the Arabs to take in to account the conflicting pressures of the period is regarded as meaningless when matched against what they regard as the calamity which eventually befell Palestine. If Britain found that events were slipping out of its control, the Arabs say, then the government in London only had itself to blame by being the power which had issued and adhered to the Balfour Declaration. The Arabs believe they have paid a double price: they have had the state of Israel forced into their midst, and have subsequently suffered in their relationship with the West from what they see as the latter's bias towards the Israelis.

As pressures on Britain built up after the First World War, colonial officials on the spot and their masters in London continued to insist that there was no intention of allowing a Jewish state to be created, but the task of convincing the Arab population became increasingly difficult. At the Arab Bureau in Cairo, General Clayton sent weekly reports to London on developments in the region. On 5 November 1918, he recorded 'certain indications of Arab propaganda in Palestine emanating from Damascus. This is not likely to have any appreciable effect on the population.' A week later, Clayton reported that in Haifa 'some uneasiness is caused by fear of Zionism and a movement is on foot for organisation of Moslems out of adherence to the Shereef'. In the weeks which followed Clayton observed 'apprehension' among both Muslims and Christians 'as to Zionist intentions in Palestine', combined with 'fear of Jewish supremacy'.

By March 1919, Clayton was reporting that 'anti-Zionist propaganda has increased considerably in Palestine lately and feeling is now running very high among Moslems and Christians who fear that political and economic advantages may be given to Jews in the [post-First World War] peace settlement. This feeling is increased by the rash of actions and words of the Jews themselves.' More specifically Clayton said there were 'considerable grounds for belief that anti-Jewish riots are being prepared in Jerusalem, Jaffa and elsewhere'.[31]

His prediction was accurate, and the trends he observed in 1919 continued up to the establishment of the state of Israel. The intention here is not to follow the events step by step: many books, written from different perspectives, have done this. Nevertheless, certain developments of this period highlight the attitudes of some of the parties involved, attitudes which have contributed to the belief in the Arab world that the West is inherently biased in favour of Israel – a conviction which is well founded, although at times expressed in an exaggerated way.

The main Western supporter of Israel (in political, financial

and military terms) in the second half of the twentieth century
has been the United States. In the years before the creation of
the Jewish state, Washington was seldom more than an
observer of events in the Middle East. For only one brief period,
at the end of the First World War, did the Americans become
involved in the politics of the region.

On a number of occasions during 1918, President Woodrow
Wilson enunciated four sets of principles which encompassed
his vision of the post-war world. The President stressed the
need for autonomous entities to be ruled on the basis of popular
consent. 'Peoples and provinces are not to be bartered about,'
he said. 'Every territorial settlement involved in this war must
be made in the interests and for the benefit of the populations
concerned.' Britain and France publicly endorsed this principle
in November 1918, stating – in what amounted to a bare-faced
lie about their intentions in the Middle East – that they had
no desire 'to impose on the populations of these regions any
particular institutions'.[32]

Echoes of the Wilsonian principles were still audible when
world leaders met at a post-war peace conference in Paris in
February 1919 where the future of the Middle East and other
regions was discussed. Emir Feisal, one of the sons of King
Hussein of Hejaz whose presence at Paris had been arranged
by Britain, made an impassioned appeal for the independence
of all Arab countries, including Palestine. He called for a commission of inquiry to go to Syria to find out what the people
living there wanted. Britain and France pretended to support
the move. In fact, each continued to covet Palestine for itself.
With London and Paris unable to agree, it was decided that an
American team should undertake the mission.

Two men, Henry King and Charles Crane, were sent, and
reported back in August 1919. The King–Crane Commission
found that the people of Syria did not want to see Palestine
broken off as a separate entity, nor did they want to become
the subjects of a foreign mandate. The view of the inhabitants
of Syria was that if a link with a foreign country was necessary
they would prefer the outside power to be the United States.
If that were not possible they would choose Britain. Under no

circumstances would they accept a French presence in their country. The French were enraged by this finding and accused British officials – almost certainly with justification – of having manipulated the witnesses to the Commission. The affair worsened still further Anglo–French relations.

From a Palestinian perspective, the most interesting findings in the King–Crane report relate to the role of Zionism. British officials may still have been trying to persuade the Arab population that Jewish supremacy was not the goal of the Zionist movement; but to the two Americans, this was clearly the aim. As a result, they recommended 'serious modification of the extreme Zionist program for Palestine of unlimited immigration of Jews, looking finally to making Palestine distinctly a Jewish State . . . The fact came out repeatedly in the Commission's conference with Jewish representatives, that the Zionists looked forward to a practically complete dispossession of the present non-Jewish inhabitants of Palestine, by various forms of purchase.'

Referring to the Wilsonian principle of 'consent of the governed', the Commission report then turned to the wishes of the non-Jewish inhabitants – nearly 90 per cent of the total population. King–Crane found that they were 'emphatically against the entire Zionist program. The tables show that there was no one thing upon which the population of Palestine were more agreed than upon this.'[33]

These latter findings seemed to express clearly and accurately the wishes of the Arabs of Syria and Palestine, judging by the reactions of the inhabitants of the area to the events of the subsequent decades. But the King–Crane findings were ignored totally by Britain and France, and were not published until December 1922. The Arabs assume that an inherent Western bias, first towards the Zionist movement and later towards Israel, has been part of a fixed policy. The British and French reaction to the King–Crane commission was interpreted in this light. However, the way in which the Commission's evidence was received in London and Paris provides yet another example of the muddle out of which the state of Israel eventually emerged.

In April 1920, as part of a compromise with France over the
control of territory, Britain was appointed by the League of
Nations as the mandate power in Palestine, 'responsible for
putting into effect' the Balfour Declaration. Widespread rioting
and clashes between Arabs and Jews occurred in May, and
martial law was imposed. Sir Ronald Storrs, the Military Governor of Jerusalem after its capture from the Turks, and then
Sir Herbert Samuel, a non-practising Jew who was the first
High Commissioner for Palestine, did their best to reconcile the
two sides. They were unsuccessful: the British, having chosen
a path blocked by opposing moral claims, were in a hopeless
position. Storrs said that 'two hours of Arab grievances drive
me into the Synagogue, while after an intensive course of
Zionist propaganda I am prepared to embrace Islam.'[34] The
British soldier on the street, meanwhile, 'felt himself
surrounded, almost opposed, by an atmosphere always critical,
frequently hostile, sometimes bitterly vindictive and even
menacing'.[35]

The rioting and general disorder led to the first of a series of
White Papers on Palestine in which Britain tried, by shuffling
the cards in different ways, to make the pack look acceptable
to all sides. The first document, the Churchill White Paper of
June 1922, said the tensions in Palestine were being caused by
Arab apprehensions 'based upon exaggerated interpretations
of the meaning of the [Balfour] Declaration favouring the
establishment of a Jewish National Home in Palestine'.

Given the evidence both of the King–Crane Commission
and of what the Arabs of Palestine could see happening around
them, it is not difficult to imagine how the impression of
double-dealing took shape in Arab minds. This feeling will have
been further enhanced by a section in the same White Paper
which dismissed the Arab insistence that independence for
Palestine was implied in the ambiguously worded letter sent
in 1915 by Sir Henry McMahon, the British High Commissioner
in Egypt, to the Sherif of Mecca. The British government document said the letter had excluded 'the portions of Syria lying
to the west of the district of Damascus' – that is to say all of
Palestine west of the River Jordan – from the areas where

independence would be granted. Despite this ruling in the White Paper, Arab historians have continued to insist that the understanding of the Sherif and others was that Palestine was to be granted independence.

The confusion stems partly from the wording of the McMahon letter. Looking at the map, the area to the west of Damascus would seem to be roughly what is present-day Lebanon, rather than Palestine. However, the Arabs have never accepted the explanation that the controversy was the result of confusion and misunderstanding. There is evidence to back the Arabs' view. As one assessment of the period says, 'Balfour admitted frankly that the West had deceived the Arabs but thought that it was in everyone's higher interest that it should do so.'[36] In 1919, five years after the McMahon letter was sent to Sherif Hussein, Lord Balfour wrote in a memorandum that 'so far as Palestine is concerned, the powers have made no statement of fact that is not admittedly wrong and no declaration of policy which, at least in the letter, they have not always intended to violate.'[37] The publication of statements of this kind has only strengthened the sense of bitterness and injustice which the Arabs have felt towards West over the Palestine affair.

Despite the Arabs' displeasure at the section in the 1922 White Paper about independence for Palestine, the document contained assurances which helped to restore relative calm there. The British government rejected categorically interpretations of the Balfour Declaration which suggested that Palestine would become 'wholly Jewish'. The White Paper also denied reports that the British government had plans for 'the disappearance or subordination of the Arabic population, language, or culture in Palestine'. In this period of calm after the 1922 White Paper, the Arabs were relieved to see a drop in the rate of immigration. After reaching a peak of 34,386 in 1924, it fell to 3,034 in 1927. The worldwide economic recession also meant that more Jews were leaving than entering Palestine.[38]

The calm lasted only until 1929 when in further outbreaks of rioting 230 people – Jews and Arabs in roughly equal

numbers – were killed. There was evidence that the trouble
had been stirred up by Jewish groups, and British officials in
Palestine urged their government to distance itself from the
Zionist movement. Arabs expressed even more vehemently
than before their fears of growing Jewish supremacy, including
the acquisition of land by the Zionists. A senior official was
sent from London to investigate the claims. His report formed
the basis of the Passfield White Paper of October 1930 which
urged both a restriction in the number of Jewish immigrants
to Palestine and a curb on the sale of land.

This was a document which appeared to take into account
the grievances of the Arab population and was a genuine
attempt to find a way of keeping the balance in Palestine. But
any sense of balance would give the Arabs at least an equal
share in an independent state, and thus thwart the aims of the
Zionist movement. So, the formidable Jewish lobby with its
unique network of personal contacts around the world was set
to work. The day after the publication of the White Paper a
chain of connections was established. One historian has
recounted the sequence of events thus, 'Baffy Dugdale, Balfour's niece, contacted the Conservative politician, Leo Amery.
Namier [a Jewish official in the Foreign Office who had first
shown Weizmann a copy of the White Paper] used the Prime
Minister's son, Malcolm MacDonald, to get through to 10
Downing Street. On 6 November Ramsay MacDonald proposed
a meeting between the Zionists and a Cabinet subcommittee,
chaired by Arthur Henderson, assisted, at Weizmann's request,
by Malcolm MacDonald. The Zionists mounted an orchestrated
campaign, and there were anti-British demonstrations
throughout the Jewish world.'[39]

The campaign, like the one which preceded the publication
of the Balfour Declaration, was successful. On 13 February
1931 the Zionists got what they wanted: a letter from the Prime
Minister which effectively dismissed the recommendations of
the Passfield White Paper. The British government, it said, 'did
not imply a prohibition of acquisition of additional land by
Jews'; also the British 'did not prescribe and do not contemplate any stoppage or prohibition of Jewish immigration in

any of its categories'. The Arabs, ever since, have called the MacDonald commitment the 'Black Letter'.

In the 1930s, violence in Palestine worsened, with Arabs, Jews and British falling as casualties. In 1936 the British government sent another team to Palestine to see whether a way could be found to restore order. The Peel Commission published its findings in July 1937, concluding that the national aspirations of the Arabs and the Jews were irreconcilable. 'To foster Jewish immigration,' the report said, 'in the hope that it might ultimately lead to the creation of a Jewish majority and the establishment of a Jewish State with the consent or at least the acquiescence of the Arabs was one thing. It was quite another to contemplate, however remotely, the forcible conversion of Palestine into a Jewish State against the will of the Arabs.'[40]

The Peel Commission decided that the competing moral claims could be addressed only if Palestine were partitioned. The Arabs rejected this scheme; and the Zionist Congress accepted it only with a slim minority. The British government decided the matter when, in November 1938, it declared its opposition to the principle of partition.

Of interest in the workings of the Peel Commission is the manner in which the Jews argued their case. The hardline Zionist leader Ze'ev Jabotinsky said it was 'quite understandable that the Arabs of Palestine would also prefer Palestine to be the Arab State No. 4, No. 5, or No. 6 – that I quite understand; but when the Arab claim is confronted with our Jewish demand to be saved, it is like the claims of appetite versus the claims of starvation.'[41] The tone of the language – especially at a time of increasing persecution of Jews in Europe – was bound to touch the emotions of a Western audience. Arabs would have found it difficult at that time to match the power and appeal of the argument. Even today, Arabs are frustrated by the way in which the West, in their opinion, seems to be bewitched by the arguments of Zionists. One Arab historian, writing in 1988, just before the collapse of communism in the Soviet Union, asserted that, 'Zionism can exert a form of pressure on the authorities and on public opinion in the United

States and western Europe (and perhaps even in the Soviet Union) that is much more effective than any lobby.'[42]

The Jewish lobby was quick to respond in 1939 when Britain made another attempt in the form of a White Paper to find a peaceful settlement for Palestine. This recommended that the number of Jewish immigrants should be severely restricted, taking into account 'the strongly expressed will of the Arab people' on this subject. At the same time, the document said the British government were 'conscious of the present unhappy plight of large numbers of Jews who seek a refuge from certain European countries, and they believe that Palestine can and should make a further contribution to the solution of this pressing world problem'.[43] But the days in which Britain could claim the moral authority and political influence sufficient to orchestrate a just and fair settlement of the Arab–Jew problem were at an end. Signs were emerging that a solution could be found only on the basis of a winner and a loser. The Jewish Agency spoke out with a flourish of emotive eloquence to try to ensure that the Zionists in Palestine were victorious. Responding to the immigration restrictions recommended by the 1939 White Paper, the Agency spoke of 'this darkest hour of Jewish history' in which 'the British government proposes to deprive the Jews of their last hope and to close the road back to their Homeland. It is a cruel blow, doubly cruel because it comes from the government of a great nation which has extended a helping hand to the Jews, and whose position must rest on foundations of moral authority and international good faith.'[44] The appeal to Britain's moral authority showed a deft touch, by flattering the ego of the mandate power at the moment when its authority was so obviously ebbing fast.

Life for the British officials and troops in Palestine became difficult and dangerous as the mandate period dragged on. In 1987, at the start of the Palestinian uprising (intifada) in the occupied West Bank and Gaza Strip, Israeli security forces found out that policing a civil rebellion is a thankless, frustrating and ultimately demoralizing task. As at the time of the intifada, so during British mandate rule, excesses were committed by troops trying to establish order. Complaints of theft and

vandalism committed by troops searching houses were frequently made. A doctor from Britain, working at Hebron in
1938, recalled receiving at his hospital early one Saturday
morning 'a series of casualties inflicted by the British, presumably on curfew breakers. A great number of broken crowns
were treated during the day at the public clinic and at this
hospital.' The same doctor quoted a seventy-five-year-old Palestinian describing how British troops had assaulted and abused
his family, and stolen their money. Before leaving they had
smashed windows and glasses. The old man said 'the Turks
were unjust and cruel and I hated them. During the war I
hoped the English would win, for they were famed for their
greatness and justice. But never in my experience of the Turks
have I witnessed such a scene. The Turks, brutes though they
were, were angels compared to you English. Why don't you
massacre all the inhabitants of Palestine and have done with
it?'.[45]

Such experiences at the hands of the British inevitably
increased the sense of injustice felt by Palestinians towards the
mandate power. In a similar way, the lack of Western action
to restrain the Israeli military authorities in the occupied territories in the closing years of the century has left Arabs – not
just Palestinians – feeling bitter.

By February 1947, Britain had admitted defeat in its attempts
to find an equitable solution to the Palestine problem – or, as
the Arabs view it, the British abandoned their moral duty –
and handed over the issue to the United Nations. On 14 May
1948, Sir Henry Gurney, Chief Secretary of Palestine had his
bags packed, along with those of the High Commissioner Sir
Alan Cunningham. 'Practically no sleep last night,' he wrote
in his diary, 'since soon after midnight firing started and went
on in the usual stupid way until about 4.00. As the sun came
up over the Mount of Olives, the shooting stopped and we
got up and dressed for the last journey ... At 8.00 the High
Commissioner inspected the HLI guard-of-honour at Government House, and left a few minutes later, the Red Cross having
taken the place of the Union Jack.'[46]

Britain's role in the birth of the Jewish state will remain a subject for debate for many years but, no matter how complex and muddled the subject might seem to Western minds, in the view of the Arabs the issue is clear: Britain was responsible for an act which caused and continues to cause deep emotional pain. 'The establishment of the state of Israel,' Mustafa Hamarneh, Professor of Modern History at the University of Jordan in Amman, said in 1991, 'as far as we are concerned here in the fertile crescent, is viewed as really a radical uprooting of an entire culture. This was not done by Jewish boy scouts hanging around there; it was basically done by the Jews, by Zionism, in close cooperation with Great Britain, and with the backing and support of Britain and the rest of the Western world.'[47] The bitterness is deep. Aside from expressions of despair and anger, Arab reaction to the presence of Israel has contributed greatly to the negative and derogatory way in which many Westerners view the people of the Middle East – a factor which is as important as the Arabs' attitudes to the West in determining why the gulf between the two regions remains wide. The emergence of the Jewish state has led to wars; the Arabs have almost invariably lost them. Palestinian frustration has at times spilled over into hijacking and other acts of terror directed at civilian targets, sometimes not directly connected with the Middle East dispute. Different Palestinian factions involved in acts of terror at various periods have enjoyed the financial and material backing of Libya, Syria, Iraq and Yemen. The accumulated effect of these developments, often reported prominently and sensationally in the Western media, has been the close identification in Western minds of the Arabs as a whole with terrorism. As this perception (which is examined in more detail in later chapters) has become established in the West, so the frustration of the Arabs at what they regard as the double standards in Western policies has increased. Double-dealing is identified in many areas of Western policy, but the most glaring one relates to the Arab–Israeli dispute and, in particular, to the way in which Israel's policies of territorial expansionism have never been seriously challenged by the West.

After the Iraqi invasion of Kuwait in August 1990, the Arabs

watched the United Nations Security Council issue a string
of resolutions condemning the Baghdad government and
ordering it to withdraw from occupied territory. There was no
surprise in the Arab world when President Saddam Hussein
reminded the West that a number of UN resolutions condemning Israel's capture of Arab territory in the war of 1967 still lay
on the shelf, ignored by the Jewish state. Iraq, he said at one
stage, might be prepared to withdraw from Kuwait if the
Israelis pulled out of occupied Arab land. This linkage of
thought, which was rejected out-of-hand by both Israel and
the West, did not seem illogical among Arabs outside the Gulf
region. The logic persists today – regardless of how President
Saddam Hussein may be judged for his thrust into Kuwait and
the subsequent humiliation he brought upon himself and the
Arab world. The argument is all the clearer in Arab minds
because of the way in which the West persuaded the international community that it was acting on behalf of the United
Nations in organizing the military rout of Iraq. The Western
coalition claimed to be going into action on behalf of the principle that the world must stop powerful countries swallowing
up weak ones. The Arabs wondered why the West could not
take the same collective action on behalf of the displaced Arabs
of Palestine. Of course, even as they posed the question, they
knew the answer. Western 'speechmakers were treading warily
round a three-letter word, trying not to mention it. Oil became
"resources" or "vital Western interests".'[48]

The West's flimsy assertion that the Gulf war was fought on
the basis of lofty principles served only to embitter further the
mass of Arab people. The imposition by the United States,
Britain and France of no-fly zones in northern and southern
Iraq in the aftermath of the war – moves which did not have
specific authorization by the United Nations Security Council
– was backed up by military strikes on Iraqi targets in January
1993. This uncompromising approach to Baghdad was con-
trasted by the Arabs as a whole with the failure of these same
countries to enforce a UN resolution ordering Israel to take
back more than 400 Palestinians who had been expelled from
the occupied territories the previous month. The shelf of UN

resolutions relating to Israel's occupation of Arab land continued to collect dust. The two resolutions quoted most frequently, 242 and 338 (which envisage a settlement of the
Arab–Israeli conflict on the basis of land being exchanged for
peace), were brought down from the shelf for the opening of
the Middle East Peace Conference in Madrid in October 1991.
The invitation sent by the Americans and Russians to the
Israelis and the Arab parties to the Middle East conflict stated
specifically that a settlement should be based on the principles
of resolutions 242 and 338. Israel accepted the invitation to
attend – but then promptly rejected the principles enshrined
in the UN resolutions. To the Arabs, after decades of Western
double-dealing, the failure of the United States (the only power
in the world able to exert pressure on the Jewish state) to
chastise the Israelis for taking this negative position caused no
surprise.

The Arabs shrugged their shoulders in a similar way when
Washington declined to pressure the right-wing Israeli government led by Yitzhak Shamir to halt the construction of new
Jewish towns and settlements in the occupied territories while
peace talks were proceeding. The subject came up during a
discussion broadcast by Amman Radio two months after the
opening of the peace process. The tone of the conversation is
typical of many of its kind and highlights once again the difference in Arab and Western perceptions. Rami Khouri, the host
of the programme, raised the issue of a UN Security Council
resolution which forbids the construction of settlements, on
the principle that such action on occupied territory is in breach
of the Geneva Convention on Human Rights. Khouri asked his
guest, Ibrahim Matar, a Palestinian economist from Jerusalem
and an expert on Israeli settlement policy, why the resolution
was not implemented. 'Well,' Matar replied, 'the United States
has had a double-standards policy with certain Security Council
resolutions. There are many resolutions regarding the illegality
of the settlements, regarding the illegality of the annexation of
Jerusalem and the Golan Heights and so on. What we need is
the implementation of these resolutions.'

Khouri suggested that this international paralysis on the

question of the Palestinians 'just heightens the feeling in the Arab world that we continue to suffer from two standards of morality'. Matar replied: 'That is exactly right. It is basically a decision by the United States government whether they want to continue with this double-standard morality or whether they want to apply one same morality for all.'

To put the matter bluntly, the arrogance displayed by the West in helping to create the state of Israel on land which it did not own continues to be displayed today in its assumption of moral superiority to the Arabs. The Arabs themselves resent and dispute the rights of the West in both instances. Mohamed Heikal has argued that what Arabs regard as this sense of arrogance was born out of deep-rooted Western attitudes to the region which made the creation of Israel possible and which still persist at the end of the twentieth century. The establishment of the Jewish state in the Middle East 'could only have been possible if the Arab world was projected to western public opinion as an object rather than a subject of history – as indeed it was. Thus the groundwork was laid for the Sykes–Picot treaty, by which Britain and France carved up the Arab world, and the Balfour Declaration, by which Britain gave herself the right to dispose of an Arab country to satisfy a religious-cum-racist myth.'[49] This is one part of the legacy with which Arabs have to live towards the end of the century; the other part is the painful realization that collective ineptitude in the face of developments around them, and political divisions among the various regimes have combined to weaken their ability to control their own destiny and have allowed them to be used and abused by outside powers.

The collective failure of Arab action against Israel contributed to the decision taken by leaders of the Palestine Liberation Organization (PLO) in 1993 to recognise formally the Jewish state and accept an autonomy agreement for the West Bank and Gaza Strip. The hope of Palestinians was that this arrangement would lead eventually to the creation of an independent state in these areas; but no guarantee of this was included in the accord. Also, as the many critics of the deal pointed out at the time, the crucial question of the future status of Jerusalem

was left for discussion at a later stage. The Palestinians insist
that it must be their capital when a state is created. The Israelis,
of all political persuasions, insist that an undivided Jerusalem
will always remain the capital of the Jewish state. Whatever
its eventual outcome, the agreement signed in September 1993
put an end to lingering hopes that joint Arab action might be
taken to recover occupied land. It also amounted to capitulation
by the PLO in the face of Israeli doggedness and the failure of
the international community, led by the West, to enforce in
full UN Security Council resolutions relating to Israelis occupation of Arab lands. In other words, the PLO was implicitly
accepting for the first time the double standards of the West
and trying to achieve what it could within that limitation.

In Lebanon, too, one of the countries to emerge out of the
Sykes–Picot agreement, Arabs have accused the West of
double-dealing and have been made to realize painfully their
own shortcomings. In comparison with the attention focused
over the years on UN Security Council resolutions 242 and 338,
number 425 has had little public exposure. This last resolution
demands the withdrawal of Israeli forces from southern Lebanon following the Israeli invasion in March 1978. The Lebanese authorities have argued that Israel's failure to comply with
resolution 425 makes impossible their task of re-establishing
their authority over the whole country after years of civil war,
internal fragmentation and foreign occupation. The American
government was prepared, in 1990, to reverse its policy of
trying to reduce Syrian influence in Lebanon because it wanted
the support of Damascus in the military build-up in the Gulf
against Iraq. The United States was also prepared to back Syria
in implementing a package of internal reforms for Lebanon
worked out at Arab League-brokered talks in Ta'if in Saudi
Arabia in October 1989; but it was not prepared to pressure
Israel to pull out of the south of the country. Marwan Hamade,
a Cabinet minister from the Lebanese Druze community, said
the Lebanese were happy 'with the support the United States
brought to the Ta'if agreement, to the process of internal
national reconciliation. But we are still very unhappy at the
negligible amount of pressure the United States are putting on

Israel to implement resolution 425. The United States, who have been so swift to act in the Gulf on behalf of the United Nations are very slow and reluctant to move when Israel is involved. I think it is high time that the United States forgets about double standards and starts implementing UN resolutions everywhere in the world, not just where it pleases them.'[50]

Double standards are perceived by the Arabs too in matters other than those directly related to the military conflict with Israel. There is the question, for example, of hostage-taking in Lebanon. The kidnapping of Westerners in Beirut in the 1980s was a subject of major concern for governments and the public in Europe and the United States. But minimal attention was paid in these countries to Arab hostages in the Middle East – either those caught up in the Lebanese civil war, or others kidnapped by the Israelis and their client militia in southern Lebanon. Nor was there any understanding in the West of the anger felt in the Middle East at the way Arabs in general were identified with hostage-taking, while the kidnappers of Westerners in Lebanon belonged to Iranian-backed groups acting on behalf of Tehran.

When Western hostages were eventually freed their movements were beamed by satellite around the world, they were provided with the best medical care that money could buy, and they found themselves celebrities for life. For Arab detainees dumped into the hands of the International Committee of the Red Cross in southern Lebanon, there was no USAF Wiesbaden or RAF Lyneham to provide medical checks, no lucrative publishing contracts or offers of lecture tours, and no certainty that they would not be abducted once more in the months ahead.

When in the summer of 1989 Israeli troops sent a force into a village in southern Lebanon to kidnap a Shiite cleric, Sheikh Abdul Karim Obeid (to put pressure on Shiite groups in Lebanon which were said to be holding missing Israeli servicemen), there were protests from the international community. But the Israeli action was never regarded as being so unacceptable that it would lead to the breaking of diplomatic ties or anything stronger. Yet it is difficult to imagine an Arab government being left unpunished after sending a group of commandos into Israel to kidnap any Jew, let alone a Jewish rabbi. Instinctively, one knows that different rules would apply. 'Everyone forgets,' an Arab columnist wrote at the start of the 1990s, 'that Israel was and remains a part of the West planted in the region.'[51] And the blame continues to be laid by the Arabs at the feet of Balfour and the British.

The Balfour Declaration led to the birth of the current Middle East crisis which has caused four wars and created a region of chronic instability on the doorstep of Europe. Britain and other Western states remain trapped by a dilemma of their own making which has haunted them throughout the second half of the century. The Palestinians' demand for self-determination based on secular, nationalistic grounds is recognized as fair and legitimate. The existence of hundreds of thousands of Palestinians who have lived as refugees since 1948 illustrates graphically that demand. Yet the West is also concerned to protect Israel, partly from a desire to redress the horrors inflicted on the Jewish populations of Europe by the Nazis during the Second World War and partly out of recognition of Jewish demands for statehood based on religious grounds.

Sir Mark Sykes, it should be recalled at this point, predicted calmly in December 1917 that the effect of the Balfour Declaration on the Arabs would be 'transient' if Britain strove to reassure the Arabs of its support for their liberation. The important word in that sentence is 'if'. The reality was that in the aftermath of the First World War, while circumstances had forced changes in the shape of the Sykes–Picot accord and while it was becoming clear that the implementation of the Balfour Declaration might cause some problems, Britain and France were still determined to go ahead with the reconstitution of the Middle East along lines which suited them.

CHAPTER THREE

Disintegration and Division

'The Arab nation consists of all who speak Arabic as their mother-tongue, no more, no less.' This unambiguous definition was made by one of the leading and most influential exponents of Arab nationalism in the decades after the First World War, Sati' al-Husri.[1] But the twentieth century is ending with the Arab nation fragmented into twenty-one independent states (twenty-two until the merger of North and South Yemen in May 1990), each with its own national identity and trappings. Within the family of Arab nations there are also many splits, leaving the people of the region with a sense of dejection and alienation from the principles of Arabism. The Iraqi invasion of Kuwait in 1990 and the subsequent splits which emerged in the region dealt a hard blow to the waning sense of a shared political identity among the Arabs.

For the Arab people from Morocco to the Gulf, the common linguistic, cultural and historical inheritance is appreciated and treasured. But the bond is not strong enough either to smother inter-Arab political rivalry and enmity or to remove the barriers erected by the individual nation states along the boundaries imposed, in many instances, by colonial powers.

The barriers are real. The Arabs run up against them every day. The appearance and decor of border checkpoints in the Arab world vary considerably, reflecting the wealth or poverty of the countries, but in every country the same scenes are visible: lines of people, resigned to long delays as they queue to face rigorous questioning by immigration officials.

For a foreigner with the correct documents the process will

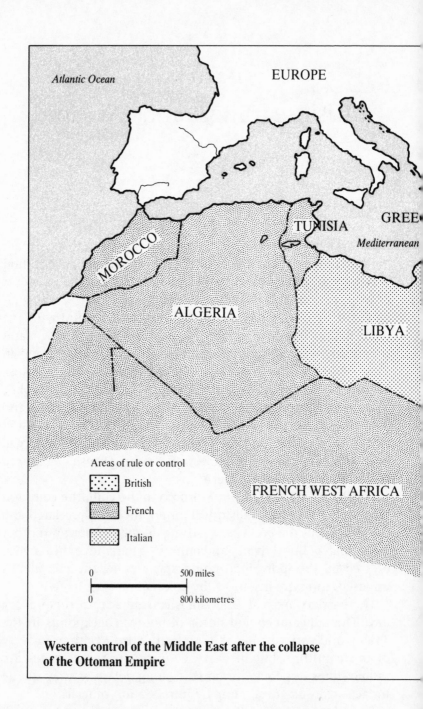

Atlantic Ocean

EUROPE

MOROCCO

TUNISIA

GREE

Mediterranean

ALGERIA

LIBYA

Areas of rule or control

British

French

Italian

FRENCH WEST AFRICA

0   500 miles

0   800 kilometres

Western control of the Middle East after the collapse of the Ottoman Empire

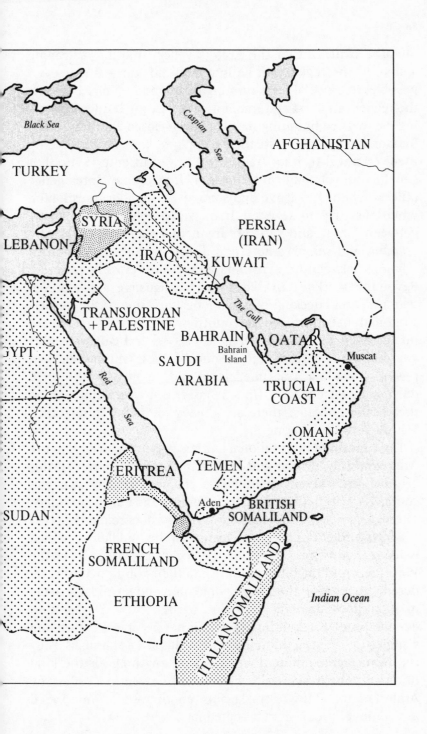

often be swift. But for the Arab traveller, entering or leaving a state in the region can be long and difficult – if it is even possible. Because of long-running rivalry and enmity between the regimes in Syria and Iraq, for example, the border separating the two neighbouring states has been closed for many years. Syrians have a stamp in their passports expressly forbidding them to travel to Iraq; Iraqis are allowed to enter Syria, but run the risk of tough interrogation from Syrian intelligence officers when they leave and some even tougher questioning when they try to re-enter Iraq. Arabs crossing the border between Jordan and Syria are frequently subjected to lengthy searches and interrogation, and during periods of tension in relations between Amman and Damascus the crossing is closed. Egyptians working in Libya face exhaustive questioning, searches, and checking of documents each side of the border. Arab nationals from certain countries, like Syria or Libya, are unable even to apply for visas to visit several Gulf states. 'If you cannot travel freely and conduct business within your own region,' a leading Arab intellectual said, 'then where the hell do you go? Europe? The United States? But we are not wanted there either, because there are already too many immigrants. It is all very humiliating.'

The concept of international borders was introduced into the Arab world by Britain and France in the first quarter of this century. The second quarter was characterized by struggles conducted within these borders to remove the European rulers. The struggles were successful; but the borders remained.

Arab disunity has become a feature of the Middle East which is recognized as much outside the region as within it. In the West the Arabs' inability to unite and their failure over several decades to marshal their huge population and formidable array of modern armaments into line against the one common enemy, Israel, is taken for granted; it has become a truism and a subject of sneering humour. 'The Arabs are a shambles, they can never agree among themselves on anything,' is the kind of remark one hears. Iraq's invasion of Kuwait in 1990 – one Arab state marching to war against another – was interpreted as additional proof of an accepted fact.

Western minds are sometimes puzzled by the lack of cohesion in the Arab world; but the reasons for disunity are not often the subject of analysis beyond, perhaps, a racist slur on the character and temperament of the Arabs. Among Arabs themselves there is also a growing acceptance that unity is no more than a dream, but this has not diminished the bitterness felt towards the West for its perceived role in encouraging the fragmentation of the region. Mahjoub Omar, an Egyptian political commentator, believes that the way in which the nation states were imposed on the Arab world was inappropriate. 'I am not against the concept as such – provided it comes at the right time. I do not believe in jumping the historical phases. We might have reached the nation-state phase after enough internal and external struggles. But it takes time. You cannot import it or impose it.' As a result, Omar said, Arab people 'have the right to blame the West for the lack of unity because they divided the Arabs'.[2]

At the end of the First World War, the people of the Arab region felt a greater sense of cohesion and collective identity than ever before. The extent to which the Arab Revolt contributed to Allied victories over the Turks remains a matter of debate. Sati' al-Husri was prepared to accept the argument that after the defeat of Germany in 1918 the collapse of the Ottoman empire would have been inevitable 'whether or not Sherif Hussein revolted against it'. But Husri argued that the importance of the Arab involvement, at whatever level, in the military campaign was considerable because 'the very fact of the revolt, of the existence of an Arab army in Syria, established the idea of Arab independence and produced a natural hostility when that independence was forcibly destroyed. In this manner the revolt, minor as it was on the stage of world power transformations, served to awaken the national feelings of the Arabs.'[3]

The 'forcibly destroyed' independence mentioned by Husri is a reference to a four-month period in 1920 in which Damascus was the capital of the self-proclaimed kingdom of Syria, with Feisal (the son of King Hussein of the Hejaz) on the throne. But with the two major European powers, Britain and France, tussling for control of the territories of the former

Ottoman empire it was perhaps inevitable that the frail flower
of Syrian (and, by extension, Arab) independence would soon
be crushed under foot.

The tussling took place at Peace Conferences held in Paris,
London, San Remo and Sèvres between January 1919 and
August 1920. The participants cynically disregarded the Wilsonian principles of self-determination for peoples liberated
from Turkish rule to which they had loftily promised to adhere.
They simply took out rulers and drew lines on the map at their
convenience. They showed little consideration for the needs or
welfare of the population, and paid only scant attention to
tribal or natural geographical borders. Some of the scenes at
these conferences would have been considered farcical if their
effects had not been so drastic for millions of Arabs. David
Fromkin has captured the mood in his account of the proceed-
ings. He quotes an Italian diplomat writing that 'a common
sight at the Peace Conference in Paris was one or other of the
world's statesmen, standing before a map and muttering to
himself: "Where is that damn'd . . . ?" while he sought with
extended forefinger for some town or river that he had never
heard of before.' Lloyd George, who kept demanding that
Britain should rule Palestine from (in the Biblical phrase) Dan
to Beersheba, did not know where Dan was. He searched
for it in a nineteenth-century Biblical atlas, but it was not
until nearly a year after the armistice [after the First World
War] that General Allenby was able to report to him that
Dan had been located and, as it was not where the Prime
Minister wanted it to be, Britain asked for a boundary
further north.'[4]

The biggest problem in the Middle East which Britain and
France had to solve during the Peace Conferences concerned
the future of Syria. British troops had remained there since
the ending of the First World War and British officials were
supporting and advising Emir Feisal ibn Hussein who was the
nominal ruler. France demanded that Britain should withdraw
and honour the commitment within the Sykes–Picot agreement for Syria to come under French control. The British
government stood firm. It even overcame French objections

and secured an invitation to the Paris conference of 1919 for Emir Feisal (but only as a representative of the kingdom of Hejaz). Feisal argued at the conference for Arab independence in a broad sweep of territory at the eastern end of the Mediterranean. After citing linguistic and ethnic links binding the people there, the Emir reminded Britain of promises made during the war. He said the Arabs had fought valiantly in the Allied cause, losing some 20,000 men. Now that the war was won 'the Arabic-speaking peoples thought themselves entitled to independence and worthy of it'.[5] Britain presented a similarly constructed argument to the French, adding for good measure that France had played a minimal role in defeating the Ottoman army. The British government also pointed to evidence that the people of Syria did not want a French presence in their country.

In the end, European pragmatism prevailed at the expense of the Arabs. With the French having conceded Palestine and Mosul (the latter was eventually incorporated into Iraq) to Britain, the British government felt it had no choice but to honour its earlier commitment to France. Aside from all other considerations 'if it came to the point, Britain would always prefer her need for good relations with France to her desire to establish an Arab State in Syria; and the Zionists could bring greater pressure to bear in London than could the Arabs'.[6] By the end of 1919 British troops had withdrawn from Syria. British ministers suggested that by so doing they had honoured their commitments both to France and to the Arabs, but 'it was a disingenuous claim. The British pretended that Feisal headed a great Arab army in Syria, but government officials were aware that this was a pretence without substance. For the British army to leave was to leave Feisal to the mercy of the French.'[7] (The overstated involvement of Arab forces in the revolt against the Turks and the grossly exaggerated version of the role played by T.E. Lawrence, who was an official at the Arab Bureau in Cairo, have become part of a romanticized Western vision of the Middle East, enshrined in the film *Lawrence of Arabia*.) Britain, before withdrawing its troops from Syria, had persuaded Feisal to visit Prime Minister Georges

Clemenceau in Paris and reach a compromise with the French. The Feisal–Clemenceau agreement envisaged total French control of the coastal districts of Syria (present-day Lebanon, where French troops were already stationed), with France providing guidance to the rest of the country, which was to be governed from Damascus.

In Syria, though, there was no mood for compromise. In May 1919, a General Syrian Congress had been formed. At a meeting in Damascus, spurred on by nationalists, it had called for complete independence for the whole of Syria (including Palestine). It also rejected plans being drawn up by Britain and France to assume mandatory powers over the region. Feisal's frequent absences abroad, discussing the future of Syria with European leaders, meant that he was out of touch with the strength of nationalist feeling at home – especially within the Congress. Syrian schoolchildren today read in their History textbook that 'news of Feisal's planned agreement with France reached Syria before he did, and the people greeted the accord with extreme anger. Demonstrations were held, calling for unity and independence.'

On 8 March 1920, as Britain and France were agreeing that the mandate for Syria should go to the Paris government, the General Syrian Congress met again. It cut the ground from under Feisal's feet, preventing his making any compromises with the French. The Congress declared Feisal King of the independent state of Syria (including, according to an account in the Military Museum in Damascus, 'all the lands extending from the Taurus mountains to the Gulf of Aqaba, and from the Mediterranean to the Euphrates'), and rejected both the appointment of a mandatory power and the division of the country.

Britain and France refused to accept the declaration of independence; and in May 1920 the Supreme Council of the League of Nations announced new proprietary arrangements for the Middle East. Iraq and Palestine were to be under British mandates; Lebanon (as a separate state) and the remaining territory of Syria were given to France. The French immediately expanded the territory of Lebanon, incorporating the Syrian city of Tripoli within its borders where it sits, uneasily, to this day.

The first attempt by the Arabs to establish independent nationhood in Syria was crushed in a matter of hours in July 1920 in the barren hills west of Damascus. This was the Battle of Maisaloun – another name that conjures up in Arab minds images of European treachery. The Arab army in Syria, led by officers who had served with the Ottoman forces, vowed during the brief life of the kingdom to fight to protect its independence. But when, on 14 July 1920, the French army commander in Lebanon, General Gouraud, sent an ultimatum to Damascus ordering Syrian acceptance of the League of Nations mandate, Arab officers realized that they faced a formidably superior opponent. At the last moment, King Feisal and his ministers accepted the ultimatum; but because of cut telegraph lines their message never reached the French military headquarters. French forces, consequently, advanced towards Syria. Alarmed by the advance, the Syrians sent Sati' al-Husri to negotiate with General Gouraud. The French commander would not compromise, and demanded further concessions of the Syrians which Husri took back to Damascus. To have accepted the new conditions 'would have met with resistance in the aroused Arab capital, and the government simply failed to act on the demands by the time the deadline expired'.[8] The Arab army was left with no choice but to go into battle. Its commanders knew they faced certain defeat. The French-led force, which included troops from Senegal and countries of north Africa, and was backed by tanks and aircraft, easily crushed the Arabs in a number of brief encounters. According to the account in the Military Museum in Damascus the Syrian force consisted of 'less than 2,000 soldiers, recruits and volunteers, with insufficient weapons and ammunition'.

The final battle came on 24 July 1920 at Maisaloun, close to the modern Damascus–Beirut highway. The remnant of the Arab army found itself trapped in a gently sloping pass, with a large, inhospitable hill blocking its retreat. In contrast to the surrounding terrain, which is barren and rocky, the soil in the pass at Maisaloun is red and rich. Hidden among conifers is a memorial to the battle which snuffed out Arab independence. The gatekeeper at the memorial, Jima'a, told me that the last man in the area who remembered the battle had died in the late 1980s. But it was well known, he went on, that a strong French force had come from Lebanon and defeated the Arabs in clashes in various places. Finally, the Arab commander Youssef al-Azmeh and about twenty of his men found themselves trapped in the pass. 'Youssef al-Azmeh was put up against a tree and shot,' Jima'a said, 'and he was buried here.' The memorial to the commander, and the battle in which he and his men were defeated, is a slab of brown marble on a raised plinth shaded by a plain, silver-painted panoply. A curtain of conifers keeps the memorial to the Arabs' defeat out of the view of motorists on the new highway.

At the Military Museum in Damascus, where an ancient acacia tree drops leaves on to a 155mm canon used by General Gouraud's forces at Maisaloun, the official account says the battle 'opened the road to Damascus to the armies of France and smashed the dream of the first national and independent Arab government'. The occupation of Syria was carried out in accordance with 'the hatched colonialist plot to divide up the lands of the Arabs'.

The arrival of the French army in Damascus marked the start of two decades of colonial rule in Syria, scarred by violence and bitter local opposition to the foreign presence. According to a later assessment of this period, 'from the Syrian and Arab perspective, indeed from the perspective of an impartial observer, France's conduct in Mandated Syria was inexcusably heavy-handed'.[9]

The French military authorities in Damascus sent Feisal into exile. The British government felt embarrassed at its role in the Syrian affair, and did its best to placate the Arab leader whom it had befriended and encouraged. Feisal travelled by train to Palestine. The British High Commissioner there, Sir Herbert Samuel, decided that Feisal 'should be received on Palestine territory, not as a defeated fugitive, but as respected friend; ordered a guard of honour to parade when his train arrived; went, with Storrs, to meet him at a stopping place on his way through'.[10] The British Colonial Secretary, Winston Churchill, acknowledged that French military operations in Syria had been 'extremely painful', but went on to say that the importance of links with France 'have to prevail, and we were not able to do anything to help the Arabs in the matter . . .'.[11]

Feisal's predicament – a leader without territory and without people to lead – was part of a legacy of embarrassment felt by the British towards the whole of the Hashemite family of Mecca. There was also the question of what would happen to Feisal's brother, Abdullah ibn Hussein. When the Syrian Congress met in Damascus to proclaim Feisal King, a group of leading Iraqis had declared their country an independent monarchy with Abdullah on the throne. It was a declaration which never became effective because Iraq, since 1917, had been under British control. When British forces captured Baghdad, Sir Mark Sykes, with his usual idiosyncrasy, advised the War Cabinet that the city 'would be a centre of education and civilization for all the Arabic-speaking world: if it is restless, hostile, or sullen, our influence will wane; if it is friendly, our influence will wax. It will never accept our dominion, but if we play our cards properly by means of "advisers" instead of "rulers", and back Arab nationalism, we shall have a permanent footing at little cost.'[12] But there was a considerable cost, and the footing was certainly not permanent. Iraq was run by a rigid administration imported from imperial India and, in the summer of 1920, after the announcement that the country was to come under a British mandate, the colonial authorities were faced with the difficult and costly task of quelling widespread rioting.

In March 1921, a new formula for Iraq was agreed upon at a meeting in Cairo attended by Churchill and British officials in the Middle East. It was decided that Feisal should be made King of Iraq, in part to compensate him for his humiliation in Syria. To justify the imposition of an Arab leader from the western edge of the Arabian peninsula as ruler of the people of Iraq the British government gave instructions that 'every effort would be made to make it appear that the offer came from the indigenous population rather than from Britain'.[13] In reality the Iraqis were looking to one of their own notables to rule them, and the announcement in August 1921 of over-whelming support for the new king in a referendum could have fooled few people. In that same month Feisal was crowned King of Iraq, with the name of the country changed formally from Mesopotamia. Despite his questionable creden-tials King Feisal proved, in the view of one Iraqi academic to be 'one of the wisest, most liberal and most compassionate leaders the country ever had. He understood the complexity and the mosaic of the country like no other leader since.'

In establishing a monarchy in Iraq Britain felt that its debt to Feisal had been paid; but there was still the future of Abdul-lah to be resolved. While Churchill, then Colonial Secretary, was meeting his advisers in Cairo, Abdullah had arrived in the territory which was eventually to become Transjordan, leading a force of tribesmen with the apparent aim of attacking the French in Syria to avenge the humiliation of his brother. Chur-chill travelled to Jerusalem and had several meetings with Abdullah at which it was agreed that the latter would become Emir of Transjordan (modern-day Jordan, the land to the east of the river of the same name) on a temporary basis until France could be persuaded to allow him on to the throne of Syria. The haughty manner in which British officials dealt with matters of such magnitude is well illustrated in Storrs's account of Churchill's stay in Jerusalem. The Colonial Secretary seemed impatient to get the business settled – the business being a decision on the fate of millions of Arabs – so that he could enjoy and capture on canvas the sites of Jerusalem. Storrs remembered the Churchill visit as being 'brief but memorable. By his swift momentous decision to accept and install the Sherif Abdallah as Emir of Transjordan, he created in a few minutes a new Principality. So appreciative was he of the beauty of the Temple Area by moonlight that he seemed thereafter to grudge every moment spent away from his easel.'[14] In May 1923, Transjordan became an independent state separate from Pales-tine, and therefore not covered by Britain's obligations towards the establishment of a homeland for the Jews. In 1946 Trans-jordan became independent, with Abdullah as King.

The fates of Feisal and Abdullah were settled, but there still remained the problem of persuading King Hussein of the Hejaz to accept the new arrangements in the Middle East agreed at the Cairo conference and during Churchill's meetings with Abdullah. T.E. Lawrence, an advisor on Arab affairs in the Middle East Department of the Colonial Office, was sent to Jeddah in the summer of 1921 to try to speak to the King. Obtaining his agreement was not easy; Hussein, his subsidy from Britain cut, was bitter about the exclusion of the Hashemites from Syria and Palestine. The old man might have served British interests once but, by this time, his worth was evaporating as fast as Lawrence's patience. 'His ambitions', Lawrence reported to London, 'are as large as his conceit, and he showed unpleasant jealousy of his sons.'[15]

Britain's plan at various times during the First World War had been that Hussein might replace the Ottoman Sultan as Caliph of Islam once the Turks had been defeated. However, there was no enthusiasm in London when in 1924, after the Turkish leader Mustafa Kemal Pasha (Ataturk) abolished the Caliphate, Hussein declared himself Caliph.

The move also brought to a head old enmity and rivalry within the Arabian peninsula between the Hashemites and supporters of Abdel Aziz ibn Saud who was recognized by the British as Sultan of Nejd and Dependencies – a large area of central and eastern Arabia. Ibn Saud and his followers were members of the puritanical Wahhabi sect of Sunni Islam and fierce warriors. Hussein's claim to be Caliph led them to attack the Hejaz with a view to bringing the sacred Islamic cities of Mecca and Medina under Wahhabi protection. Hussein abdicated in favour of his son, Ali, and went into exile in October 1924. One year later Ali abandoned Hejaz, allowing the forces of ibn Saud to take control of most of the Arabian peninsula. In 1932 Nejd and Hejaz were merged into the kingdom of Saudi Arabia – but not before further adjustments had been made to borders in the region. Problems arose because the tribes of the Arabian peninsula wandered freely over wide areas of desert and made the idea of a defined border inconceivable. Despite these difficulties, 'the British protectors of Iraq and Kuwait were determined to establish a frontier beyond which Wahhabi power would not be allowed to expand. At Uqair, the seaport of al-Hasa on the Gulf, Sir Percy Cox, British High Commissioner of Iraq, reached an agreement with ibn Saud whereby a large slice of territory claimed by Iraq was allocated to the new kingdom of Iraq. In order to placate ibn Saud, some two thirds of the land that had been considered to belong to Kuwait at the time of the 1913 agreement with the Ottoman government became part of the Nejd. An embarrassed Cox later explained to the Emir of Kuwait that nothing could be done to prevent ibn Saud from taking the territories if he wished.'[16]

Supporters of ibn Saud also carried out frequent raids across the border into Transjordan, backing a claim to a strip of land at the northern end of the Red Sea, including the port of Aqaba. This had been incorporated into the borders of the new emirate in order to give it access to the sea. British troops supported by air power helped the tribes of Transjordan repel the Wahhabi attacks; and Britain stuck to its insistence that Aqaba should remain within the emirate. The loss of Aqaba became a source of bitterness between the Saudis and the Hashemites, and it contributed to the rivalry and hostility between the two clans which has continued with greater or lesser intensity since then. This rivalry has been a constant impediment in the way of moves towards Arab unity – as have disputes between Saudi Arabia and Yemen over disputed border territory, despite the conclusion of an agreement in 1934 supposedly delineating an agreed joint frontier.

In these various ways, the new lines appeared on the map; to this day some of them, like those separating Jordan, Syria and Iraq, look unnaturally rulered and clinical, defying rational justification based on either geography or demography. The outcome of the new borders was that British control extended in a large circle from Egypt and Sudan, passing through Aden to the Gulf sheikhdoms and up to Iraq; then down through Transjordan to Palestine. French control passed through most of north Africa (only Libya was under Italian colonial rule) into Lebanon and Syria. Many changes had been made to the crude divisions envisaged by the Sykes–Picot agreement but the colonial powers achieved in the end what they had set out to do: they established their grip on the region in such a way that they could keep their rival interests in check.

The Middle East that they created was hopelessly unstable, and signs of the instability soon became visible. By 1922 British politicians and officials were beginning to have doubts about the wisdom of some of the appointments which they had made around the region. They decided that Feisal was treacherous, and Abdullah lazy and ineffective. Yet 'in Iraq and Transjordan, Feisal and Abdullah were the rulers whom Britain had installed; Britain had committed itself to the Hashemite cause'. Britain had also lost enthusiasm for the cause of Zionism, so it was hardly surprising that in the years which followed 'British officials were to govern the Middle East with no great sense of direction or conviction.'[17] Because the conviction began to ebb, Britain and France gradually lost the will to resist the national- ist movements which sprung up all around the region demanding independence.

Britain felt the full force of nationalist passions for the first time in Egypt, where its policy-makers and administrators for the region had their headquarters. Even before the outbreak of the war there had been more than just faint stirrings of nationalist discontent. But British officials chose either to ignore the signs or to dismiss them as being the product of a few hotheads. They also ignored the social grievances of poor Egyptians, who constituted the large majority of the popu- lation. During the war, while some cotton magnates and entre- preneurs became rich, most Egyptians suffered – from rising prices or from conscription as labourers with the Allied army. When British troops invaded Egypt in 1882 they promised that the occupation would not last long. The British had been reluc- tant to commit their troops in the first place, and 'knew that the acquisition of Egypt and its incorporation into the empire was out of the question. For one thing it would almost certainly have provoked a European war for which the British govern- ment, with its small army and its continued preoccupation with Irish affairs was quite unprepared.'[18] One month after the invasion, in response to a question in the Commons as to whether Britain contemplated an indefinite occupation of Egypt, the Prime Minister William Gladstone replied, 'Undoubtedly, of all things in the world, that is a thing which we are not going to do.' At the end of the First World War, with martial law lifted, the Egyptians waited for Britain to act in the spirit of the Wilsonian principles and grant the country what they regarded as its long overdue independence.

The Egyptians were disappointed. Word spread in Cairo that Britain had realized the strategic importance of Egypt during the war and was therefore planning to remain, keeping control of the country's legislature and finance. Sa'ad Zaghloul, who had established himself as the leader of the nationalists during the brief session of the consultative assembly just before the outbreak of the war, demanded of the British authorities in Cairo to be allowed to attend the Paris Peace Conference to argue Egypt's case for complete independence. Zaghloul said he planned to lead a delegation of nationalists to Paris. The Arabic word for delegation is 'wafd' – and this is the name which was adopted for the political party which was formed around Zaghloul and which dominated Egyptian politics in the post-war decades. Zaghloul's demand to be present in Paris was turned down flat. A similar request from the Prime Minister, Rushdi Pasha, was rejected. The British Foreign Secretary, Lord Balfour, justifying his rejection of Egyptian nationalist demands to Sir Reginald Wingate, the High Commissioner in Cairo, said 'the stage has not yet been reached at which self-government is possible'.[19]

The stand taken by the British government led to widespread protests across Egypt. In response Whitehall relented, giving permission for the Prime Minister to travel to Paris, but turning down the latter's demand that Zaghloul be part of the delegation. In March 1919, with tension in the country rising, the government resigned. The British authorities, in an attempt to regain the initiative, arrested Zaghloul and deported him to Malta. Their moment of self-congratulation was brief: when news of Zaghloul's fate spread, intense violence erupted and went on for months. Muhammed Hussein Heikal, an Egyptian politician and writer who lived through the troubles, described how they started. News of Zaghloul's arrest, he wrote, 'passed quickly round Cairo and then spread like lightning around the regions'. Heikal remembered seeing a crowd of 'students, workers and effendis' gather at Al-Azhar square in Cairo, some of the demonstrators carrying large branches which they had broken off trees along the streets on the way there to attack passing vehicles. Heikal's account continued: 'I said at the time: "The human animal has been released from his bonds."' Within a few hours 'an astonishing revolution had spread everywhere'.[20] The explosion of four decades of anti-British frustration became known as the 1919 Revolution.

The British, once again, were taken by surprise at the depth of support for the nationalists and by the extent of the violence. The trouble was often exacerbated by over-reaction on the part of British and Australian troops who were embittered by their long wait for demobilization following the ending of the First World War and resentful at being ordered to carry out police work. Thomas Russell, head of the Cairo police, in a letter home on 9 April 1919, wrote 'today, I fear, will be known as a bloody day in Cairo, to history. The town has gone clean mad and for two days the whole city has been given over to frenzied demonstrations . . . Yesterday was bad but today is far worse; the roughs of the town are out, tearing down telephone wires, barricading streets and pillaging.'[21]

Britain responded to the mass violence by relieving Sir Reginald Wingate of his duties and replacing him with General Edward Allenby, fresh from his successes in leading the liberation by the Allies of Palestine and Syria from Ottoman rule. Allenby ordered tough measures to be taken to bring the troubles under control; but he recognized at the same time what his predecessors had been unable or unwilling to see – that denying Egyptian nationalist aspirations was not a workable basis on which to govern the country. Allenby arranged Zaghloul's return from exile. This, unfortunately, changed little. The British government stood as firmly opposed to Egyptian nationalist aspirations as ever, and Zaghloul was no less vociferous in his demand for independence. Rioting resumed and Zaghloul was deported once more. But Allenby stuck to his principles and, in the face of much opposition in London, succeeded in February 1922 in securing from the British government a declaration of Egyptian independence – with strings attached. Britain retained sweeping rights on matters of security and defence, and on the future of Sudan, but Sultan Fuad became King of Egypt.

For the next three decades, Egypt 'was governed by an uneasy and ultimately unworkable balance of forces'[22] made up of the monarchy, the Wafd-dominated parliament and the British authorities. This messy and painful arrangement was resolved only after the 1952 revolution which eventually brought President Nasser to power and heralded the end of the British presence there.

The 1919 Revolution, which forced Britain in the direction of granting a measure of independence to Egypt, was the first success chalked up by nationalists in the Arab world. But it was a distinctively Egyptian affair; nationalist leaders had the limited goal of removing the colonial presence from within their own borders. Nationalist struggles in other countries in the following years were frequently conducted in the name of pan-Arabism but, in practice, the struggles achieved only national independence, leaving the region as a patchwork of sovereign states and destroying the dream of a unified Arab world.

Egypt at this time made no pretence of being part of a pan-Arab nationalist movement. It followed its own course because up to 1922 and well beyond this date it did not consider itself part of the Arab world, but rather as a country with a distinctive past which could trace its origins back to the time of the Pharaohs. Sati' al-Husri happened to be in Cairo during the 1919 Revolution. Because he was 'deeply moved by the spirit of patriotism and sacrifice which he witnessed at that time, Husri believed that the Egyptians were bound to the rest of the Arab world by feelings of Arabism and opposition to foreign rule. He was thus profoundly affected by Egypt's apparent disavowal of Arabism and her lack of concern over the French occupation of Syria. For the next forty years, Husri wrote article after article urging the Egyptians to assume their destined role in the Arab nationalist movement.'[23] Sa'ad Zaghloul, when approached by Arab leaders in 1919 with a view to coordinating a position at the Paris Peace Conference, rejected the suggestion on the grounds that 'our case is an Egyptian and not an Arab one'.[24] The Egyptian author, Taha Hussein, who is regarded as one of the greatest Arab writers of the twentieth century, went so far as to declare in the 1930s that Egypt could be considered part of Europe on the basis of its culture and temperament, having retained its distinctive identity from the Pharaonic era.

The exclusion of Egypt from the cause of pan-Arab nationalism during the important years of the anti-colonial struggles in the Middle East is of huge importance, and it is understandable, with the benefit of knowing how events shaped themselves, that Husri should have been so distressed at the indifference he encountered in Cairo. From the point of view of a supporter of Arabism, to have the region's most powerful and, at the time, richest country turning its back on the regional movement was a major handicap. Jamil Matar, who runs a political research centre in Cairo, says Egypt did not need to look for a modern identity in the region because it had had one of its own 'at least since the time of Muhammed Ali in the nineteenth century. Also the Egyptians are not very ideologically oriented. They have behaved in a nationalist way most of the time, but it has always been pragmatic. When we look back at Muhammed Ali's son Ibrahim, we find he adopted the Arabist point of view when he went to Syria because he found out that an Arab base of influence was going to be useful for Egyptian hegemony in the area.'[25]

Examples of Egyptian pragmatism have continued to appear in the last half of this century. In late 1977, President Anwar Sadat was able, with minimal opposition expressed within his own borders, to break the most sacred of taboos and begin talks with the enemy in Jerusalem, a city regarded by the Arabs as being under Zionist occupation. About a year and a half later, shrugging off the condemnation of his peers around the region, he became the first Arab leader to sign a peace treaty with

Israel. This move led to the political isolation of Egypt within the Arab world for a decade. It has been argued that Sadat's policy of making peace with the Jewish state led directly to his assassination in October 1981. But at no stage in his life was the sense of outrage expressed throughout the Arab world matched by public disorder within Egypt. The prospect of winning American financial support was too appealing. It is an inescapable fact, too, that while intellectuals and others in Egypt have continued to criticize the signing of the peace deal with Israel, the treaty survived the change of presidency and looks set to survive into the twenty-first century.

Egyptian pragmatism could be seen also in the early 1990s, as foreign forces gathered round the banner raised by the United States in preparation for the military assault to liberate Kuwait from Iraqi occupation. President Husni Mubarak had no hesitation in committing his country to the cause, despite widespread distaste at the move expressed on the streets of a number of Arab capitals. It seemed that for most Egyptians – at least for most of those whose concerns extended beyond the daily problems of staying alive – Mubarak had taken the only sensible course, given the country's financial dependence on the United States.

Egypt's confidence in the closing decade of the century to act according to its own interests is based on its size and on the status which it has acquired as the leading country in the Arab world. Egypt acquired this status in the 1950s during the Nasser presidency. After many years of concentration exclusively on the liberation of their own country from Britain, Egyptian leaders sought to play a part within the Arab world – to take up the cause of pan-Arabism. To do so they had to look to the two main centres of Arab nationalism: Damascus and Baghdad.

The Syrian capital was where 'the idea of the Arab nation first became explicit'.[26] The French colonial authorities did not hesitate to send in the army to break up nationalist demonstrations but the mandate power was faced by a formidable nationalist movement which demanded independence for a state incorporating both Palestine and Transjordan. In the opinion of Jamil Matar, 'Nasser fused the anti-British feeling in Egypt which had existed before the 1952 revolution with the wider nationalism which was a Syrian invention, a Syrian ideology.'[27]

As nationalist leaders in Syria found difficulties operating under the restrictions imposed by the French occupation, the centre of anti-colonial, pan-Arab thinking and activity shifted for a time from Damascus to Baghdad. In the aftermath of the Arab revolt, nationalist groups still felt an attachment to the Hashemites and, in particular, towards Feisal, the King of Iraq. The new kingdom, 'although more backward politically and socially, obtained relative independence earlier than the new states created out of Syria'.[28]

King Feisal had been imposed on Iraq, but the monarchy provided a unifying focus for the various groups in the country, notably the Kurds in the north and the large Shiite Muslim population in the south. By the mid-1920s Britain was beginning to relax its tight grip on Iraq, while insisting, despite nationalist opposition, on keeping important security and defence rights. In 1930 an Anglo-Iraqi treaty was signed; Britain, aware by this stage of Iraq's huge potential as an oil producer, secured a twenty-five-year special alliance with Baghdad. Even though Iraq became nominally independent in 1932 and joined the League of Nations, the alliance remained valid.

Nationalists in Iraq felt aggrieved at the way Britain had contrived to keep a foot in the door after independence. So the struggle to remove the presence of foreign troops and officials continued in Iraq as elsewhere. Iraqi nationalists also joined in calls for support for the Arabs of Palestine in the light of the increase in Jewish immigration and the continuing expropriation of land. Nationalists around the region stressed also that one of their goals was pan-Arab unity. In practical terms, this last objective was to be achieved first through a 'reunion of the States of geographical Syria, then a federation of Syria and Iraq; then a looser link with other Arab States'.[29] The assumption was that it was only a matter of time before individual states won their independence, after which the reconstruction of the Arab nation would begin.

Even as late as 1950, Sati' al-Husri, after examining the roots
of divisions within the Arab world, was predicting an eventual
and inevitable union. At a speech in Cairo he blamed the division of the Arab world on 'the bargaining and ambitions of
the foreign states' without regard to 'the views and interests
of the people of the countries'. But he went on to ridicule the
prospect of the people of Syria forming 'a true nation different
from the people of Iraq or Lebanon', concluding that 'the differences we see between the people of these states are temporary
and superficial.'[30]

In the same year, Husri said he heard a group of young men
wondering among themselves how the Arabs lost the battle of
Palestine against the newly-created nation of Israel in 1948,
'even though there were seven Arab states'. Husri's answer
was that their logic was flawed. The Arabs had lost the battle
precisely 'because' there were seven Arab states.[31]

Four years later, with Arab unity remaining elusive, Husri
addressed the failure of states in the region to rebuild the Arab
nation. 'We rose up against the English,' he wrote, with a tinge
of melancholy, 'we revolted against the French . . . We revolted
against those who requisitioned our land and tried to drive
us out.' Arabs suffered torture in this process, casualties were
inflicted on them and many people were killed. Despite all this,
'when we freed ourselves from the yoke of the foreigners we
began to sanctify the borders which they had established in
our lands after they had broken the links between us.'[32]

Efforts to mend the links continued during the 1930s and
1940s, even as states were winning independence. At a meeting
in Jerusalem in 1931, for example, nationalists drew up a
covenant which declared that 'the Arab lands are a complete
and indivisible whole, and the divisions of whatever nature to
which they have been subjected are not approved or recognized
by the Arab nation.'[33] Such declarations fired the imagination
of new generations of Arabs. Hazem Nuseibeh was a student
at the American University of Beirut in the early 1940s. Among
the students, drawn from all over the Arab world, there was
some support for the Communist Party and some for the Syrian
Popular Party (which envisaged a reunited Syria leading a loose

grouping of Arab states), but 'Arab nationalism was the majority view. Of course we were idealistic, but we were just waiting
to graduate so that we could all go back home and start building
the structures and functions of Arab unity. We were impatient
to get going. We were sure about it because we had inherited
the legacy of the Arab rebellion. Everyone believed we were
one country, one nation, one people.'[34]

As Nuseibeh and his colleagues were dreaming of the future,
Europe was involved in the Second World War. Britain, as it
had done in the previous war, looked to the Arabs for support.
The British aim was still to secure continued safe passage for
its ships through the Suez Canal. But new factors had emerged
since the previous world conflict: the realization of the growing
importance of Arab oil; and the perceived threat of Soviet infil-
tration into the region. Also, in the short term, Britain felt its
interests in the Middle East were threatened by the 'growing
influence of the Axis powers and by the Arab nationalist movements' in Iraq and elsewhere which were hostile to the colonial
power.[35] To counter the possible dangers Britain came up with
the idea of encouraging the creation of an institution to promote Arab unity (and, by implication, friendly Arab ties with
Britain). By encouraging unity between regimes which were
sympathetic to Britain the government in London believed it
could eliminate all its concerns in the Middle East. This was
perhaps the first example of the West making mutually beneficial deals with regimes without regard to the interests of the
Arab people.

Britain's ideas about Arab unity were first revealed by the
Foreign Secretary Anthony Eden in May 1941. In the course
of a speech in London he said 'many Arab thinkers desire for
the Arab peoples a greater degree of unity than they now enjoy.
In reaching out towards this unity they hope for support. No
such appeal from our friends should go unanswered. It seems
to me both natural and right that the cultural, and economic
ties, too, should be strengthened. His Majesty's Government
for their part will give their full support to any scheme that
commands general approval.'[36] Four years later, the League of
Arab States was formed. The creation of this body might have

been judged by some as an important step along the road to
Arab unity. But Hazem Nuseibeh is among those Arabs who
viewed the manner of its formation – and in particular Britain's
motives for supporting it – as a move which forced the implied
acceptance of the borders drawn by the colonialists and therefore dealt a blow to the cause of pan-Arabism. 'Unfortunately,'
Nuseibeh said, 'Mr Anthony Eden came and he saw that [Arab]
unity was going to follow immediately after states gained their
independence. So he made his famous declaration that the
British government looks with favour on the unity of the Arab
world. But actually this pre-empted the real unity. Reuniting
Syria would have been the first step – further cooperation
would have followed.' Nuseibeh admits, whatever role Britain
may have played in encouraging the process, that the newly
independent Arab states were quick – in Husri's words – to
'sanctify' existing borders. Nuseibeh's answer to the question
posed earlier about why independent Arab states did not unite
is similar to that given by other intellectuals in the region.
'Once you create an entity,' he said, 'it has a tendency to self-
perpetuate itself. And this is what happened in the various
former provinces of Syria and elsewhere. The territories
became independent. Each had its own head of state, its own
flag, its own borders, its own currency, its own local pride.
Now we are unable to unify anyone.'[37]

   The formation of the Arab League revealed the kind of rivalries which have bedevilled inter-state relations ever since. Arab
states came together to form the League, as one observer said,
'not in amity, but in a contest of wills and struggle for prestige
between the then Prime Ministers of Iraq and Egypt, Nuri Pasha
al-Said and Mustafa Pasha al-Nahas'.[38] Egypt, encouraged by
Britain, took the initiative in early moves to bring together the
seven Arab states which were independent at the time. It might
seem ironic that the one nation which had distanced itself from
the pan-Arab cause should have found itself playing this role.
But there was a reason: Britain decided that 'Egypt – the site
of the Middle East Supply Centre and focus of the Allied war
effort in the region – would make the best headquarters for
any Western-sponsored Arab federation ... Reluctantly Nuri

al-Said and other Arab leaders came to accept the inevitable: there was no alternative to Egypt.'³⁹

Both Iraq and Transjordan had welcomed Britain's support for the concept of Arab unity. Each put forward its interpretation of how unity should be achieved. Nuri al-Said called for Iraq to be joined in union with a reunified Syria. Egypt and the Arabian peninsula would be excluded. Cairo, not surprisingly, rejected this plan. King Abdullah responded to Britain's initiative by repeating his demand for the reunification of Syria, and called on Syrian leaders to help him achieve his aim. The Transjordanian initiative came to nothing because 'Syrians suspected his motives and argued that Abdullah's kingdom should be annexed to the Syrian republic since it had been a Syrian province during the Ottoman empire.'⁴⁰ Against the background of these squabbles, Egypt took the opportunity offered by Britain to assert a claim to be the leading Arab powerbroker. Nahas brought together officials from Saudi Arabia, Syria, Iraq, Lebanon, Yemen and Transjordan, along with representatives of the Palestinians, to discuss the formation of the new grouping. The pact of the Arab League was signed in Cairo on 22 March 1945. The League has provided a useful forum for the Arabs; but judged from the perspective of those seeking full unity it has inherent flaws. Far from breaking down frontiers the Arab League pact stresses 'the independence and sovereignty' of individual states. It also undermines the prospect of common Arab action by stating that majority decisions taken by the League 'shall be binding only upon those states which have accepted them'. In other words, states which choose not to vote on a resolution can disregard it.

The sanctification of borders and state institutions has proved to be irreversible. During the Nasser era, when the cause of Arab unity was pursued with more vigour and enthusiasm than at any time before or since, popular response within the Arab world was enormous. The Voice of the Arabs radio station beamed Nasser's ideas into households all around the region. In this way, the President talked directly to the people, by-passing leaders and regimes. But nationalist sentiments have proved no more effective than the bond of common language and culture in breaking down borders or destroying the vested interests of individual regimes. By the 1950s, independence and sovereignty were firmly entrenched. The humiliating defeat of the Arabs by Israel in the 1967 Middle East war crushed both President Nasser and the pan-Arabism for which he had stood.

Another obstacle blocked the path of pan-Arabists in the period before 1967: the differing nature of the independence won by individual states. Arab countries under colonial rule had looked forward to the day when they would be free and independent. But 'to be independent, in the language of the time, was to have internal autonomy and be a member of the League of Nations. But it did not exclude (in fact it almost implied) a permanent relationship with the former occupying power: the maintenance of military bases and economic and cultural links, the subordination of policy in major matters of foreign relations.'[41] It goes without saying that it was invariably in the interests of the former ruling powers to encourage the development of the individual states in small, manageable units, rather than allowing the birth of a large, unwieldy and possibly (to Western interests) threatening union of Arab countries.

A common view among Arab people (as distinct from the regimes and those associated with them) is that the region has never fully shaken off the controlling hand of the West, the presence of which is blocking any prospect of Arab union. Mahjoub Omar believes that 'those countries which emerged after colonization are still not fully independent. Our ex-colonists were not that stupid; they left, yes. But they built something to represent their interests. We have elites – military sometimes, nationalist sometimes, tribalist sometimes – and they find that to be a ruler in this international order you have to keep your nation state, your flag, your chair at the UN, your membership of the International Monetary Fund, and so on.'[42]

The region in the Middle East where the hand of the West can be seen most clearly is the Gulf, which was distanced to a large extent from the Arab nationalist movement both by its geographical position and because of the tiny size of the indigenous population. The latter factor ruled out the whole concept of a mass movement. Saudi Arabia was unique in never coming under direct foreign control, while the Gulf sheikhdoms had long-standing arrangements with the British (beginning with Muscat in 1798) 'which kept local power in the hands of those who signed the treaties with Britain'. The discovery of oil by British and American companies was the most important factor which mitigated against Arab national-ism taking root in the Gulf, once mutually beneficial arrange-ments had been made with the firms concerned. As a result, 'for a period of time, some of these statelets showed a certain sympathy for the Arab national movement', while they quar-relled with dominant British or American transnational oil companies, and while they 'feared absorption by neighbouring big countries. Such sympathy was most noticeable in those statelets, usually built around trading and fishing ports, where there happened to have been a tradition of enterprise and a budding local bourgeoisie.' There were pro-Nasser demon-strations in Bahrain in 1956, and keeping the lid on anti-Western sentiments felt by sections of the population there has been a task of the security services ever since. In general in the Gulf, as oil production developed, so the attention of the sheikhdoms was directed more at establishing trading and marketing relations with the West than with political causes in the region. Leading the way was a new power in the Arab world, Saudi Arabia, 'whose pull towards identification with American interests and designs and away from the twin causes of Arab national liberation and national unification became more and more difficult to resist'.[43]

In the second half of the twentieth century the West's desire to obtain a secure flow of oil from the Middle East came to dominate its policies in the region, relegating to second and third places moves to check the expansion of Soviet influence and the continued support for Israel. Up to the October 1973 Arab–Israeli war, when the Arabs succeeded briefly in cutting supplies as a weapon against the West, the future of oil was closely linked with nationalist themes. 'Arab Oil for the Arabs' was a common slogan during the Nasser period. Since 1973,

splits within the Arab world and the waning of the pan-Arab
movement have left most ordinary people in the region with
a feeling of dejection and despair. They are resigned to
accepting the fact that oil, contrary to their hopes and expectations, will not be the means by which the majority of Arabs
will acquire economic security and regain self-esteem. Instead
it will bring riches to a small minority of Arabs who have signed
lucrative contracts with the West. The ruling establishments in
the Gulf and in all other Arab states have vested interests of
one kind or another which they want to protect. The prospect
of any government abandoning its privileges for the ideals of
regional unity is regarded by Arabs everywhere as unrealistic.
Yet that does not mean that all Arabs have abandoned the
ideals of Arabism. Many believe that Islam will provide the
inspiration, leading to the overthrow of corrupt secular
regimes. In time, the argument goes, Islam will dominate the
Middle East, making national boundaries unnecessary.

Islam played an important role in the long struggle for independence in Algeria. In the countries at the western end of the
Arab world, the campaigns to end colonial rule were motivated
by the desire for national liberation, as distinct from the pan-
Arabism espoused in Syria and Iraq. France had captured
Algeria in 1830, Tunisia in 1881 and Morocco during the 1920s.
The nature of the French occupation of north Africa differed
considerably from the rule by France and Britain of other Arab
states further east. Large numbers of French farmers, businessmen and others settled in Algeria, Tunisia and Morocco.
Their presence 'threatened the population of north Africa with
permanent subjection and the gradual loss of their lands; it
made it more difficult for them to obtain or the French government to grant independence; and it led to the creation of a
French administration (whether direct as in Algeria or indirect
as in the other two) geared to the needs of the French communities more than of the indigenous population.'[44] The
trauma of this disruption and destruction of the patterns of
traditional life is still felt in the three north African countries
(in particular in Algeria) many years after independence was
won.

At the beginning of the twentieth century, French-educated Algerians and Tunisians began asking their colonial masters politely whether there was any chance of their being given improved positions within their own countries, without posing any threat to French domination. Their requests brought no significant change. Around the time of the First World War, the thoughts of intellectuals in Algeria and Tunisia turned towards the broader goal of independence, a move which gained momentum after 1918. For Algerians, to a greater degree than anyone else, more than a century of forced immersion in the French language and culture gave lingering attachments to their Arab and Islamic heritage a special poignancy as a sense of national identity was reborn. Once they began to see themselves as Algerians, rather than French, 'the nationalists felt the need to reassert their link with the past before it was too late.'[45] The full-scale battle for independence, launched in 1954 by the Front de la Libération Nationale (FLN), was in part inspired and encouraged by the secular pan-Arab nationalism of President Nasser of Egypt; but the war, in which one million people died before independence was won in 1962, was fought in the name of Islam.

National liberation movements in Morocco appeared in the 1930s and developed full impetus after the Second World War. Tunisian efforts were led by Habib Bourguiba, founder of the Destour party, with strong trade union backing. In Morocco, support rallied round the Istiqlal (Independence) party, which enjoyed the support of Sultan Muhammed V. After initial attempts by the French to quash the two movements, both countries won independence in 1956. There was talk at this period, as there is still, of the need for unity among the states of north Africa. But here again, borders and separate state institutions born out of the colonial era appear to have been sanctified by post-independence regimes.

The extent to which the former colonial powers were directly responsible for the continued fragmentation of the Arab world after independence is debatable. What counts is the Arab perception of that role in the context of the Arab–West divide. Unassailable, surely, is the charge levelled at the European

powers by those groups whose claims at the end of the First
World War could not be accommodated within the patchwork
of states stitched together by Britain and France. The
Armenians, for example, came to the post-war conferences
with demands for a vast state on territory of the former Ottoman empire with outlets on the Mediterranean, the Black Sea
and the Caspian Sea. Although the Armenians admitted that
they did not constitute a popular majority in the area that they
claimed, their delegation 'laid the blame directly on Turkish
atrocities before and during the war'. The Armenians asserted
that once their state was established, exiles from around the
world would return, increasing the numbers. The European
powers 'showed a great reluctance to make any specific commitment on the Armenian question. Although pledged to the
general concept of an Armenian state, neither Britain, France,
nor Italy had any desire to become too directly involved in the
actual creation and support of the state', on the grounds of
finance and out of an unwillingness to take on the rigours of
the military and political commitment which would be needed.
In addition there would be the danger of alienating 'not only
the Turks but the whole Muslim population of the Near East'[46].
This lack of support from powerful nations was crucial. The
Treaty of Lausanne of July 1923 which ended the Graeco–
Turkish war recognized Turkish sovereignty over most of what
is present-day Turkey, and 'the long-suffering Armenians lost
their hopes of independence in the process'.[47]

The Lausanne Peace Conference also reversed a commitment
made to the Kurds – a mountain people inhabiting an area of
territory split between Iraq, Syria, Turkey and Iran – which
had been made at the post-First World War Peace Conference.
In Iraq, the Kurdish people, like other tribes, have launched
periodic revolts against the central authorities in Baghdad.
These uprisings have always been crushed. Under the regime
of President Saddam Hussein the relationship between Baghdad and the Kurds changed: the latter suffered massacres and
persecution at the hands of the Iraqi army and no longer feel
themselves to be fully integrated into the country. The Kurdish
cause has frequently been a pawn in both regional and inter-

national rivalries. Apart from a period after the 1991 Gulf war when the Kurds, under the strong but false impression that the West was making good its errors of the past by backing their armed revolt against the regime of President Saddam Hussein, the Kurdish question has never received the spotlight of international attention.

It was, perhaps, too late in the latter half of the twentieth century to start changing the lines drawn on the map by the colonialists on the basis of old claims. President Saddam Hussein tried to justify his invasion of Kuwait on the grounds that the emirate had been carved unnaturally out of Iraq to suit the interests of the colonial powers. He said he was merely re-attaching the branch, Kuwait, to the stem, Iraq. The Western-led international community insisted that there would be no re-drawing of lines and the Iraqi army was driven out of Kuwait. Saddam Hussein's argument appealed to a large number of Arabs, not because they were particularly keen to see colonial lines rubbed off the map, but because it seemed to them that Israel – since 1948 – had been doing precisely what the international community was forbidding: drawing new lines on the map, after the gradual acquisition of Arab lands in a series of wars.

CHAPTER FOUR

Defeat and Despair

The names are inscribed in gold lettering on glass and mounted against a green background. More than two thousand names appear, in thirty-six neat columns. This is a list of Jordanians killed in war (a small fraction of the total, according to independent assessments), and is found in the Martyrs' Memorial Museum in Amman, at the top of a carpeted corridor which winds and climbs around the walls of the giant stone building. All the way up the corridor one passes displays illustrating the various important events in Jordan's history in which the military were involved. Most of the space is dedicated to the years of the Arab revolt and the creation of the state of Transjordan – the pre-1948 period. Since then, Jordan's external wars have been fought exclusively against Israel. These were not occasions of triumph for the Jordanians any more than for other Arabs involved.

The first Arab–Israeli conflict, the Palestine war of 1948, is given a brief mention in the museum. One is told that '4,500 men of the Jordan army saved Jerusalem and forced enemy troops in the Jewish quarter to surrender' and that 'Jordan's forces took up positions at the strategically important positions at Latroun and Bab al-Wad controlling the road from the coast to Jerusalem – and cut enemy lines of communication. During the severe fighting in this area, the enemy suffered a signal defeat.' The account is highly selective, referring only to isolated events in the opening days of the conflict: the subsequent rout of the Arab armies by the Israeli forces is omitted.

The Six-Day Arab–Israeli war of June 1967, in which Jordan

LEBANON

SYRIA

Mediterranean
Sea

● Haifa

Sea of
Galilee

Nazareth

Nablus

River Jordan

Tel Aviv
Jaffa
(to Arab state)

Jerusalem

Jericho
● Amman

Bethlehem

Hebron ●

Dead
Sea

Beersheba

TRANSJORDAN

::::: Jewish state under UN plan

0   30 miles

0   50 kilometres

EGYPT

UN partition plan
for Palestine: 1947

Gulf of Aqaba

Arab land occupied after 1967

lost control of East Jerusalem and the West Bank, receives no mention in the museum. A general book about Jordan issued by the Ministry of Information in Amman says only that in June 1967 Jordan 'was forced to enter a war with Israel, the result of which was the loss of a precious part of the homeland'. At the Military Museum in Damascus, the official account of the 1967 war is that 'the Zionist enemy was able to achieve a temporary victory' because of both 'its aerial superiority and the imperialist and international support' which it received.

Coming to terms with defeat would mean coming to terms both with the failure of Arabs to sink their differences in a common cause and with the existence of the state of Israel. Of all the Arab governments, only the Egyptian has concluded that joint Arab military action will never succeed, and has accorded formal recognition to the Jewish state. The PLO, despite considerable opposition within the Palestinian movement, did the same in 1993. The inability of Arab regimes as a whole since 1948 to devise a way of inflicting military defeat on Israel is a source of profound depression and despair among the non-Israeli inhabitants of the region. Frustration at Arab impotence is matched by resentment at Western support for the Jewish state – as strong as ever, more than forty years after the creation of Israel. An Arab political commentator summarized the overwhelming popular view expressed from one end of the region to the other when he wrote: 'Israel was, still is and will remain a Western body implanted in this region.'[1] The role of the West in supporting Israel is interwoven in Arab minds with the trauma of defeat and the knowledge that so many lives were thrown away in fruitless attempts to challenge the military superiority of the Jewish state. It is estimated that in the 1967 war alone at least 26,000 Arabs were killed.[2]

Five full-scale wars have been fought between the Arabs and the Israelis – in 1948, 1956, 1967, 1973 and 1982 – the last resulting from the Israeli invasion of Lebanon. Interspersed with the wars have been frequent smaller-scale, but still significant, military encounters, mostly involving Israel and Arab groups based in Lebanon. The Middle East wars (with the exception of that of 1973) have led not just to huge losses of life and the further erosion of Arab morale and self-esteem, but to the steady accumulation by Israel of territory and to the continuing displacement of Arab families.

One can find some of these families at sixty-one camps administered by the United Nations Relief and Works Agency for Palestine Refugees in the Near East (UNRWA) in Jordan, Syria and Lebanon, and in the Israeli-occupied West Bank and Gaza Strip. Around 800,000 Palestinians live in these camps, while a further 1.5 million are registered with UNRWA as refugees living outside. The camps and their inhabitants are tangible reminders both of military defeat and of the collective failure of Arab regimes to shape the region to the satisfaction of its inhabitants. Palestinian leaders argue that the continued existence of the camps is necessary to remind the world of their people's plight and to stress their determination to return eventually to their homes. While the political symbolism of the camps may be acceptable, some Arab intellectuals have questioned the need to keep the refugees living in the kind of squalor that one finds in these camps. 'There is plenty of money in the Palestinian community scattered around the world,' one Arab intellectual said. 'The Palestinians have a responsibility to lift themselves by their own bootstraps.' Until September 1993 the possiblity of wealthy Palestinians donating money to rehouse and resettle refugees was remote, not least because the leaders of the community, and even the refugees themselves, would have regarded such gestures as a sign of defeat, suggesting that the struggle to regain lost territory had been abandoned. The acceptance by the PLO of the autonomy agreement for the occupied territories in 1993 marked the formal abandoment of the struggle to recover those areas of Palestine incorporated into Israel in 1948.

The refugees, victims of circumstance and of political manipulation, feel neglected both by Arab governments and by the world outside, in particular, the West. 'Britain alone should be paying for the education of all these children,' a teacher at a school in the Baqa'a camp north of Amman said. 'Britain is the country responsible for all this.'

For young children in the Baqa'a camp, school provides a

few hours each day of escape from the difficulties of life centred
on the 100-square-metre shelters allocated to each family. The
youngsters learn with enthusiasm. 'Farisa finds a coin,' the
children in one English class were declaiming in unison when
I was shown in. Youthful enthusiasm and a desire, no doubt,
to demonstrate newly acquired skills had prompted one student
to write in English on the wall outside the classroom 'Easy
come, easy go'. But long before those children reach adulthood
they will realize that the message contained in that English
aphorism is inappropriate for the Palestinian people in exile.
Easy come, perhaps, but certainly not easy go. 'Britain and the
West dumped us here,' Ali, who was born a refugee in 1950,
said. 'It was Britain and other countries which gave Palestine
to Israel on a golden platter.' Over the years Ali's family, like
many others, found themselves scattered around the countries
of the Arab world in search of jobs. 'Probably God chose it for
the Palestinians,' he continued, 'to remain homeless because
he wanted them to build other Arab countries. If you went to
the moon you would probably find a Palestinian there.'

Life in Baqa'a is tough, but nothing like as difficult as in the
camps in the occupied Gaza Strip or in Lebanon. The rigours of
camp life in Lebanon have been compounded by the country's
involvement in wars, both internal and external (involving
Syria and Israel). There have also been long and bruising
clashes on Lebanese soil between opposing factions within the
Palestinian movement.

The despair caused by defeat is felt not just by Palestinians
but by the Arabs as a whole. An Egyptian economist and
political commentator Fawzy Mansour has written of 'the
implantation of Israel in the heart of the Arab world' and 'the
progressive infirmity with which the Arab world seems to have
been stricken' in the years since 1948. In that period, the
Jewish state had 'fought four wars with its neighbours,
interspersed with countless raids, strikes, incursions and campaigns, and in all four major confrontations the Arab side has
been defeated.'[3]

The first defeat came moments after the state of Israel had
been created. Early in the 1940s, even though the Arabs were

becoming increasingly alarmed by the stream of Jewish immigration into Palestine, many still felt that the creation of a state
for the Jews could be avoided. Hazem Nuseibeh recalled being
a student at the American University of Beirut in those days.
It was an era when dreams of imminent Arab unity in the
new post-colonialist world precluded serious thought about the
implications of events in Palestine. 'I do not believe that Zionism was very much on our minds in those days,' he said. 'We
understood that there was a Jewish national home being built
in Palestine. But the Jews then still represented a minority,
albeit a sizeable one. It never occurred to us that six or seven
years later they would create a state which would totally oblit-
erate our national existence. Not in our dreams or nightmares
could we imagine that this could happen.'4

During the Second World War thousands of Jews sought
refuge from the Nazis in Palestine; many entered illegally
despite British attempts to control the flow of immigrants.
British troops and police found themselves trapped hopelessly
in the middle of the intensifying violence between Jews and
Arabs. Public opinion in Britain demanded the withdrawal of
British troops. With increasing concern being expressed in Arab
capitals about the tightening of the Zionists' grip on Palestine,
Britain in February 1947 handed the problem over to the
United Nations. Six months later a Special Committee on Palestine (UNSCOP) made a majority proposal that two separate
states should be created, one Arab and one Jewish. Jerusalem
would be administered by international trusteeship. The proposal envisaged the Jewish state acquiring 55 per cent of Palestine, even though the Jews were still a minority (680,000,
against 1.3 million Arabs). While Zionist leaders were not
happy at the prospect of Jerusalem being put beyond their
jurisdiction they accepted the partition plan. The Arabs rejected
it. As always they 'bitterly opposed partition but they were
especially outraged because the proposed Jewish state would
include almost as many Arabs as Jews'.5 In September 1947
Britain announced that it would be relinquishing its mandate
for Palestine the following April; and in November the United
Nations General Assembly endorsed the partition plan in a

motion passed by 33 votes to 13. All Arab and some Asian states voted against it, as did Greece and Cuba. Britain was among the nations which abstained. The vote 'confirmed Arab fears, and seemed to presage the establishment of an alien and hostile Zionist state in their midst'.[6]

As the day approached when Britain was to pull out of Palestine the violence intensified still further, reaching the level of civil war. The two armed Zionist underground groups Irgun and the Stern Gang joined forces with the Haganah, the Jewish army, to take over vacated British positions and force as many Arabs as possible out of their homes by direct violence and by intimidation. On 9 April 1948, Irgun terrorists massacred 250 Arabs in the village of Deir Yasin, near Jerusalem – an event which has never been forgotten in the Arab world. (Arab retaliation for the Deir Yasin massacre came four days later when 77 people – mainly Jewish doctors and nurses – travelling in a convoy to Mount Scopus in Jerusalem were killed in an ambush.)[7] The Deir Yasin massacre was perhaps the most gruesome act perpetrated against the Arabs of Palestine at the time, but Zionist fighters also used force to break down resistance in parts of Jerusalem, Jaffa, Acre, Haifa and Tiberias. During this period tens of thousands of Arabs fled from their homes. When the battle for Jaffa ended in April 1948, for example, only 3,000 out of the original Arab population of 70,000 remained.[8] Most families left their homes in the belief that they would be able to return after a short time, once the troubles had subsided. Many are still waiting in exile – at the Baqa'a camp in Jordan, at Shatila in Lebanon, and elsewhere. The overwhelming majority of refugees came from towns and villages which have been inside the borders of Israel since 1948. They have no prospect of returning home; and even if a Palestinian state is established in the West Bank and Gaza Strip, there is unlikely to be space to accommodate them.

The United States, which had backed the 1947 partition plan, watched with horror the breakdown of law and order. With no provisions in the plan for the mechanics of dividing Palestine, Washington indicated that it would no longer support the forcible partition of the land. But the Zionists, with their final goal in sight, refused to allow last-minute dithering in the American capital to ruin their plans. In the United States, 'the Zionists mounted mass public rallies, lobbied [President] Truman, [Chief of Staff] Marshall and congressmen and ran advertisements in the press. They were in a strong position: New York [where a high percentage of voters were Jewish] with its forty-seven electoral votes was seen as the key state in the forthcoming presidential election.'[9] Not for the first time or the last, the Jewish lobby acted decisively and effectively. One of the most important weapons in the armoury of that lobby has always been the ability to set up lines of communication to those holding key positions of power. There was no one in a better position to help the Zionists at crucial moments in 1947 and 1948 than President Truman. He faced opposition from the State Department which argued against partition on the grounds that it would 'place the United States in the position of favouring the creation of a state against the wishes of its indigenous inhabitants'. But Truman used his influence to make sure that the Jewish lobby's views won the day. Study of his private correspondence 'suggests that the President had no particular sympathy for the Jews. But he wanted to be re-elected. In his diagnosis the Jews in the United States could do that.'[10] The birth of the Jewish state on 14 May 1948 marks the point, therefore, when American and Israeli interests became enmeshed and when the United States began taking over from Britain and France as the Western power with which the Arabs would have to deal – by way either of cooperation or confrontation – for the rest of the twentieth century. 'Jewish Palestine State Is Recognized by U.S. – Jerusalem Battle Starts', banner headlines in the New York Herald Tribune declared, 'Bagpipes Skirl, Snipers Duel As Britain's Mandate Ends'.

Within hours the confrontation had developed into something much more serious than the duelling of snipers. On 15 May, troops from Syria, Lebanon, Transjordan, Iraq and Egypt crossed into Palestine. While the populations of the states from which the troops were drawn far exceeded that of Israel, the size of the combined force facing a Jewish army of some 60,000 men was no more than about 18,000.[11] In the years leading up to the creation of the state of Israel, the Jewish population had organized itself into a powerful underground force which became the army of the new nation. Another of the Israelis' strengths lay in the fact that many of its men had had considerable battle experience fighting with the Allies during the Second World War. By contrast, the Arab soldiers were inexperienced, and the individual units from the different countries lacked coordination. But they went into battle encouraged by a fever of popular enthusiasm and support throughout the region. The assumption among the majority of Arabs in this conflict, as in others which followed, was that victory was inevitable. The Arabs enjoyed some early successes, notably in cutting the main road between Tel Aviv and West Jerusalem – one of the few events in the campaign acknowledged by the military museum in Amman. The cutting of the road put West Jerusalem under partial siege (only partial because the Jews were able with difficulty to keep a secondary line open between the two cities).

One month after the outbreak of hostilities a four-week ceasefire was secured by a United Nations mediator, Count Folke Bernadotte of Sweden. During the lull in the fighting the new Israeli army smuggled, by ship and by plane, large quantities of weapons and ammunition into the country and reorganized for the next round of hostilities. The size of the Arab force was increased to 45,000 while the truce held, but little was done to improve the coordination between the various units. As soon as the fighting resumed the Israelis moved fast, breaking the blockade of West Jerusalem and capturing Nazareth and other areas of Galilee. Count Bernadotte proposed a modified partition plan in which 'Jerusalem was to be an international city under United Nations control; the Negeb would go to the Arabs together with Lydda and Ramle; in return Israel would get Galilee. Bernadotte stressed that the Arab refugees should have the right to return home.' The day after this plan was submitted to the UN, Bernadotte was murdered by the Stern Gang.[12] Four decades later its leader, Yitzhak Shamir, became Prime Minister of Israel.

The Palestine war ended in the opening weeks of 1949, and in the months which followed armistice agreements were

signed with Egypt, Lebanon, Jordan and Syria (but not with
Iraq which had also taken part in the war but did not share
borders with Israel). The outcome, from the Arab perspective,
was a catastrophe. The Palestine war has been referred to by
the Arabs ever since simply as 'the disaster' – al-Nahda. The
minimal aim of the Arab armies had been to secure the 45
per cent of the territory of Palestine allotted to them in the UN
partition arrangement. In the end, land was lost. The new map,
when compared with the original UN partition plan, showed
that Israel had managed to expand the area of its territory by 21
per cent, giving it control over 80 per cent of the former mandate.
The Arab view was that the 'implant from the West' had been
allowed to trample on UN agreements (even though the partition plan had been rejected by the Arabs at the time) and
impose its will on the indigenous population without the world
appearing to care. The mould for the next five decades of Arab–
Western distrust over the question of Israel had been cast.

Another aspect of the 1948 trauma for the Arabs, which
has lingered for the subsequent fifty years, relates to the mass
uprooting of 800,000 people – half the population of Palestine.
Most of these people, and their descendants, are still living in
refugee camps. The widespread indifference in the West then
and in the following years to the plight of the refugees is in
stark contrast with the concern for the welfare of the displaced
Jews of Europe. The Arabs believe that the roots of indifference
lie in Western racism towards them, and in an instinctive desire
to protect Israel at any cost. The real reason, though, seems to
be linked to the overwhelming sense of guilt felt by Western
nations following the Western history of anti-Semitism, culminating in the persecution and extermination of the Jews in
Europe by the Nazis. The British Foreign Secretary in 1949,
Ernest Bevin, was correct when he said young Arabs 'consider
that for the Arab population, which has been occupying Palestine for more than twenty centuries to be turned out of their
land and homes to make way for another race is a profound
injustice'. The Foreign Secretary marvelled that the conscience
of the world was so little stirred by the tragedy of the Arab
refugees.[13]

In the months after the ending of the Palestine war, the Arabs began asking themselves what had gone had wrong. Among ordinary people 'blame was divided between Britain, the United States and the Arab leaders whose incompetence and divisive rivalries had contributed to the miserable Arab performance'.[14] Arabs pointed to the fact that the United States (and in particular President Harry Truman) had played an important role in enabling the state of Israel to be created when it was. The Arabs also accused the British of having allowed the Jews to stamp their authority on Palestine in the closing days of the mandate at the expense of the indigenous population. But the Arabs could not lay the blame for their military defeat in the Palestine war only on external factors. The conflict exposed the painful reality of disunity. As the leading proponent of Arab nationalism Sati' al-Husri said, the disaster occurred precisely 'because' there were seven separate Arab countries facing the Jewish state.[15] The lack of planning and coordination on the part of the leaders gave the Arab soldiers little chance of success. More seriously than this, there were major differences in the aspirations of the various leaders. Before the war started King Abdullah of Transjordan, for example, had been having secret contacts with Zionist leaders in an attempt to set up 'what amounted to a strategic alliance which would enable him to take over the Arab part of Palestine and exclude the Palestine nationalist leaders, such as the Husseinis, who were hostile to the Hashemites'.[16] The plan was scuppered by the Palestine war. As this conflict was nearing its end in December 1948, King Abdullah made another move which enraged many Arabs and served to hamper still further attempts to reach agreement on coordinated action against Israel. The king organized 'a ceremonial conference at Jericho where Palestinian and Transjordanian delegates favoured the joining of Palestine and Transjordan as an indivisible Hashemite Kingdom of Jordan'.[17] In this context 'Palestine' meant the eastern half of Jerusalem and the territory on the western bank of the River Jordan. This area remained under Jordanian control until the 1967 Middle East war.

In the years immediately after the 1948 'disaster' Arab

opinion was radicalized.[18] The defeat appeared to be the direct result of a lax and disorganized Arab stand in the years during which Zionist Jews were working and fighting for the creation of Israel. The unwillingness of the politicians to face the reality of what was happening in Palestine before 1948 seemed to have been mirrored by the failure of Arab military leaders on the battlefield. In Egypt, 'younger officers who served in the war became convinced of the criminal incompetence' of their rulers. Supplies of food and medicine 'were inadequate, while arms were obsolete and in some cases worthless. Senior officers gave contradictory and meaningless orders, while some showed downright incompetence.'[19]

The humiliation of 1948, in all its aspects, 'started a far-reaching debate on the reasons for the Arab failure'.[20] One of the leading contributors to this debate was Qustantin Zurayq, a Syrian academic, who wrote a book entitled *The Meaning of the Disaster*. He argued that a true Arab nation with the ability to confront the Zionists did not exist, adding that only a complete transformation of all aspects of life in the region to take account of modern developments would enable the Arabs to confront the dangers, as he correctly predicted, of continued Israeli expansion. The Zionist victory in 1948, he went on, had its origin not in 'the predominance of one people over another, but in the preference of one system over another. The reason is that the roots of Zionism are deeply embedded in modern Western life. In the meantime, we continue to live far away from this life, expressing hostility to it. They live in the present and the future, whereas we continue to dream our dreams of the past and anaesthetize ourselves with its former glory.'[21]

Forty years later the same debate was continuing. Fawzy Mansour wrote that 'the past, a very much idealized past needless to say, often presents itself with a persistence and vigour nowhere matched in the rest of the world as a viable substitute for the present.' This backward-looking attitude, he argued, has hampered genuine analysis of Arab failings in war, and 'following every defeat, an apparently valid excuse for the defeat was proffered: the fact that the Arab governments and armies were controlled by the imperialist powers in 1948; that they did not have time to digest new weapons recently made available to them in 1956; that a corrupt and inefficient bureaucracy disaffected by radical social transformations had managed to entrench itself in high command in 1967. With every excuse came the implicit or explicit promise that if the Israelis came again (as they were sure to do), the Arabs would not this time be caught off guard. But when the next round came, the Arabs found themselves confronted with an even greater defeat, a less plausible excuse and still greater imperialist–Israeli gains.'[22] Another Egyptian commentator, Jamil Matar, writing twenty-five years after the 1967 defeat, also denounced the tendency among Arab regimes to find excuses for defeat and ascribe every setback to some kind of conspiracy. 'The word "plot" is always used by those who have been politically or militarily defeated to cover up for their inadequacy. They do not want to admit that their enemy's political strategy is superior to theirs . . . the idea of the plot has led in turn to an extension of the repercussions of defeat.'[23]

The Arab disaster in June 1967 was the most costly and most humiliating of all the defeats at the hands of Israel. It changed the face of the Middle East and left a wound on the Arabs' consciousness which shows no signs of healing. Fouad Ajami, a Lebanese American academic, wrote a book which examines Arab political thought from 1967 onwards. He described his study as a 'chronicle of illusions and despair'.[24] The despair felt by the Arabs after 1967 was captured in a poem by the Syrian poet Nizar Qabbani called 'Footnotes to the Book of the Setback'. (President Nasser, in the wake of the humiliating defeat had euphemistically described the outcome of the war as 'a setback'.) Qabbani's poem 'was banned throughout the Arab world, and as a result was smuggled into every Arab country, printed surreptitiously and learnt by heart. It released a flood of political frustration and anger that found expression in what is now known as Al-Adab al-Huzairani (The June Literature).' [25]

1
Friends,
The ancient word is dead.

The ancient books are dead.
Our speech with holes like worn-out shoes is dead.
Dead is the mind that led to defeat.

2
Our poems have gone sour.
Women's hair, nights, curtains and sofas
Have gone sour.
Everything has gone sour.

3
My grieved country,
In a flash
You changed me from a poet who wrote love poems
To a poet who writes with a knife.

4
What we feel is beyond words:
We should be ashamed of our poems.[26]

The humiliation of the 1967 defeat was all the greater because
the Arab people had been led to believe that the war would
end in triumph. President Nasser, the hero of the Arab people
(but not of the regimes), had promised to lead the nations of
the region to an historic victory over Israel. The outbreak of
war came against the background of rising tension between
Israel on the one side, and Egypt and Syria (bound by a defence
pact) on the other. On 13 May 1967, the Soviet Union confirmed Egyptian and Syrian intelligence reports that Israel was
preparing for an imminent attack on Syria. Three days later,
Nasser requested the withdrawal of a United Nations deterrent
force which had been stationed along the Egyptian–Israel
border in Sinai since 1956. Once the UN had left, a large force
of Egyptian troops entered Sinai. The danger of war was growing fast; and the Arab people, hanging on every word spoken
by President Nasser, were confident of victory. In a speech to
senior air force officers on 25 May, the Egyptian leader
announced a move which made war inevitable: he declared
the Straits of Tiran (the entrance to the Gulf of Aqaba), closed
to Israeli shipping. He spoke of Egypt's rights and sovereignty

over the gulf 'which constitutes Egyptian territorial waters. Under no circumstances will we allow the Israeli flag to pass through the Gulf of Aqaba.' President Nasser's bellicose rhetoric continued. 'The Jews threaten war,' he said. 'We tell them you are welcome, we are ready for war, but under no circumstances will we abandon any of our rights. This water is ours . . . The army and all the forces are mobilized and so are the people. They are all behind you, praying for you day and night and believing that you are the pride of their nation, of the Arab nation. This is the feeling of the Arab people in Egypt and outside Egypt. We are confident that you will honour the trust. Everyone of us is ready to die and not give away a grain of his country's sand.'

On 30 May, Jordan signed a defence pact with Egypt. War broke out on 5 June. It was effectively over in a few hours.

> 5
> Stirred
> By Oriental bombast,
> By Antaric* swaggering that never killed a fly,
> By the fiddle and the drum,
> We went to war
> And lost.
>
> 6
> Our shouting is louder than our actions,
> Our swords are taller than us,
> This is our tragedy.[27]

Vice-President Anwar Sadat, who later succeeded Nasser as President of Egypt, said he first heard that the conflict had started when he switched on his radio on the morning of 5 June. The news report said that twenty-seven Israeli jets had been shot down. Sadat went at once to army headquarters. There he found the commander of the armed forces Field Marshal Abdel Hakim Amer standing behind his desk, 'his eyes

---

* Antar (525–615), a pre-Islamic poet and hero of a popular epic bearing his name, is the symbol of the unbeaten knight.

shifting, not concentrating on anything'. Sadat greeted him; but a full minute passed before Amer responded. Vice-President Sadat asked others present what had happened. 'The answer was the last thing I expected. With one voice they said: "The Israelis have destroyed our entire air force."'

Sadat said the shock of what had happened was devastating because a few days earlier President Nasser had been told by his senior commanders that they expected the Israelis' first strike to be against the air force and had made plans accordingly. In the event, the first attack came while Field Marshal Amer was flying back from a meeting with his commanders in Sinai. Instructions had been given to anti-aircraft missile batteries not to open fire while the Commander-in-Chief's plane was still in the air. Also the Israelis struck 'at 8.30 a.m. – the breakfast hour for our pilots after the inspection shifts. Routine had not changed, even though we were on the brink of war and the enemy might take that into account.' Field Marshal Amer's plane turned back when those on board realized what was happening and the Egyptian Commander-in-Chief 'personally witnessed the bombing of our airports'[28] from his panoramic vantage point in the sky.

All seventeen air bases in Egypt were attacked. The Egyptian planes were sitting targets for the Israeli jets. Within hours, 309 of the Egyptian Air Force's total fleet of 340 planes had been destroyed. With air cover removed the Egyptian army found itself in a hopeless position. By the third day of the war, in the face of a swift Israeli advance, the spirit of the Egyptian troops had been broken. A brigade commander recalled that 'everyone wanted to flee for his own skin. All vehicles were abandoned and the men set off on foot to cross the mountains to the west.'[29] An estimated 10,000 Egyptian soldiers were killed or died of thirst trying to get back home.[30] The Israelis reached the banks of the Suez Canal and dug in. Ships in the waterway which were caught in the crossfire sank, blocking the Canal.

On the three days which followed, Israel took the war to Jordan and Syria. East Jerusalem and the West Bank were captured, and the Syrian army was driven off the strategically important Golan Heights. The Arab armies had suffered a comprehensive defeat; the 'emotional self-intoxication'[31] which the Arab people had enjoyed before the outbreak of hostilities had evaporated.

11
It's painful to listen to the news in the morning.
It's painful listening to the barking of dogs.

12
Our enemies did not cross our borders
They crept through our weaknesses like ants.[32]

In Egypt and throughout the Arab world shock and despair were felt in equal measure. The Egyptian President addressed his people in a speech broadcast by Cairo radio and television on 9 June. On the screen 'he appeared a broken man. His features were drawn and haggard, his voice half choking and hesitant as he read the text of the speech.'[33] Nasser sought to explain the reasons for the abysmal performance of the country's armed forces. He said the attack on 5 June had been 'a stronger blow than we had expected', and went on to accuse the United States and Britain of helping Israel. It had been established, he said, 'that American and British aircraft carriers were off the shores of the enemy helping his war effort'. But, in the end, the President said he was 'ready to bear the whole responsibility', and had therefore decided to resign.[34]

The effect was immediate and astonishing. The people of Egypt took to the streets in their millions in an emotional display of support for their president, urging him to change his mind. Nasser accordingly withdrew his resignation.

On 23 July 1967, President Nasser addressed the nation again – to mark the fifteenth anniversary of the Egyptian revolution. Nasser said that because of what happened 'we must faithfully and honourably admit that the military battle did not go as we had expected and hoped', but he refused 'to apportion blame'. The Egyptian leader also repeated his insistence that, as head of state, he took full responsibility for the defeat, while once more accusing the Americans of having provided Israel with military support.[35]

The President's speech, in its feeble admission that something had simply gone wrong, in its vague allegation of foreign connivance with Israel, and in its clear unwillingness to examine where the faults lay, was typical of the tone of official pronouncements on the 1967 defeat in the Arab world in the months and years which followed the disaster. Sadeq al-Azm, a radical Syrian academic, published in 1968 a book entitled, *Self Criticism after the Defeat*. Azm made a comparison between officials of Tsarist Russia and those in the Arab world. Both had 'insisted up to the last moment that they could overwhelm their enemies. Their defeat served a harsh judgement on them: they had failed to modernize and to reform; they had fallen behind, could no longer generate power, and were unable to secure the loyalty of the populace.' Azm argued that the Russians' defeat had 'triggered the revolutionary events of 1905, fostered radical politics and set the stage for the Bolshevik revolution'. But one year after the Six-Day war, he remained pessimistic about the prospects for radical changes in the Arab world, noting 'the tendency among Arab officials, spokesmen and even some critics to lay the blame for defeat elsewhere instead of accepting responsibility'. Some people, Azm said, pointed to American and British participation in the war, others accused Moscow of 'plotting the Arab defeat. Finally, there were those who declared it was Allah's will.'[36] Some important questions were therefore left unanswered. There was no public explanation for the incompetence of military planning which led to the Egyptian Air Force being wiped out on the ground in the opening hours of war. At least one story of humiliating incompetence from that period has been told by General Saad al-Shazly, the man who eventually became commander of the Egyptian armed forces. General Shazly recalled that a prominent feature of military parades before 1967 was the appearance of trucks carrying Al-Kahir missiles. The Kahir was said to be Egypt's secret weapon – a domestically produced short-range ballistic missile. The Kahir mysteriously failed to appear in the 1967 war. When General Shazly became Chief of Staff he made inquiries into the matter, discovering 'shameful details' of wasted money, the secret suspension of production, and 'the deception thereafter by authorities afraid to admit the truth'. In 1971, General Shazly ordered a test firing of the missile. 'Al-Kahir turned out to be very primitive indeed . . . Apart from the destructive power of its warhead, Al-Kahir was medieval.'[37]

Aside from specific examples of incompetence, a more fundamental question is why President Nasser went headlong down the road to the conflict when between 40,000 and 50,000 of his troops were committed in North Yemen on the side of government forces involved in a civil war with Saudi-backed supporters of the former imamate which broke out in late 1962. Nasser talked himself and the Arab people into a war for which Egypt and the other Arab states were unprepared.

While these larger questions remained unanswered, the heads of some senior officers fell in the immediate aftermath of the military disaster. As President Nasser tried to hold his country together and began thinking of ways of rebuilding its defences, he faced pressure from within the army for the reinstatement of Field Marshal Amer. In September, 149 people, including several former ministers and ex-generals, were arrested. They were accused of plotting a limited coup to force Nasser to reinstate Amer and to call off the investigation of army officers aimed at establishing the military's responsibility for the defeat. Amer was put under house arrest and committed suicide. After a three-month trial early in 1968 'the five chief accused were all sentenced to hard labour for life'.[38]

A few individual military officers paid a price for the defeat. President Nasser, too, was made to suffer in a different way. Even though he stayed in power, he never recovered fully from the trauma of what happened during those six days in June 1967. His army carried on a war of attrition against Israeli forces positioned on the eastern shore of the Suez Canal in 1968 and 1969. But both Nasser's physical health and his mental stamina deserted him before his armed forces could be rebuilt sufficiently to try to make amends for the humiliation of the Six-Day war defeat. Nasser died in September 1970. In the decades since then, there have been few serious and detached attempts by Arab analysts to investigate either the steps which led to the war or the conduct of the campaign. There is still no inclination on the part of Arab regimes to countenance the painful self-examination or speculation of the type which fills many pages of Western publications and occupies hours of air time in the wake of a major catastrophe. The Western obsession in the later decades of the twentieth century with trying to unearth incompetence and corruption in high places has not even begun to take root in the Arab tradition.

> 19
> We want an angry generation
> To plough the sky
> To blow up history
> To blow up our thoughts.
> We want a new generation
> That does not forgive mistakes
> That does not bend.
> We want a generation
> Of giants.[39]

The despair of 1967 was ameliorated to a certain extent by the next Middle East war – of October 1973. The years between the two conflicts brought a rare period of relative harmony among most Arab countries, with radical and conservative regimes going a long way to patch up old quarrels. Jamil Matar looks back on this era as having been 'good and beneficial to the Arab system because all the Arab disputes were stopped. They concentrated for about five years up to 1973 on solidarity, with Gulf money coming to Egypt and no fights among the Arabs. Then came both the consolidation with Syria and the preparation for the 1973 war and the agreement with Saudi Arabia to support the oil embargo.'[40]

The 1973 war, launched by Egypt and Syria (after close coordination between President Sadat and President Assad), is described in the official version of history in the Arab world as a victory. This is misleading. Fouad Ajami refers to the conflict as 'the so-called victory'; but in blunt language one would be bound to describe the conflict as having ended in a resounding Arab defeat after spectacular early successes. The spectacular element of victory came in the opening hours of the war on 6 October – it was Yom Kippur, the most sacred day in the Jewish calendar when Israelis *en masse* stay at home. It was also the Islamic month of Ramadan, when Muslims fast during daylight hours and activity in the Middle East slows to a minimum. War was the last thing on the minds of the Israelis. The Egyptian army achieved that day what most people (including the Israelis) thought would be impossible. They crossed the Suez Canal and penetrated the Bar Lev Line, the defensive wall established by the Israelis. Within twenty-four hours, Egypt had despatched 90,000 men and 850 tanks across the Canal. At the same time, three Syrian divisions and an armoured brigade broke through Israel's defences on the Golan Heights. The Arabs' most effective weapon 'was the element of total surprise, which was helped by Israel's complacency'.[41]

The Jewish state had been dealt a severe blow, and for a moment it seemed to be dazed. But its military recovery 'was swift, helped by an immediate and massive airlift of the most sophisticated arms from the United States'. In the days which followed the Syrian advance was reversed, and the Israeli army inflicted heavy losses on Egyptian troops in Sinai. Eventually, an Israeli force established a bridgehead on the western bank of the Suez Canal, and 'Egypt's Third Army was surrounded and cut off in Sinai . . . Israel had snatched a stunning military victory from initial defeat.'[42] But without American support the course of the war and possibly even the outcome would have been different.

The Egyptian successes in the early hours of the war are still celebrated in the Arab world, while the later setbacks are largely overlooked. The euphoria generated by the successful crossing of the Suez Canal and the delivery of a body-blow to Israel was massive because the two actions served to bury some of the humiliation suffered in 1967. In the words of President Sadat, speaking on 16 October 1973 (just after the Israelis had crossed to the western bank of the Canal), 'the arrogant enemy lost its equilibrium at this moment. The wounded nation restored its honour.'[43] The legacy of defeat is so strong in the Arab world that moments of honour, even the briefest, are celebrated to a degree which to Western minds might seem exaggerated and excessive.

Outsiders might have difficulty, too, in grasping the extent to which Arabs associate what they regard as Western meddling in the region with the theme of defeat. Ghassan Abdallah, a Palestinian in his forties, studied for ten years in England and Italy, and has a European wife. In the early 1990s he was working with an Arab cultural foundation in Amman. He considered the recent history of the Arabs as 'a series of defeats, with short periods in between when the West was busy. It seems to us that when the West is busy with other things we can take the opportunity to try to make progress. In the 1950s and 1960s we had Nasser and the pan-Arab movement. Then when the West got its act together again after Suez they hit Nasser in 1967. Always there is this idea – we feel that the West is hitting us.' Abdallah added that the constant feeling of being knocked down had left the Arabs with 'a feeling of inferiority, a feeling that the West has been the more powerful, the more technologically advanced. That is probably why a lot of middle-class people here send their children to the West to learn the science of the invaders, of the conquerors, of the rulers of the world, if you like. Trying to play their game. But it still does not seem to work.'[44]

There is, without question, a clear disparity between the large quantity and high quality of technology and knowledge imported from the West on the one hand and the inability of the Arabs on the other to put these acquired resources to their most effective use. The results of the Middle East wars are proof enough of this. Sadeq al-Azm, in his book analysing the 1967 defeat, suggested that the rhythm of Arab life had yet to accommodate itself to the scientific age. The Arabs, he wrote, had made room in their lives 'for the refrigerator, the television set, oil wells, MIG airplanes, the radar . . . etc, but the mentality that uses these imported products remains the same traditional mentality that belongs to bedouin, agrarian supernatural stages that preceded the industrial revolution'.[45]

Another school of thought in the Arab world blames the West for deliberately preventing countries in the region (with the blinding exception of Israel) from developing the skills needed to put modern technology to its most effective use. Ghassan Abdallah spoke of 'a feeling towards the West that they will not allow us to progress. Even Iraq is viewed sometimes as a country that tried to modernize and use modern technology. My own opinion is that they used technology for the wrong purposes. But most Arabs seem to think that the West hit Iraq or destroyed Iraq [in the 1991 Gulf war] to prevent it from progressing.' This view was shared by a Moroccan commentator who argued that 'if the basis of technology is not equipment as such but the person who is able to master and control it, then Iraq was one of a few countries in the Third World, and the only one in the Arab world, whose efforts in scientific research allowed it a measure of independence and self-reliance which the West would not allow', because its efforts were directed against Israel.[46]

The Arabs' inability thus far to put modern technology to its most effective use stems also from their cultural distance from the West. The West's technological achievements are the product of a long process of industrialization, backed by an evolving and increasingly sophisticated education system. Industrialization in the Arab world is a relatively new phenomenon; and while the cream of Arab intellectuals are on a par with any in the world, education generally is of a poor standard, with illiteracy still a major problem in highly populated countries.

Iraq was one of the first Arab states to develop both its industry and its education system – which is why, before the two Gulf wars, it was a leading force in scientific development in the Middle East. Resentment was widely expressed among Arabs at the way the West homed in on and then dismantled the country's nuclear industry, on the grounds that Baghdad was close to being able to produce nuclear weapons. The attitude of the West compounded the anger still felt at the way the international community had turned a blind eye to the raid by Israeli jets in 1981 on a nuclear reactor in Iraq. This resentment stems from the fact that no international action was ever suggested against Israel's arsenal of nuclear arms and other weapons of mass-destruction. Hazem Nuseibeh said he wrote an article in 1950 pointing out that the Israelis had set up an atomic commission under the direct control of the prime minister and warning that if the Arabs did not make a similar move they would find suddenly that Israel had become an atomic power. In 1965 Nuseibeh, while Foreign Minister of Jordan, passed on to Dean Rusk, the US Secretary of State, information received from inside the Israeli nuclear plant at Dimona about progress in the weapons programme. According to Nuseibeh, Rusk 'said he had no such information. I told him we received this information from Europeans working inside Dimona and I knew what I was talking about. So he said he would examine the matter. Later the US ambassador came to me and said that every word was true.' Nuseibeh added that Israel's production of nuclear weapons and the failure of the West to check their development were among 'the basic reasons why the Israelis are so unresponsive to all peace efforts. They feel they have the technological superiority.'[47]

Resentment at Israel's favoured status as the exclusive nuclear power in the region increased after the collapse of the Soviet Union. An Egyptian commentator said that Western concerns about former Soviet nuclear experts being offered jobs in Islamic countries, or about nuclear equipment being sold to them were hypocritical as long as Israel was allowed to maintain and build up the only nuclear arsenal in the region. The sale of former Soviet technology, he noted, excluded 'new customers who are not members of the American-led nuclear club'.[48]

The perception can be summarized as one in which the West seems always to be deciding what would be best for the Middle East – or, to be more accurate, using the pretext that the interests of the region are paramount when its real motive is to promote Western ambitions there. In the popular perception, the decisions seldom seem to favour the Arabs.

Even in the 1950s, United States foreign policy in relation to Israel and the Cold War dictated the role that countries in the region should play. Any attempt by a particular state to challenge the American vision was considered insubordination. So, for example, in 1955 when President Nasser announced that Egypt was buying arms from the Soviet Union (after

America, under pressure from Israel and its supporters in Washington, had been wavering over the question of whether or not to sell weapons to Cairo), the US Secretary of State, John Foster Dulles, was enraged and speculated on how the Egyptians could be punished. America, he said, had 'a lot of cards to play with Nasser, although they are mostly negative. The waters of the Upper Nile: we can strangle him if we want to, we can develop the Baghdad group [the Baghdad Pact states], and we can ruin the cotton market; we can switch this year's economic aid from Egypt to Iraq.'[49]

The Arabs have continued in the decades since then to accuse the West of displaying an attitude to the region which at best is condescending and at worst is hostile, callous or hypocritical. 'We do not seek the destruction of Iraq,' President Bush said during the 1991 Gulf war. Rather, he went on, the Western allies wanted an Iraq which would use its resources 'to build a better life for itself'.

'What right,' an Arab academic commented, 'does Washington have to decide what constitutes "a better life" for Iraq?'

During the same war, a State Department official speculated on the kind of regime the United States wanted to see taking over from that of President Saddam Hussein. He said the main aim would be 'to find some way, perhaps through UN-supervised elections, of letting the Iraqis choose their own government. That could be a prolonged and confused process, given the level of economic chaos. But at the worst, we should have an effective veto over the future government of Baghdad.'[50] This last sentence (similar in tone to scores of others spoken at the time), with its echoes of the colonialist sentiments expressed by British and French officials in the opening decades of the twentieth century, is treated by the Arabs as further proof that Western perceptions of them have changed little during the last century.

As the Western destruction of Iraq's armaments industry continued early in 1992, another event occurred which increased Arab cynicism about Western motives in the region. The Algerian authorities cancelled a second round of voting in general elections when it became certain that Islamic funda-

mentalists would win. A Tunisian writer, in an angry commentary which described Arab popular despair, linked the
disarming of Iraq with the near-silence of Western leaders (self-
professed champions of the principles of democracy – not least
for Iraq) on the freezing of the democratic process in Algeria.
Mohammed Kreishan wrote that the two events had left ordinary Arabs with 'a feeling of bitterness and a sense of being
insulted . . . we as Arabs felt that just as we were banned from
having among us a country powerful enough to counter the
interests of this or that Western country, so we are banned from
enjoying liberty and democracy to the extent of deciding our fate
for ourselves in a manner that might not suit the interests of this
or that Western country. As they destroyed the military and
technological edge of Iraq, so in Algeria they aborted our democratic experiment. It is as though fate has decreed that we must
be without weight or dignity in perpetuity.'[51]

The difference in attitudes between the West and Arabs (outside the Gulf region) towards the humiliation of Iraq reveals
another general area of misunderstanding between the two
regions which a century of contact has failed to eradicate.
Mohamed Heikal, in his assessment of the Gulf conflict, said
that 'Americans assumed that Arabs were glad of protection
against Iraq's ambitions to dominate the region, and against its
vast chemical weapons capabilities, without realizing that the
whole affair was wounding to Arab self-respect. The constant
feeling of being infiltrated by Western interests of all kinds
tends to undermine Arab self-confidence.'[52]

All Arab analysis of the defeatism and despair which pervades their world is shadowed, consciously or unconsciously,
by the looming image of Israel, which is seen both as an interloper and as the guardian of Western interests in the region.
Professor Mustafa Hamarneh at the University of Jordan
described the existence of Israel and its occupation of Arab land
as 'a daily reminder that you cannot trust the West. Here you
have Israel, by any standards, clearly on the side of injustice,
clearly the aggressor. I mean if we change the name of Israel
to, say, France and be objective about it, people would be horrified if it was the French imposing such an occupation with its

arbitrary military laws and so on, and uprooting the people.'[53]

In southern Lebanon, too, where the population has lived under Israeli occupation and has frequently been the target for Israeli air and artillery attacks, there is a strong feeling that the West allows the Jewish state a free hand. In Lebanon, as in the Golan Heights in Syria, and in the occupied West Bank and Gaza Strip, Israel has failed to abide by a binding UN Security Council Resolution under the terms of which it is obliged to withdraw. 'The Security Council is at the service of the United States and dominated by them,' said a shopkeeper in the village of Tibnin close to the strip of land near the border occupied by Israeli troops – which Israel calls its security zone. A few days earlier the village had again come under artillery fire as punishment for the alleged involvement of the inhabitants in an attack against an Israeli position near the border. The villagers strenuously denied being involved. 'The Americans have not put pressure on Israel to withdraw. The US attitude is not balanced. We suffer and the world does not care,' the shopkeeper said.

The feeling of injustice is imbedded so deeply among most Arabs that shifts of American policy away from Israel during periods of strained relations between the two countries make little impression on them. Much more importance is attached to these changes in American attitude in the West than in the Arab world. Heikal wrote in 1992 that President Bush 'might seem marginally firmer with Israel than his predecessors, but United States policy as a whole remained massively weighted in Tel Aviv's favour . . . Forty years of tension or war with Israel and Washington's economic and military support of Tel Aviv have had a devastating effect on Arab relations with non-Arabs. When Westerners accuse Arabs of being over-suspicious, they tend to forget that the West has never shown evenhandedness on issues which affect the survival of the Arab nation.'[54] It is accepted in the Arab world that as long as the West needs Middle Eastern oil, then it will continue to view Israel as a vital defender and upholder of its interests in the region.

Arab–Western political relations may often be over-shadowed by the presence of Israel, but such a long-running relationship cannot be entirely negative. Many leading critics of American policy, like Professor Hamarneh, for example, lived and studied in the United States and speak English with pronounced American accents. Hamarneh concedes that the relationship overall is ambivalent. There is 'admiration of the technology of the West – that these people landed a man on the moon. There is admiration at how, with their technology, they have brought about improvements in the quality of life. People are very impressed by what they call ethics – of Western armies, Western institutions. That is quite impressive. People talk about how life is easy in the West; and we sort of mourn the disarray we live in. When someone like Saddam Hussein gets up and tries to rectify matters, all these issues reappear and gain force.'

Rabee' Dejani, a Palestinian who spent many years living in Europe and the United States agreed that the Arab–Western relationship was complex. Many Arabs, he said, had enjoyed their time in the West and were proud of the educational institutions to which they had been attached. Many also accepted that Westerners had helped to build some of the institutions of the modern Arab world. But Dejani added that over political matters – and especially on the question of Israel – Arab–Western relations were severely strained. At his management consultancy in Amman, after talking animatedly about a wide range of topics, Dejani's voice became quiet and he chose his words carefully as he began explaining to me the Arabs' basic attitude to the West. 'We are a society in deep and great trouble. We have a problem with self-esteem. Historically, the Arab–Western relationship was adversarial. It remains adversarial. True, it has expanded to find many areas of cooperation. However, it is characterized by antagonism. Every day, this part of the world compares its present state of affairs with its desired state of affairs. And, more than that, with an ideal state of affairs beyond the desired one. It thinks very highly of itself, yet finds itself defeated, deprived and confused. It finds parties, which it takes for granted to be inferior, in point of fact dictating the terms. And this makes it very unhappy with itself.'

'What parties?'

'The West,' Dejani answered sharply. 'The West calls the tune to which we dance. We hate the tune, and we hate ourselves for dancing.'

'You mean the cards are all stacked against you?'

'No, quite the contrary. Deep down there is the feeling that we will see the West disappear and disintegrate, and that we will ultimately triumph. Imagine a chess game. The Americans and the West are preoccupied with winning every move and celebrating along the way. You and I know that only one move counts – the checkmate. If I can checkmate you at move ten, your nine little victories will be invalidated. We are always thinking about the long run. Ultimately, what is right will triumph over what is wrong. That is why we can never accept Israel, never – regardless of any agreements that are signed. The conflict will continue in various forms until Israel is completely dismantled. It is the inherent dynamic of the Arab mind: what is not right I will not live with.'

'No matter how long it takes?'

'I just will not live with it.'

Two days later, in conversation with Sari Nasir, Professor of Sociology at the University of Jordan, the subject of Israel came up in the context of the impressive performance of Islamic fundamentalists in the previous round of general elections in Jordan in November 1989. Nasir said the fundamentalists' success was based on the fact that during the election campaign they had stressed their opposition to compromise or surrender on the question of Jerusalem. I asked him if he realistically believed that the Arabs would get Jerusalem back, and he replied: 'We will have to'.

When I raised the subject of Israel's future with Rami Khouri, a Palestinian Christian from Nazareth, he brought up the subject of the Crusades. 'When the Western Armada came to the region at the time of the 1990–91 Gulf crisis,' he said, 'instantly many Arabs, most Arabs, called this the new Crusade. Because we remember the Crusades very vividly. We walk around Arab countries – Jordan and Palestine, Syria and Lebanon – and we see their castles. Of course, they are ruins now because they could not last. Any kind of audacious, colonial, imperial experi-

ment like that could not last. The Crusaders hung on for two
hundred years, and then off they went. We look at the Arab–
Israeli conflict and say, well, it is almost a hundred years since
the birth of political Zionism – we are half-way. The Crusaders
could not sustain it in the end. And neither, of course, will the
Israelis – if they try to maintain the Crusader mentality of an
armed fortress dominating the Arabs by force. If they co-exist
in the region peacefully, with equal rights, they will reaffirm
not only their right to live in the region, but also their historical
presence as an integral part of this area of the world.'[55]

In stark contrast, then, with the overwhelming popular
mood of defeat and despair one finds a quiet certainty that one
day – one very distant day, maybe – things will change for
the better. Ibrahim Matar, a Palestinian expert on the Israeli
settlement policy in the occupied Arab territories, was asked
in a radio interview if he thought the building of new Jewish
towns in these areas was an irreversible process. In reply, he
argued that 'the Israelis have been able to reverse two thousand
years of history. They came as immigrants in small numbers
and by 1948 were able to uproot and disperse 800,000 Palestinians. Israel was built over destroyed Palestinian homes. If they
are able to reverse two thousand years of history, Palestinians
together with the Arab world are able to reverse twenty-four
years of Israeli occupation. We can reverse the process.'[56]

As Khouri indicated, inspiration for this process of thought
comes from experience of the Crusades and, in particular, from
the exploits of Salah al-Din al Ayubi who drove the foreign
invaders out of Jerusalem. In his book, *The Crusades Through
Arab Eyes*, the Lebanese writer Amin Maalouf made the same
point – that 'in the popular mind, and in some official discourse
too, Israel is regarded as a new Crusader state. Of the three
divisions of the Palestine Liberation Army, one bears the name
Hittin and another Ayn Jalut [battles in which the Crusaders
were defeated].'[57]

To the Arabs, the Crusades are significant not just because
local forces united and drove out a foreign occupying power –
even though that is very important – but also because of the
manner of the encounter between the Europeans and the

people of the Middle East and the way it is portrayed differently
in these two parts of the world. In the West, a romanticized
vision of knights in shining armour carrying the banner of
civilization to barbaric infidels lingers on. The Arabs, on the
other hand, point to the atrocities committed by the foreigners
and to their ignorance on such matters as science and medicine.
Arab chroniclers write frequently about the uncouth and vul-
gar behaviour of the foreigners (in Arabic, *franj*). 'All those
who were well-informed about the franj', an Arab wrote at the
time, 'saw them as beasts superior in courage and fighting
ardour but in nothing else, just as animals are superior in
strength and aggression.'[58] There was a general feeling too that
the franj benefited from their contact with the superior Arab
civilization, taking back home with them newly acquired intellectual and practical skills which helped to form the basis of
the flowering of European culture and scholarship in the subsequent centuries. The knowledge that the West owes this debt
to the civilization of the Middle East provides some comfort to
Arabs today, but memories of the past also point up the failure
of the Arabs to match Western standards of education. Until
Arab leaders put greater emphasis on broadening both the
scope and availability of education, there seems little hope that
the sense of inferiority, powerlessness and despair will be dis-
sipated.

Hopelessness is most striking in some of the Palestinian refugee camps. The Shatila camp, on the southern fringes of Beirut,
has found itself in the middle of several conflicts, and was
the scene of a massacre by Israeli-backed right-wing Christian
militiamen in 1982. Piles of rubble, craters and wrecked buildings are memorials to years of bombardment and bloodshed.
During the late 1980s, Shatila was besieged for many months
by Shiite Muslim militiamen and was later the scene of bitter
inter-Palestinian fighting. In the early 1990s, Syrian soldiers
and intelligence men controlled the entrance to the camp. During a visit to the UNRWA clinic at Shatila, rebuilt after the
various rounds of hostilities, I met a mother who had brought
her baby for treatment. Her family had been living at Shatila
since 1948. I asked her if she thought her son would live all

his life at the camp. She shrugged her shoulders. 'Only God knows,' she replies. 'I cannot decide this, this is not my decision. Only God knows.'

Having faith in the long-term future and taking comfort from history will deflect the thoughts of millions of Arabs only briefly from more immediate concerns, like making enough money to feed and find homes for their families. The task is made more difficult than ever in most Arab states where there are wide gaps between rich and poor, and between rulers (and their clique) and ruled. While Arab nations have suffered defeat on the battlefield, millions of Arabs face the possibility of personal defeat each day as they battle against inequality and prejudice. In the 1930s, an Egyptian poet wrote about the plight of the poor worker living in a society controlled by a rich and privileged elite. Six decades later its relevance has not diminished.

> You live in lofty buildings
> Though I am their builder,
> You spread a gilded table cloth
> Which I have embroidered.
> You own a water-wheel of gold
> And I am the one who draws it.
> God, this is not envy
> It's simply reproof.[59]

The daily battle for survival is made more difficult, and the disparities within Arab societies are reinforced by widespread corruption. Sometimes it is discreet, at other times the evidence of it is plain to see. In Beirut in the winter of 1991, an Arab Gulf state gave the Lebanese government a sum of money to pay for the mending and resurfacing of the streets of the capital which were in serious need of repair after years of civil warfare and neglect. By the time the various officials had taken their cut from the original sum, little was left for the contractor. The company went ahead and resurfaced the streets, but it could afford only inferior materials. The result was that when the heavy winter rains began, all the new surfacing was washed into the sea, leaving the streets once again looking like unmade country lanes.

When corruption has become an institution in the highest offices in the land, there is little that the ordinary person can do but join in to the best of his ability. As a character in a novel by the Egyptian writer Naguib Mahfouz says, 'there's widespread corruption, believe me. Nobody in a position of authority today thinks about anything but the rotten game of getting rich quick. We inhale corruption in the very air we breathe! How can any of our genuine hopes emerge from this quagmire?'[60]

Those in the highest authority in the Arab world are usually those benefiting most from corruption; and they have one overriding aim: to hold on to power by whatever means necessary. Consulting the people is considered neither necessary nor advisable. The people of Syria were not asked if they wanted their country to join the Western-led coalition against Iraq in 1990, any more than the men whose names are inscribed in the war memorials in Amman and other capitals had any influence over the regimes which, since 1948, have led the Arab nations from one disastrous military defeat to another. Arab leaders may take credit for their successes, but they are not accountable for their mistakes. Of all the analyses of the 1967 defeat, one of the most astute – and least likely to win favour from Arab regimes – was written by the distinguished Moroccan academic, Abdallah Laroui. He concluded that the principal factor for the Arabs' defeat in the Six-Day war lay in 'the enemy's social organization, his sense of individual freedom, his lack of subjugation, despite all appearances, to any form of finalism or absolutism'.[61]

From Morocco to the Gulf, subjugation and absolutism are common features of regimes, whether they be monarchies or republics. Leaders in the Arab world could not survive without them.

CHAPTER FIVE

Absolute Power

In the dawn light the tall buildings and minarets of Cairo are vague suggestions of shape in a watercolour painting, washed by the pale mist and smog of early morning. But soon the light hardens, revealing fully the dilapidation of the buildings; and the arteries of the city throb once more at their usual frenetic pace. Dawn on 7 October 1981 was no exception, but the difference between that day and any other was that while the sun burnt away the morning mist as usual, the city remained quiet. Cars and buses moved with relative freedom around streets which would normally have been clogged by traffic and the mass of humanity for whom the city provides shelter each night. On the road into the centre of Cairo and in the city itself there was a police presence. This was not a normal day: less than twenty-four hours earlier President Anwar Sadat had been assassinated by Islamic fundamentalists in the army while attending a military parade.

Dignitaries from around the world flew to Cairo later that morning to attend the funeral of the Egyptian President. Cairo remained sullen. The Egyptian people, on the whole, have a gentle disposition. They did not approve of the murder of their president. There was no public rejoicing, even among Sadat's many critics; and the event did not provoke a popular uprising inspired by Islamic fundamentalists against the institutions and symbols of secular power and privilege as some people had predicted. But neither did the Egyptian people mourn.

An obvious contrast came to mind. In 1970, after the death of President Nasser 'men wept, women wailed and scratched their faces'. At his funeral millions of Egyptians blocked the streets of the capital and 'every vantage point, rooftop, balcony, statue, palm tree, was black with people'.[1] A number of people are said to have been crushed to death in the crowds.

Sadat, the man who expelled the Soviets from Egypt, made peace with Israel, and liberalized his country's economy seemed to be everything the West wanted of an Arab leader, but the Egyptians did not take him to their hearts. Nasser, on the other hand, was a figure of hate in the West, while most Egyptians and most Arabs loved him. Even some of his enemies admired him for having stood up to the power of the West at the time of the Suez Crisis in 1956 and for having put both Egypt and the Arab world firmly on the map.

The writer Lutfi el-Kholi was one of the millions who wept on the day that Nasser died. 'I was very upset and very sad,' he said. But Kholi did not attend the funeral because he was in prison. 'Despite our backing for Nasser as leader of the Arabs I was also opposing him for his failure to allow democracy. Unfortunately, he imprisoned me because some of his aides bugged a meeting here in my house which was criticizing the heavy hand of the security services, the lack of democracy, and so on.'[2]

The prisons of Cairo were also full in October 1981 when President Sadat was killed. A few days before his assassination newspapers in Cairo had published a list of 1,500 names of people arrested the previous month on suspicion of having been plotting against the regime. They joined hundreds of others already in jail. The last batch included senior figures from both the Islamic and Coptic Christian establishments, and prominent politicians, as well as leading writers and academics.

The Egyptian people responded to the differences between Nasser and Sadat but, in two respects, Nasser and Sadat were similar to each other and to all leaders in the Arab world: each kept the instruments of power within his own grasp and each moved quickly and decisively against anyone suspected of trying to challenge his authority. The relationship between an Arab leader and his own people or the West is determined more than anything else by the need to keep a firm hand on

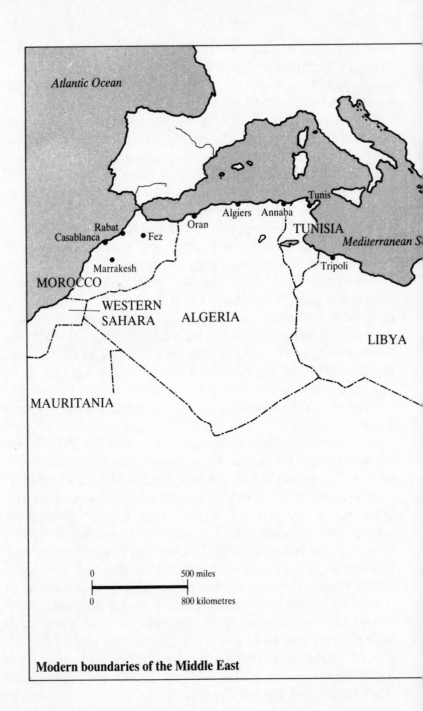

Modern boundaries of the Middle East

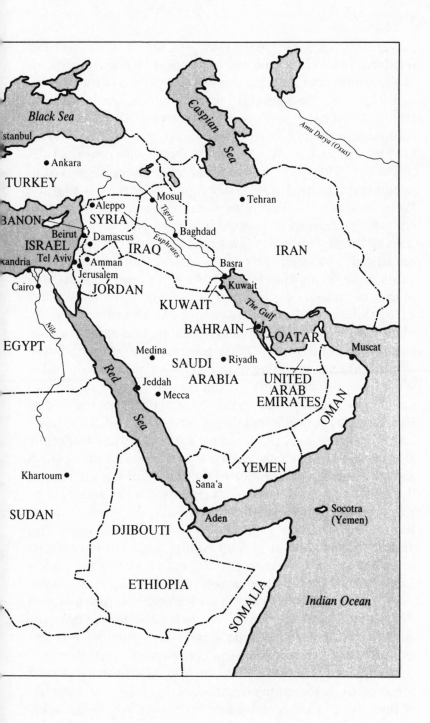

power. This fact has led to the emergence of a distinct three-tier relationship involving the outside world (normally the West), Arab regimes, and the Arab people. This pattern of interdependence is the background against which Arab–Western relationships have developed in the twentieth century. The continued existence of the framework in the Middle East towards the end of the century, when in other areas of the world authoritarian power has been crumbling, has served to widen further the Arab–Western gulf. The irony is that the West, through its close links with certain totalitarian Arab regimes for reasons of political and economic expediency, is helping the process which is keeping open this chasm in political attitudes between the two regions. As long as this chasm exists there seems little hope, in the short term, that the role of the the Arab people will be anything other than passive.

The three-tier relationship developed in the opening decades of the century when European colonial powers took control of large areas of the region. These powers were, at times, brutal and insensitive, expecting nothing but compliance from those whom they ruled. Because the rulers were foreigners the indignity felt by the Arabs was great. But the people of the Middle East are inheritors of a tradition of leadership which is characterized by toughness and brutality at the top; Arab leadership also expects subservience below. It has been said of President Saddam Hussein of Iraq, one of the most ruthless dictators of the Middle East of the twentieth century, for example, that he was 'a product of a society which looks for strength in its leaders, and does not expect them to be compassionate. This attitude, deeply rooted in Iraqi culture, stems from centuries of conflict in one of the most turbulent regions of the Middle East.'[3] The attitude is the same throughout the Arab world. Wa'il Kheir is a Lebanese university lecturer who runs a human rights organization in Beirut. He explained to me how the Arabic word for power – *salta* – has overwhelmingly negative connotations of repression. 'The very concept, in Arab minds, of having a benevolent ruler is a contradiction in terms. A ruler is bound to be something negative, and you have to keep out of his way. This concept of authority means it is a very uphill

struggle for human rights activists in the region because we
have to train people to understand that they have rights in the
first place. "Oriental despotism" seems to be a fixed feature in
our landscape.'[4]

The struggle for leadership and power is a theme running
through Arab history from the earliest centuries of Islam. The
Prophet Muhammed died in AD 623. Twenty-four years later
a full-scale civil war broke out over the question of who should
be the leader of the Islamic community. During those first
twenty-four years, as the Arab armies began moving out of the
Arabian peninsula in their campaigns of conquest, leadership
was provided by a succession of four caliphs (from the Arabic
word *khalifa*, meaning 'successor') who had been companions
of the Prophet. Two of the caliphs were murdered. In 656, a
cousin and son-in-law of the Prophet, Ali ibn Abi Talib, claimed
the succession on the grounds that it should remain among
the earliest converts to Islam. But the move was challenged by
associates of the early caliphs and those who were acquiring
power in new urban centres beyond the Arabian peninsula as
the Arab conquests spread. Forces representing the latter group
clashed with Ali and his supporters at the battle of Siffin (in
present-day Iraq). The conflict was inconclusive because, after
a time, both sides agreed that the matter of the succession
should be settled by arbitration. Some of Ali's supporters
deserted him at this stage because they 'were not willing to
accept compromise and submit the Will of God, as they saw it,
to human judgement; the honour due to early conversion to
Islam was at stake'. Ali was assassinated in his own city of
Kufa. In 680, his second son, Hussein, took up the cause and
moved into Iraq 'with a small party of kinsmen and retainers,
hoping to find support in and around Kufa. He was killed in a
fight at Karbala in Iraq, and his death was to give the strength
of remembered martyrdom to the partisans of Ali [the shi'at
'Ali – more commonly contracted to Shi'a or Shiites].'[5]

The implications of these early power struggles, which
caused the major schism in Islam between Sunnis and Shiites,
were important. Fawzy Mansour, commenting on the lack of
democracy in the Arab world at the end of the twentieth

century, noted that Islamic jurists in the early years of Islam 'studiously avoided the thorny problem of the legitimate ways of assuming power'. This meant, in effect, that anyone seizing power by any method was regarded, *de facto*, a legitimate ruler. The evolving tradition also 'outlawed the challenging of power, once established, except for serious doctrinal reasons or the equivalent, and sanctioned the most severe penalties in this world and utter damnation in the next one for armed dissent'. According to Mansour, one of the long-term effects of 'the tragic experience of early Islam' was 'to establish an in-built bias in favour of the authoritarian state and absolutist rule'. Mansour argued, too, that in the early Islamic period 'the failure to establish a generally accepted and obeyed rule of succession (a failure which continued to bedevil all ruling Arab and Islamic dynasties and, with them, their states up to modern times) involved the main Arab tribes in still more rivalries and even conflicts'.[6]

With the struggles for power continuing in the centuries after the birth of Islam, a conventional view about leadership emerged among Muslims. This was that 'the ruler possesses absolute executive power, but his use of it should be tempered by respect for the law and those who preserve it.' Furthermore the ruler 'was God's representative, answerable to God alone, and under God his own conscience was his only judge'. When it came to the attitude of the population towards their ruler, the view of the majority of Muslim thinkers over the ages was that citizens 'should protest against injustice but submit to it'.[7]

The opening centuries of Islamic history are surprisingly similar to those in early European history; in both, leaders backed by strong armies captured thrones and claimed authority in the name of the Church. In the West, church and state later separated; in Islam, spiritual and secular power remain inseparable. As Arab society developed, emphasis continued to be placed on the solidarity of the community with its strong political and spiritual leader, who represented the will of God. Christianity, on the other hand, provided a code to live by, but stressed the responsibility of individuals to be answerable to God for their own actions. In the Islamic world, the community exerted a powerful pressure on individuals to conform; in the West, the pressure came from guilt and fear of judgement after death. Muslims, too, are taught to fear judgement after death but the stress laid on this doctrine over others has been greater in Christianity. Partly as a consequence of this, a tradition of free thought and expression developed faster in Christian society than it did in the Islamic world. As the centuries passed, authoritarian rule persisted in Arab countries, while democracy, with leadership accountable to the people, was born in the West.

Authoritarian rule over such a long period has bred passivity and subservience in the attitudes of Arabs to their rulers. They fear the power which their leaders, supported by corrupt governing elites, exert over them, and feel impotent as individuals to complain or resist, no matter how great the humiliation they may suffer. Most contemporary Arab intellectuals would agree that observations on popular attitudes to leadership made by Lutfi al-Sayyid, a hero of Egyptian nationalism at the beginning of the century, during the time of British colonial rule in Egypt, are still applicable in the Middle East today. 'We Egyptians, he says, [his words paraphrased by Albert Hourani, a distinguished Lebanese-born Arab historian] are hypocritical in our desire to praise and flatter those who are strong, and that is because we do not believe in ourselves as independent human beings. We are easy-going, we say "Never mind" – *ma'laysh* – to whatever happens; that is a sort of virtue, but one which is rooted in weakness of soul. We are servile and will accept insults and humiliation rather than lose a post or make a protest.'[8] Another Egyptian, Anis Mansour, writing in the last decade of the century about the Nasser era, recalled how during that period 'tens of thousands of people went to prison and came out with reduced weight, stature and dignity. And they did not say a word . . . Some of them went to prison and were rolled around in fire and urine; they licked the earth and let dogs tear them to pieces. Then they came out thanking and praising Gamel Abdel Nasser for having punished them.'[9]

When Egypt and other countries were granted their independence after the Second World War and nationalist leaders came to power, in the words of Professor Majid Khadduri, a leading Arab academic writing in the 1980s, 'the elder politicians who were presumably in favour of parliamentary democracy in principle betrayed authoritarian propensities.' They failed to match the aspirations of the younger generation, and they would not share power with them. The elder leaders relied on land-owners and merchants for support and they 'thus appeared in the public eye as vain, self-seeking and an obstacle to progress. They could no longer carry the public behind them'.[10]

Disillusionment among young Arabs with the post-independence establishment reached a peak after the trauma of the creation of the state of Israel and subsequent humiliation in the Palestine war. The mood of popular discontent, among young army officers and the civilian population alike, was met not by acknowledgements of failure or promises of reform but by the firm and uncompromising hand of authority. Street pro-tests were dispersed with violence, while state institutions designed to provide a platform for popular grievances were clogged by the vested interests of those in power or enfeebled by corruption. The only way to oust the discredited leadership was by force, and so dissidents turned to groups of disaffected army officers for help. The old guard was removed at gunpoint. Civilian groups which had sunk their differences in the inter-ests of removing the incumbents from power frequently fell out with each other once their goal had been achieved. The result was that 'competition and rivalry among the civilian leaders to whom the young officers were expected to entrust power became so intense that the officers who seized power were bound to remain in power. In time the military regimes became self-perpetuating, because each civilian group con-sciously tried to influence a "faction" in the army to seize power by force and install a regime which would eventually give an expression to one of the ideologies that had become fashionable in Arab society.' This process sparked off a series of military coups until 'the army was brought under the control of a strong leader who dominated the officers' corps'.[11] The result was that in many Arab countries the military either brought leaders to power or the heads of state emerged from the armed services. The legacy of this can still be found at the end of the century. The list of leaders within this category is long and includes Presidents Nasser, Sadat and Mubarak of Egypt, Muammar Qadafi of Libya, Hafez al-Assad of Syria, and Saddam Hussein of Iraq.

The appearance of military men as heads of state in the Arab world did not encourage either open leadership or healthy political debate. Abdallah Laroui, the distinguished Moroccan academic, has observed that the post-independence coups in the Arab world were 'all reactions to political and military failures and were to a certain extent improvised (not as tactical moves but in as much as they did not form part of an overall strategy). As retaliatory acts without an ideological foundation, they had in the long run only a mediocre effect on political education.'[12]

All the leaders who emerged from the military share or shared a quality in common with every Arab head of state of modern times: a determination to hang on to power at all costs for as long as possible. The desire to formulate and propagate a coherent political ideology is a far less pressing concern. While President Nasser of Egypt, Colonel Qadafi of Libya and President Saddam Hussein of Iraq are among leaders who have been proponents of pan-Arab nationalism, each has made certain first of his own solid grip on power at home; and each has coveted the role of leader of a more integrated Arab world. In the end, the calls for pan-Arabism have failed because regimes have been preoccupied by their desire to stay in power.

Nader Fergany, an eminent, independent, political scientist based in Cairo, holds strong views about the process by which Arab leaders acquire and consolidate power. His refreshingly frank and outspoken analysis is such that his views seldom find a platform inside the Arab world where public criticism of ruling elites is usually forbidden. Fergany's analysis of the longevity of rule within Arab regimes would make uncomfortable reading in most palaces around the region but few Arabs would honestly dispute his conclusion. 'I think the vast majority of Arab people,' Fergany said, 'are outside the political process. The standard democratic procedure is that people elect governments to take care of their interests and direct their society to attain the goals of the people; in turn people have control over the next government in the sense that they evaluate them periodically and if they do not like their achievements they change them. We, in this part of the world, have an opposite situation where somehow somebody – and I mean a person, not a party – plus, maybe, a small clique reaches the pinnacle of power, and regardless of how they get there, they are there for good. If you look at most Arab regimes now, the chances are, with the exception maybe of Lebanon, that whoever is at the top of power will remain there for life. Whether it is by revolutionary decree, or by elections that are rigged, or by a parliament electing someone for life. You end up with a power vacuum around one person who has been transformed into a mini-god.'[13] The Arab leader – president, king or emir – becomes a remote and exalted figure, demanding public shows of obedience and respect, and assuming for himself what seems like a divine right to deliver bounty or punishment as he sees fit. The contrast with Western attitudes in this respect is striking.

Arab leaders are able to behave in this fashion because state institutions designed to guard against abuses of power either do not exist or have been corrupted by the ruling elite. The leader, living in his sheltered world, surrounded by sycophants, is free to act in any manner he chooses. But the danger of a rival appearing on the scene and the possibility of a coup to unseat him always remains. For this reason, Arab presidents and monarchs do not tend to appoint strong vice-presidents or surround themselves with people who could challenge their position. In fact, a major deficiency inherent within the whole system of leadership in the Arab world – in republics, kingdoms and sheikhdoms – is the absence of clear rules of succession. In the early 1990s, for example, it was not clear who would be the next ruler of (among others) Libya, Syria, Oman and the United Arab Emirates – four countries with widely differing systems of leadership.

The fear of a military coup haunts all regimes in the Middle East, even those under civilian rule. In Khadduri's view, it is 'small wonder that in most Arab lands the question of the survival of the regime has become a top priority'. As a result, 'often the goals of reform and development have been subordinated to the requirements of security'.[14] Abdallah Laroui has written, on the same theme, of politics in the Arab world being 'reduced to the level of shortsighted tactical manoeuvring subservient to egotistical interests'.[15]

These interests have to be protected at all costs and by whatever methods, no matter how brutal. It is the rule, rather than the exception, for opponents of Arab regimes to be imprisoned, deported or put to death. Even those within the ruling clique have to be careful not to step out of line. In 1984, in the middle of the Iran–Iraq war, Ayatollah Khomeini suggested that a settlement between the two countries might be achieved if President Saddam Hussein of Iraq (the man responsible for starting the conflict) stepped down. At a cabinet meeting in Baghdad attended by the Iraqi President, the Minister of Health, a British-trained surgeon, Dr Riyad Ibrahim, broached the possibility of Saddam Hussein leaving office as a temporary measure in the interests of ending the bloodshed. After the meeting, Dr Ibrahim was arrested, tried and executed. Unconfirmed reports said that Saddam Hussein pulled the trigger.

There are many examples of arbitrary decisions taken by Arab leaders – usually less brutal but no less effective than that concerning Dr Ibrahim. Senior members of the Syrian establishment recall an occasion when President Assad summoned his Prime Minister Abdel-Rauf al-Kassem with the intention of asking him to form a new Cabinet. The Speaker of parliament, Mahmoud al-Zubi, was also present. The Syrian President said that the previous Cabinet had made mistakes and needed to be changed. 'We all make mistakes,' the Prime Minister is quoted as having said. At which point, President Assad turned to the Speaker and ordered him to form the next government. In Arab society anyone with even limited power or influence who challenges the opinion of the head of state can expect, at the very minimum, to be stripped of his privileges. For this reason, throughout the Middle East, the educated liberal elite tends to be used by the regimes to explain policies and plans but is excluded from the decision-making process. This is true even in more superficially modern Arab states popular with the West. In 1986, the Saudi Minister for Oil, Sheikh Ahmed Zaki Yamani, was peremptorily dismissed after twenty-four years in the job when he told King Fahd that it was impossible for the country simultaneously to seek higher oil prices and to export larger quantities of oil, as the monarch was demanding. As one Arab intellectual said, 'when the advice or opinions of the educated elite differ from that of the ruling elite, the former are more often than not fired. The other depressing thing is that very few of the educated elite who have got to high posts have avoided getting corrupted. They have used their posts to accumulate wealth, sometimes unlimited wealth. This is not just the case in Saudi Arabia and the Gulf states, it is the same in Algeria, Libya, Syria – everywhere.'

Totalitarian rule, with its inherent obsession with security, leaves open the possibility of arbitrary decisions being taken which affect not only the country itself but also the states around about it. Yezid Sayigh, a Palestinian academic at Oxford University, has argued that 'because real power in most Arab countries rests with narrowly based elites (drawn from family, tribal, ethnic or sectarian minorities, and almost invariably unelected and too often supported by Western nations), incumbent regimes wield a disproportionate impact on the functioning and stability of the regional state system as a whole. The ability of Iraqi President Saddam Hussein almost single-handedly to launch his country into two vastly debilitating wars within a decade reveals this relationship most starkly.'[16]

Saddam Hussein's success in remaining in power for so long despite having made two catastrophic miscalculations which cost tens of thousands of lives is also a stark illustration of the determination of Arab leaders not to leave office. In general, regimes in the Arab world have changed when a leader has died, has been assassinated, or has been overthrown in a military coup. The number of military coups has declined steadily in the post-independence era, but the possibility is still there. In 1989, for example, General Omar Hassan Ahmad Bashir seized power in Sudan. On occasions, too, leaders have been removed from office by what one might call gentlemanly coups. In Abu Dhabi, in 1966, British political agents in the Gulf connived with Sheikh Zayid al Nahyan to force the ruler of the emirate, his brother Sheikh Shakhbut, to relinquish his powers. The latter had refused to allow the modernization and development of Abu Dhabi following the discovery of large oil reserves and, in the face of growing discontent among his citizens, had dismissed demands that he should abdicate. Sheikh Shakhbut's palace was surrounded by troops, but still he refused to leave. In the end, soldiers were sent in; Sheikh Shakhbut put up some resistance, but the troops 'managed to manoeuvre him out of the palace. A car, waiting at the front door carried him to the airport where a special plane was ready to take him directly to London.'[17] A similar sequence of events, also with British involvement, brought Sultan Qabous of Oman to power in July 1970 when his father Sultan Said was overthrown.

These were quiet coups, but still the threat of military action and the physical presence of troops at the palaces were needed to force the incumbents to leave. Examples of Arab leaders finding themselves in a position where they had no choice but to stand down because their power base had crumbled, the method by which leadership often changes hands in the West, are rare. But there were two notable occasions when this happened: in Saudi Arabia in the 1960s, and in Algeria at the start of the 1990s. The first case involved King Saud who was forced to abdicate in December 1964. His profligate lifestyle (including an addiction to alcohol),[18] his squandering of public money and his interference in the affairs of other Arab states had such disastrous consequences that 'the position of the whole Saudi House seemed to have been undermined, which prompted the leading members of the family to force him first to relinquish some of his powers to the Council of Ministers, headed by his brother Feisal, and then to abdicate in favour of Feisal.'[19] Early in 1965, 'accompanied by a huge retinue, apart from his harem, and teeming progeny, Saud departed for exile in Greece, grudgingly recognizing Feisal as King before he left.'[20]

The incident in Algeria concerned President Chadli Benjedid. In January 1991 the first round of voting in general elections brought unexpected success to the Islamic Salvation Front (FIS). With the FIS looking set to sweep to power in the second round of voting, the army-led establishment in Algiers, without putting tanks and soldiers on the streets, pressured the President into resigning, to be replaced on a temporary basis by a seven-member High Executive Council. The leading figure in the council was the Defence Minister General Khaled Nazzar. The army took this step because it 'had no desire to see its considerable influence questioned by the Islamic fundamentalists'.[21]

In both the Saudi and Algerian examples, even though the circumstances in the two countries at the time and the nature of the regimes were different, the reasons behind the moves were the same: those in each of the ruling cliques with vested interests in keeping the regimes in power felt that their privileged positions might be threatened unless their leaders stepped down. Because each man had been put into power by the ruling clique in the first place, his power-base assured by them, each also accepted that he could not survive when that backing was withdrawn.

The ruling clique often encompasses people far outside the narrow confines of government. Regimes should not be thought of only as governments, but rather as a combination of a political apparatus and an attendant structure involving economic, social and other interests. The aim of those with vested interests in the regime, according to Fergany, 'is not just staying in power for the sake of it, but because attachment to the governing structure is a means to an end. The end is the benefits derived from staying in power.' Fergany's view is that the continued fragmentation of the Arab world is in the best interests of the individual regimes, even though cooperation and unity would benefit the Arab people. 'If people had control of their destiny in each Arab country we would not have these regimes that are in the long run, by design or default, really working against the best interests of their countries.'

Regimes face possible challenges, then, both from military coups and from popular uprisings. To minimize the chances of the latter possibility, Fergany argued, regimes have three instruments at their disposal: control of prestige; manipulation of the mind; and repression.

Fergany explained the workings of the first instrument of control in the following way: 'All Arab regimes, regardless of their bent, have a great deal of control over the distribution of economic benefits and social prestige in society. Even when there are attempts at privatization of economic interests, the government in a country like Egypt tries to keep a great deal of economic control over its privatization process. For example, the Business Sector Law which was issued in Egypt leaves the appointment of the heads of the holding companies – in fact the entire general assembly of the holding company and the heads of affiliated firms – to the prime minister. Which really means that thousands of major posts are under the control of the government. It is also very difficult for any person to succeed in a business venture unless he has the cooperation of the bureaucracy or the power structure: the bureaucracy in terms of bribery, commissions and so on; the power structure in terms of facilitating getting round red tape.' Aside from business matters, Arab regimes also have control over 'all institutions which grant intellectual and social status outside government, over universities, over social institutions and the media. These are all channels of access to social power and prestige and they are very well controlled and manipulated in such a way that only those who are conforming to the line of the government are given access.'

The extent to which the Egyptian government interferes in non-governmental institutions was the subject of comment by another political scientist in Cairo, Ahmed Abdallah. He said that the 20,000 charitable, social, cultural, religious, scientific, artistic and environmental associations in Egypt 'could have provided a fair base for encouraging citizens to take part in public life'. This had not happened for three reasons. Firstly, the Ministry of Social Affairs 'retains the right to veto candidates to the associations' councils' under a 1964 law aimed at tightening government control over them. Secondly, while the associations are not allowed to engage in political action the regime 'welcomes pro-government activity by whatever association

while it censors those who take anti-government stances (like
university professors' clubs, which are registered as associations
and have become strongholds of the Islamic movement).
Thirdly, most associations are dominated by 'local elites which
monopolize power' and disregard the interests of members. As
a result, most Egyptians believe these associations serve as a
vehicle for the interests of only small groups and do not regard
them 'as an arena for their own participation in public life'.[22]

Control of access to positions of prestige applies also to
writers and artists in the Arab world. Journalists who have
prepared articles which do not conform with the thinking of
the regime have found that their material has not got into
print, and that they have not been asked to write any more –
even though they have not necessarily been sacked. This was
the experience of the Egyptian writer, Muhammed Sid Ahmed.
During the Sadat presidency, he worked for the semi-official
daily *Al-Ahram* and was critical of the President's policies. 'I
was pushed out of *Al-Ahram* for years,' he said. 'By "out" I
mean I was still on the payroll but nothing of mine was published. As the game is played, you see, there are ways by which
you come to understand whether or not you are in their good
books.'[23] In similar fashion, authors whose works have dis-
pleased particular governments have found their names
excluded from lists of invitees to seminars and book fairs, or
have been passed over in the filling of academic and other
posts.

The second instrument of power in the hands of Arab rulers,
the manipulation of the mind, was described by Fergany as
being 'even more pernicious than the first'. The process begins
with deficient education systems. Those who begin schooling
do not necessarily finish it, and those who complete the course
'do not necessarily get educated in the sense of mastering
elements of reading, writing and arithmetic. So you have this
basic environment of illiteracy which guarantees that the population is generally lacking in social awareness. In addition, if
you take the content of the education system, it has been
known for years that it does not instil critical faculties, but is
based on rote learning and memorizing.'

Fergany insisted that shortcomings in the education system were found far beyond the borders of Egypt – even in the wealthy Gulf states, where schooling is freely available to everyone. In the Gulf, he said, 'while education is generally widespread, the quality is very poor.' There is 'something that works against good education in Arab societies, whether they are rich or poor. This is related to social incentive. Any society has an incentive system, a system of rewards and punishments. I think that in both rich and poor Arab countries now the system of social incentives punishes education, it punishes knowledge, it punishes using critical faculties, it punishes merely having a critical faculty.' Fergany added that, in terms of both earnings and prestige, education had a negative effect in Arab society. A peasant child in Egypt who works in the fields as he grows up stands to earn more money in the long run than one who goes through the education system, finds himself unemployed for several years before getting, if he is lucky, a low-paid job. Conversely, for an Arab in the Gulf there is no earnings incentive to spend many years being educated – especially in societies where 'social prestige is no longer related to how enlightened or educated you are, but to what car you drive and what kind of position you have.'

Whether or not Arabs receive formal schooling they will receive informal education through the mass media. In Fergany's view, throughout the Arab world, there is 'pervasive state control over the mass media – television, radio and written journalism, in that order because television is the most influential, broadcasting second, and in a generally illiterate society newspaper reading is very limited. So, with the informal education system – the mass media – we have general and persistent bombardment of the minds of the people, from the very young to the very old, of the line of the government. There are also many other variants on the technique, like great emphasis on national sports and on a general type of trite material aired to divert people from the big issues. And when the big issues are tackled, they are tackled from one point of view.'

Criticism of the indifferent quality of state-controlled mass media is voiced by Arab intellectuals throughout the region. ('Arab regimes want to distract people from serious topics; they do not want people to give a damn about politics,' a Syrian student told me.) News broadcasts, in particular, invariably fail to satisfy the appetites of concerned or inquiring minds. Most Arab countries devote a long section of their television news broadcasts each evening to the actions of the head of state, regardless of how mundane or uninteresting those actions were on a particular day. News about other events and developments within the country or elsewhere is usually, at best, sketchy if there is any element of controversy in them. It is common, therefore, for Arabs to hear first about major events taking place on their doorstep from the Arab language services of the British Broadcasting Corporation, the Voice of America or Radio Monte Carlo. During the early years of the Palestinian uprising (intifada) in the Israeli-occupied territories, which began in December 1987, coverage was much more extensive and detailed in the West than in the Arab world. ('It is well known,' an Arab from north Africa commented, 'that government and popular support for the intifada was greater in Italy than in all the Arabs states put together because we hardly got to hear about it.') Arab regimes found themselves in an awkward spot. While they wanted to show support and sympathy for the Palestinians, they did not want to encourage the principle of people rising up in rebellion against those in control. If the example of unarmed Palestinians being prepared to challenge a strong occupation force was shown too widely it might put ideas into the heads of other Arabs and encourage them to rise up against their own governments.

Of all the Arab states only Lebanon has experienced the phenomenon of unfettered broadcasting. During the civil war, private radio stations were set up by the various warring factions, partly with the purpose of disseminating propaganda and disinformation, but with the much more important role of providing fast and detailed reports of where fighting was taking place, where bombs had exploded and who had been killed and injured.

State broadcasting organizations may, for a certain time, by

showing football matches, soap operas and quiz shows, be able
to divert the attention of the people from the difficulties of
daily life or the complexities of politics. In the same way, the
control of economic and social prestige may, for a while,
buy the loyalty of key sections of the population. If these two
instruments fail, the regime can always fall back on the third:
repression. Nader Fergany's belief is that under the weight of
deepening economic crises in the Arab world, combined with
increasing disparities in income and wealth, regimes may find
themselves resorting more and more to this third instrument.
Social inequality in Arab cities is striking. 'You just have to
stroll through the streets of the new chic areas of Cairo and
look at the Mercedes and BMWs. Each is half a million Egyptian
pounds. So on the one hand there are people who have to
make do on forty or fifty pounds a month, if they can get it
after a long spell of unemployment; on the other hand, there
are people who flaunt half-million-pound cars and things like
that.' The Egyptians have coined a neat term to describe this
phenomenon. In Arabic it is *al-istihlaak al-istifzaazy* – which
could be loosely translated as 'the provocative flaunting of
worldly goods'.

When the need arises to use the third instrument of state
control there is no limit to the power which the regimes have
given themselves. 'Looking at the record of human rights in
the country, you find that, starting with the legal system,
through the adminstrative procedures, to the actual practice of
the security forces, you live in a very strict police state when
the government decides that the situation warrants it.' Fergany
added that on Egyptian streets there was already 'an undeclared state of war in which members of the extreme Islamic
groups assassinate influential members of the regime or the
security forces, or vice versa. This is going on all the time. And
I am sure that with the deepening economic crisis and with
the nationalization, so to speak, of the political process so that
there is no possibility of changing government in a peaceful
way, there is going to be increased social conflict – perhaps
mass popular unrest or much more violent conflict than we
are witnessing now.' In June 1992 the liberal elite in Egypt

were shaken by the murder by Islamic fundamentalists of Farag
Foda, a leading secularist writer and critic of fundamentalism.
The incident prompted an alarmed comment from Hala Mustafa, an expert on Islamic fundamentalism at Al-Ahram Center
for Strategic Studies. She considered the murder of a writer
because of his liberal and secular opinions 'a dangerous tendency, because one used to say that those [fundamentalist]
groups were in conflict with the government. But now it is not
so: they are targeting any kind of view which is contrary to
theirs.'[24]

Fergany asserted that the three instruments of state control
were used not just in Egypt but extensively throughout the
region – only with variations. 'The difference is in the relative
emphasis placed on each of the three instruments. If you go
to Iraq, for example, there is very effective use of, or strong
reliance on, all three to an extreme. I mean sheer physical
oppression is at a maximum, 100 per cent. You might have in
other countries the use of the instruments ranging between 40
and 50 per cent. But what I am saying is that the reliance on
them does not go below a certain threshold which could
threaten the continuity of the regime. It is the combination of
the three instruments and the level of reliance on them that
gives the regimes their different looks.'

During the twentieth century, Arab regimes have resorted
on a number of occasions to measures of extreme repression
– as in Syria in February 1982 when the security forces moved
against Sunni Muslim fundamentalists in Hama, killing several
thousands of people; or in northern Iraq over a long period
beginning in the 1970s when the Baghdad government tried
to quell uprisings by the Kurds, using both heavy conventional
and, later, chemical weapons, and killing thousands of people.
Nevertheless, extreme examples are rare. Regimes aim to prevent matters reaching such a pitch by reliance on their state
security services (*mukhabarat*). Through networks of informers
they monitor the mood and watch the activities of the population with the aim of trying to find and eliminate possible
threats to the regime. The further removed a leader is from his
people, the greater his need for information from the security

services. Even President Nasser, the hero of the Arab people, relied heavily on the mukhabarat. 'Lacking a trustworthy, powerful mass organization, Nasser had to fall back for the protection of his power and enforcement of his daring measures and policies on the state apparatus, more particularly on the various security services attached to his state.'[25] The danger, of course, is that the security services themselves could get too powerful and become a threat to the leadership. To protect against this, Egypt, Syria, Iraq, Libya, Yemen and other Arab states have several internal security departments, whose brief is to report on each other as well as on the civilian population, the armed services, or on whatever area of society they specialize. Egyptian leaders, for example, 'have at their disposal three competing intelligence services. The Defence Intelligence Department which reports to the Minister of War. The National Intelligence Service under the direct control of the President. And the Secret Investigations Department run by the Minister of the Interior . . . The reports of each service go to the President. If two report a rumour, while the third does not, it is at once suspected that there is a conspiracy in the third to suppress it.'[26]

The brief of the security services is also to watch out for agents from other Arab countries sent to foment trouble. In the context of the three-tier structure mentioned earlier, even if the relationship between a regime and its people is kept tightly under control, leaders have to keep a constant watch on developments and new political alignments beyond their borders – not just in the West, but also within the Arab world. Inter-Arab alliances, sometimes tactical and short-lived, play an important part in the efforts of regimes to stay in power and enhance regional and international prestige. For this reason, President Assad of Syria steadfastly supported Iran during the eight-year-long war with Iraq, and was the only Arab state to do so. Syria's decision was based on long-standing rivalry with Iraq (each country being governed by rival wings of the Ba'ath party) and the mutual hatred of Presidents Assad and Saddam Hussein. Syria was prepared to endure the condemnation of other Arab states for backing a non-Arab Shiite fundamentalist regime because its higher interest was in ensuring that Iraq did not emerge as the victor from that conflict. A militarily strong and politically powerful Iraq could have represented a challenge both to the security of Syria and to President Assad's desire to become the chief regional powerbroker. For similar reasons, the Syrian regime was prepared to risk its relationship with Iran and support the Western-led coalition in the 1991 Gulf war.

Ethnic groups within Arab states have on occasions found themselves pawns in the power games of the ruling regimes. In the early 1970s, the Iraqi Kurdish community was involved in a series of violent confrontations with the army as part of its struggle to win full autonomy in the north of the country. The Kurds were being supported by Iran (under the Shah at that time) and Israel, and were using Iranian territory as a sanctuary. As the conflict developed and spread President Saddam Hussein judged that a point had been reached at which his regime could come under threat, so he 'decided on drastic action. In March 1975 he accepted public reconciliation with the Shah at an Algiers summit meeting of OPEC states.' The Shah agreed to cut off aid to the Kurds and close his country's borders to them. The Kurdish revolt collapsed. In return, though, Saddam Hussein had to make a major concession on a border demarcation dispute with Iran. This dispute re-emerged five years later and was the pretext on which Iraq began its war with Iran.[27] But, in the short term, the deal with Iran achieved its aim in ensuring the survival and the continued stability of the Baghdad regime.

The West supports the structure of the three-tier relationship by making deals, both short and long term, with Arab regimes as a political expedient and without considering the wishes of the people. In doing so, the West is prepared, if necessary, to disregard blatant abuses of human rights and the absence of democratic freedoms – failings which have frequently been condemned elsewhere in the world. During the Gulf crisis of 1990 and 1991, the West was anxious to broaden as much as possible the base of the military force being assembled in preparation for the attack on Iraqi troops in Kuwait. Of particular importance was the need to bring as many Arab countries as possible from outside the Gulf region into the alliance. When President Assad offered to send a token force to the Gulf, the Western powers accepted with alacrity; the presence of Syria, it was said, gave the alliance the credibility it needed. In return, the West quietly dropped the accusations that it had for many years been making against the Damascus regime – that it supported terrorism, abused human rights and suppressed democracy. The massacres at Hama were overlooked. The Syrian people, who were not consulted about the Gulf policy and silently opposed it, were amazed at the sudden transformation in the relationship between their government and the West. Even a figure within the Syrian establishment expressed, privately, his astonishment. 'Assad, up to the Gulf crisis,' he told me, 'was called by the West a terrorist, a dictator, a despot. What happened? President Assad has not changed his being – he has been like this since he took over officially in 1971. What has made him now the godfather of peace in the area? His image has been polished by the Americans. How can the Americans justify this on the grounds that they are defending the worst and most corrupt kind of monarchies in the Gulf?'

In punishing Iraq for aggression in an area of vital economic interest, the United States's desire to add international respectability to its cause made the concession to Syria worth any temporary embarrassment. In the *Realpolitik* of the Middle East, as long as Arab leaders are not accountable to their people, both the regimes in the region and the West can shrug off difficulties of this kind.

Abrupt reversals of alignment have occurred in Western–Arab relations as much as between powers inside the region. In the earlier Gulf conflict, for example, Washington was giving support and encouragement to the Iraqis in their war with Iran. When the extent of United States involvement became clear in the early 1990s, it was discovered that in 1984 – the year when the Iraqi health minister was murdered for expressing a view considered unacceptable by President Saddam Hussein – the State Department, in a secret memorandum outlining United States policy towards the Gulf war, said that 'victory by either side would have a seriously destabilizing effect on the region ... We must therefore seek means to bolster Iraq's ability and resolve.'[28] Declassified documents also showed that in 1982, in addition to providing Iraq with top-secret intelligence information, Washington decided to take Iraq off its list of countries supporting terrorism. Until the invasion of Kuwait in 1990, senior United States officials consistently denied that there was evidence showing Iraq to be continuing to support groups considered by Washington as terrorists, despite the existence of reliable reports to the contrary. But one month after the occupation of Kuwait, Deputy Secretary of State, Lawrence Eagleburger, described Iraq as 'a country which has repeatedly provided support for acts of international terrorism'.[29] As part of its policy of support for Baghdad in the 1980s, Washington deliberately ignored atrocities being committed by the regime there. The US State Department rejected the findings of its own Bureau of Human Rights which said in 1988 that Iraq had consistently and grossly violated human rights and had used chemical weapons against the Kurds.[30] Sam Gejdenson, a Democratic congressman heading a committee investigating US–Iraqi relations before the Gulf conflict, said (in an interview with the *New York Times*) in June 1992 that the US government had taken no action 'to send a signal to Saddam that our outrage was so great – when he gassed the Kurds, when he harboured terrorists – that it would cost him the friendship of the United States. It is worse than paying no attention. Those paying attention at the highest level were trying to coddle Saddam.'

Within the Arab world, too, there is a widespread feeling that the Washington–Baghdad relationship at this time, (within the framework of the three-tier relationship, and at very heavy cost to the Iraqi people) went a long way towards sparking off the 1990 Gulf crisis. 'President Saddam Hussein would not have reached that degree of chauvinism if it had not been for the backing of the United States,' Professor Aziz Shukri, head of the Department of Law at Damascus University said, echoing a commonly expressed belief in the region.[31]

The intensity with which the West concentrated on the flaws of the Iraqi regime after the occupation of Kuwait caused considerable anger to many Arabs living outside the Gulf region. This was because they saw the way in which the West ignored the violation of human rights by other regimes in that area. 'Admittedly, human rights were and are violated in Saddam's Iraq,' an Egyptian commentator wrote. 'But this is also true of two thirds of the member states of the United Nations, among them some other Gulf countries, with which Europe and the United States have normal, and in many cases, cordial relations. This Western selectivity did not escape the notice of Arab public opinion.'[32] A member of the board of the Arab Organization for Human Rights, which is based in Cairo, said he felt it was 'so hypocritical as to be disgusting that the United States and other Western powers had gone to war in the Gulf ostensibly under the banner of human rights, having taken totally different stands over Israeli violations of Palestinian rights, and the rights of people living under regimes they support – like Egypt* and Morocco.'†

International human rights organizations have often taken the West to task over its attitude towards its major ally in the region and its chief supplier of oil, Saudi Arabia. In May 1992, the New York-based organization, Middle East Watch, pointed out that while the United States publicly pushed for democratic reforms in Cuba, Iraq, Kenya and elsewhere, it had 'remained mute towards one of the most singularly undemocratic nations in the world, its longtime ally Saudi Arabia ... Although the United States, by virtue of a long and intimate relationship with Saudi Arabia, has been in a position to help effect an improvement in the dismal human rights record, the US has rarely criticized Saudi violations.'[33]

A similar charge was levelled by a member of the Arab Organization for Human Rights against Western attitudes

---

* According to the Arab Organization for Human Rights, in 1991 there were 640 political prisoners in Egypt; incidents of detainees being tortured by the security forces increased.

† According to human rights organizations, more than 750 political prisoners are being held in Morocco. *Independent*, 16 June 1992.

towards another Gulf state. 'Bahrain,' he said, 'has a terrible
human rights record, but is looked on by the West as a bastion
of freedom simply because British and American businessmen
can have their liquor there and are not harassed. They have
their nice fancy beaches, and that is all they care for.'

For a Westerner, Bahrain, with its long tradition of British
influence up to and beyond the granting of independence in
1971, seems to be a comforting oasis of liberalism in a region
where legal regulations and social customs tend to inhibit the
lifestyle to which many foreigners are accustomed. But for Bahrainis who are not in full support of the policies of the Emir
and his government – or who are suspected of being opponents
of the regime – the penalties are harsh. Bahrainis have found
the treatment handed out by the security services all the more
offensive because, at least up to the early 1990s, a Briton still
organized the internal security branch of the Bahraini police
force, the department accused of dispensing rough justice. The
Arab Organization for Human Rights reported in 1991 that it
had received 'numerous complaints to the effect that detainees
and prisoners were subjected to acts of violence, torture and
ill-treatment'. A year later there was little change in the picture.
'Prisoners', the Organization said, 'are habitually subjected to
torture and ill-treatment after being arrested . . . and torture
is habitually used to induce those accused to give information
or make confessions to be used as grounds to convict them.
There are other situations in which detainees are subjected to
torture or the threat of it to force them to cooperate with the
authorities.'[34]

The human rights reports also point to a number of cases in
which the Bahraini authorities have confiscated passports from
their citizens, and in which citizens living abroad have not been
able to return home. This was the fate of Abdel-Hadi Khalaf,
a professor at Lund University in Sweden. During a brief period
after the declaration of independence from Britain in 1971
Bahrain allowed a National Assembly to convene. Khalaf, a
leftist, was one of the youngest and most outspoken members
of parliament. When the assembly was dissolved and the constitution suspended Khalaf was imprisoned for a time before

going into voluntary exile. The Bahraini authorities subsequently refused to renew his passport. In March 1992, Khalaf flew back to Bahrain and was detained for questioning at the airport for eighteen hours before being put on a flight to London. He was not allowed to contact his family in the country while at the airport. Khalaf later set out the details of his case and those of other alleged breaches of human rights by the Bahraini authorities in a letter to the Emir. The letter was published by an Arabic-language newspaper in London. Khalaf openly admitted that he was a member of the Bahraini opposition and had wanted to return to his home country. He said he was willing to face any legal charges which might be brought against him. Khalaf described his interrogation at the airport as 'tragi-comic' because the two Bahraini policemen involved 'could not hide their embarrassment at the duty they were carrying out – the main part of it being to translate the questions connected with the investigation, which had been written in English, into Arabic. (Can you imagine, Your Highness, from English to Arabic, and we are in an Arab country which has been independent for twenty years?).' Khalaf told the Emir he was writing directly to him because he was afraid that if His Highness ever heard about the case some of the true meaning of the report might get lost in translation from Arabic to English, or vice versa.

Western anxiety about possible public criticism of the regimes in the Gulf is intense. In 1991, during a visit to Bahrain I was discussing with a British diplomat the rash of border disputes in the Gulf – including the one between Bahrain and Qatar – and what these lingering disputes showed about the lack of success in moves towards greater regional cooperation. 'Yes, but I really do not think it would be wise of you to write about it,' the diplomat said. 'They are very sensitive about issues of this kind.'

Fear, rather than a respect of sensitivity, has discouraged forthright analysis and criticism within the Middle East of the machinations of Arab leaders – either of the way they rule their own people or how they deal with outside powers. While in some countries, like Egypt, criticism of the regime is allowed,

negative comments about the president are not. When relations
between two Arab nations break down it is not unusual for
the official media in each to declare war, with stinging abuse
directed at the respective leaders and regimes. In general, however, mention of leadership is couched in tones of sycophancy
more than calm objectivity. Abdallah Laroui has chided Arab
intellectuals for not playing a sufficiently active role in working
for change and reform in Middle Eastern society. 'All too long,'
he wrote, 'has the Arab intellectual hesitated to make radical
criticisms of culture, language and tradition. Too long has he
drawn back from criticizing the aims of local national policy,
the result of which is a stifling of democracy and a generalized
dualism.'[35]

Some Arab writers and other intellectuals have made public
calls for greater democracy. But most are realistic enough to
realize that a radical change of this kind 'is dependent on the
existence of well-defined classes or class alliances, whose interests are best served by democracy and who are capable of
imposing it and are willing to practise it'.[36] The reality is that
those with vested interests in the status quo in the various
Arab states – the regimes and their supporters outside, the top
two elements in the three-tier relationship – have nothing to
gain and everything to lose from encouraging the development
of politically aware and active electorates. 'Look what happened in Algeria in January 1992,' a senior Egyptian official
said to me, referring to the success of Islamic fundamentalists.
'If that is the result of democracy, then forget it.' A similar
shocked reaction came from Western states which had been
proclaiming the need for greater democracy around the world.
The Algerian experience presented the West with a dilemma:
should they support the introduction of democracy at all costs,
even if the results threatened Western interests in the Middle
East? As the Algerian authorities stepped in to suspend the
democratic process their unease increased. The *New York Times*
commented that 'Western governments, the Bush administration included, have been shamefully reluctant to condemn
an illegitimate and unwise move . . .'

A number of countries, Jordan and Egypt among them, have

made small moves towards granting greater democratic freedoms. The Jordanian parliament, elected in November 1989 in an unprecedented fair poll, witnessed lively debate, much of it critical of government policies. Despite the outward appearances of parliamentary life in certain Arab states, politicians' freedom of manoeuvre is constrained by the hand of the ruling elite. Even more significantly, the Arab people's experience of democracy is, at best, limited. In the view of Mona Makrem Obeid, a member of parliament in Egypt, democracy should evolve from the roots of society rather than be imposed from above. 'It is no use saying that Egypt is a democracy because we have a parliament, elections and so on. Democracy is a culture that you have to acquire, that you have to learn through experience. Small organizations and associations allow you to get the gist of it, to know how to run a campaign, how to differ without getting at each other's throats. Egyptians and other Arabs are not being allowed to get that experience.'[37]

Radical moves towards full and free democracy in the Arab world do not seem likely in the near future, nor is there much prospect of a softening in the relationship between regimes and the ordinary people. The Syrian intellectual, Sadeq al-Azm, in his bitter analysis of the Arab defeat in the 1967 war with Israel, summed up the relationship between states and people in the Middle East. It is a definition that has needed no altering in the years since it was written. 'Remote and hostile,' he said (his words paraphrased), 'the Arab state is disconnected from its citizenry. The latter wish only to be left alone, and they shelter themselves from the capricious will of the state.'[38] One result of this cold and remote relationship is a widespread lack of respect among ordinary Arabs for their leaders. King Hussein of Jordan and Sultan Qabous of Oman are among the exceptions in having loyal followings at all levels of society. The King has a reputation for hard work and for being sensitive to the needs and aspirations of his people. His pragmatism and adroitness was demonstrated well in 1991, when Jordan refused, despite its reputation as a friend of the West, to join the anti-Saddam Hussein coalition against Iraq. This stand reflected exactly the wishes of the people (and those of most other Arabs) and although it resulted in economic suffering and political isolation for the country, King Hussein won enormous respect from his citizens and from Arabs throughout the region for having shown courage in the face of international pressure. Sultan Qabous's following is more limited – but he has won the respect of the Omanis for his care in making sure that the whole nation benefits from its oil revenues while maintaining the character of a traditional society.

Hussein and Qabous are rare examples. 'There is an almost total disenchantment with rulers in the Arab world,' a Palestinian businessman told me. A young Syrian, in response to a question about the qualities of leadership in the region said 'nepotism and loyalty are the only things that count. It is just like in society at large. If my relative needs a job and there is someone else more qualified, I will still feel happier having my relative.' A Lebanese student said Arabs 'have no respect for their leaders. All the leaders seek is self-glorification.' At a social gathering in Amman, attended by Arabs from six different countries, I asked those around me whom they considered to be the best leader in the region. 'He has not been born yet,' one man replied. The rest chuckled and agreed that this was the best answer they could give. What qualities did they want to see in their leaders? An Iraqi doctor replied: 'The most important thing would be an ability to respect the intelligence of his people and not to insult it.'

That gathering was in December 1991, just after the referendum in Syria which, official figures said, gave President Assad 99.9 per cent backing for a new term in office. The campaign leading up to the referendum effectively brought the country to a halt for two weeks as workers, students and schoolchildren paraded through cities, towns and villages in officially organized marches in support of President Assad. Portraits of the Syrian leader seemed to cover all available wall space. President Assad, smiling, serious, in military uniform or civilian clothes, also stared at one from shopfronts and car windows. A giant portrait covered the whole frontage of a five-storey building in a main square in Damascus. Flags and banners carrying slogans of support hung across the streets. '"Yes" to Hafez al-Assad, a thousand times "yes" to the hero of war and peace'. The officially whipped-up frenzy of street demonstrations all round the country, with car-horns blaring, and slogans chanted by the crowds, were shown at great length each night on Syrian television. 'With our souls and bodies we will sacrifice ourselves for you, O Hafez, protector of our nation and symbol of its struggle'. The chants went on hour after hour, day after day. But the mood of many of the people out of range of the television cameras was strikingly subdued. It was marked more by resignation than jubilation. A high-school student told me he was taking part only because a rumour had gone round that anyone not attending the demonstration would not be allowed to sit his final examinations.

All the fanfare and frenzy were unnecessary: the Syrian people knew the result would be no less than 99 per cent support for the President whatever they did. The moment the outcome was made public the damp Damascus evening was illuminated by signs reading *Mubaruk* – Congratulations. Everything had been prepared; and the marches and fanfares continued, this time in celebration. The fact is, the people could do nothing but accept the charade. Jamal Atassi, a former Syrian minister, dismissed the whole referendum as an effort 'aimed at sanctifying the system and the president. Those who rule this totalitarian state see the people as objects to be manipulated, and they use these spectacles to justify their hold on power.'[39] Cynicism over the integrity of the democratic process – even in a country like Egypt where a semblance of democracy has emerged in recent years – is intense. Saeed al-Ashmawi, a senior judge in Cairo, blamed 'the totalitarian regime of the Nasser era' for the passivity of the people at election time. 'They believe that their votes will never be effective and that the result of the election is known before they give their votes.'[40]

Over the decades, the inability of ordinary Arabs to have any say over their destiny has bred not only contempt for their leaders but apathy towards politics in general. In part, this is the result of the regimes' policy of discouraging mass political enlightenment and debate. 'The various types of political process in the Arab world', Nader Fergany said, 'are centred on persons and cliques. They have definitely strengthened the role of the central power structure vis-à-vis the power of the people. One result is apathy. All you have to do is to look at popular reaction to the Gulf crisis [of 1990–91], for example, and compare it with what used to happen thirty or forty years ago. Then, when some event took place in, say, Damascus you would find demonstrations across the Arab region from the Gulf to Morocco.'[41]

In April 1992, during the political tussle over the fate of the two Libyans accused of involvement in the Lockerbie bombing, anti-Western demonstrations took place in Tripoli. One British newspaper reported the incident with the headline: 'Arab States Braced For Trouble After Tripoli Riots'. But that headline described an Arab world of an earlier era: in the 1990s, to the dismay of the Libyans, popular anger towards Western attitudes was not translated into street protests.

Mass apathy in the Arab world is born in large measure, too, out of the difficulties which millions of people face in their daily lives, especially in countries with large and growing populations and faltering economies like Egypt and Sudan. 'The Egyptian intelligentsia are more radical than the people,' the writer Muhammed Sid Ahmed said. 'The people cannot afford to be all that much politicized because their priority is to get their daily bread.'[42]

CHAPTER SIX

Oil Wealth and Poverty

As recently as the 1960s the drive from the Gulf emirate of Abu Dhabi to neighbouring Dubai was something of a desert adventure. Where a fast highway today whisks cars between the two cities at top speeds, in those days a four-wheel-drive vehicle was needed to guarantee safe passage through the desert sand. As the heat built up during the morning, so the sun began to play tricks on the traveller, offering the false prospect of lakes of shimmering water through the distant haze over the yellowy sand.

Abu Dhabi, Dubai and the other emirates of the Gulf, along with their giant neighbour Saudi Arabia, form the heart of the 'yellow' desert lands of the Arab world. Ignoring the fertile region of Yemen in the south-western tip of the Arabian peninsula, you have to travel a thousand miles or more to the north or north-west to find the 'green' cultivable area — the Nile valley and the Fertile Crescent curving up through the Jordan valley and the eastern coast of the Mediterranean over into Lebanon, Syria and further into Iraq. In many senses the 'green' and the 'yellow' are different worlds. Muhammed Sid Ahmed, an eminent journalist, speaking at the start of the 1990s, singled out the inherent tension of the green–yellow relationship as one of the main reasons for the failure of the Arabs to cooperate and unite in the last quarter of the twentieth century. In earlier decades, he said, the '"green" was everything, while the "yellow" was marginal. Certain nation states with large populations were built up in the "green". Then Israel was implanted into the heart of the "green", so it became all the more a central part.' According to Sid Ahmed's theory, the countries all around Israel developed their armies with the intention of confronting the Jewish state. Military coups were staged in most of the states around Israel – Egypt, Syria and Iraq. But the new republics, with their leaders coming from the military, failed to defeat Israel. Both because of this failure and 'because of a God-send called oil in the "yellow", the epicentre moved there from the "green". There they have enormous wealth; here we have enormous economic problems. Here the military are in power; over there, people are dead afraid of the military. So this dichotomy came into being, taking various expressions.'[1]

The countries of the 'yellow' feared the influence of the military regimes because these seemed both to threaten traditional forms of leadership and to offer nothing to their people except misery – the result of harsh dictatorships and rampant corruption. There was no political model in the 'green' that offered the people in the 'yellow' any more attractive systems of government than those already established in the Gulf.

Muhammed Sid Ahmed's portrait of the 'yellow–green' divide needs qualification. Iraq, Algeria and Libya straddle both categories. As major oil and gas producers, all three would fit theoretically into the yellow category. They are disqualified because they are ruled by regimes in which the military is dominant. Also, in contrast to the Gulf states, Iraq, Algeria and Libya have experienced anti-Western revolutions, and their relations with Europe and the United States are not close. In these respects, and in that they have large populations, Iraq and Algeria could be considered possible candidates for the 'green'. Libya, however, with its small population, its maverick leadership and its geographical position so far from the Gulf, falls uneasily between the two categories. These anomalies apart, Sid Ahmed's argument is based on the fact that the greater part of Arab oil wealth is to be found in Saudi Arabia and the desert emirates of the Gulf where about one tenth of all Arabs live, while the greater part of the Arab population is to be found in countries devoid of abundant natural resources.

As much as the glittering high-rise blocks seem like part of a mirage to those who knew Abu Dhabi before the oil boom, when there was nothing to see but a few small buildings clustered around the ruler's fort, so a journey into rural areas of Iraq or Egypt can seem unreal. Here the trick of the mirage is to make one believe that time has been frozen at some point well before the start of the twentieth century. I drove up into the fertile land of the Nile delta early one summer morning and, north of Kanatir, I stopped to look at the river which was like a misted mirror, the surface rippled at one spot where a group of women were washing clothes. Other women, barefoot – some in bright, long dresses, others in black – approached through the palm trees, carrying their washing in big baskets on their heads. A donkey cart passed by, loaded with cauliflowers, followed by a donkey laden with green vegetation. A boy in a pale blue *jellabah* squatted on top of the pile of greenery, holding a stick in his left hand and gazing with curiosity at the foreigner. From close by came creaking sounds of wood and rope as a buffalo, with a beam from a waterwheel attached, plodded in slow paces through its lazy, circular course, its vision blocked by huge brown eyepatches made out of matted palm leaves.

For the peasants of the Nile delta, as much as for the millions of people living in slums around the major cities in the region, the hope that Arab oil money might be spent on alleviating the hardships of their daily life evaporated even before the last quarter of the twentieth century began. But for a time, up to and after the Arab–Israeli war of October 1973, they were enticed and fooled by a mirage which showed prosperity being shared and Arab political differences being forgotten in the interests of new harmony. For a time, the Arabs were united in standing up to the West. Within a matter of months, however, the West had reasserted itself in its relationship with the fragmented Arab world.

Western interest in exploiting oil resources in the Middle East was aroused early in the century. The Anglo-Persian Oil Company was extracting oil from Iran before the First World War and by the outbreak of the Second World War Iraq was also a major oil exporter – a concession having been granted

to the Turkish Petroleum Company (later to become the Iraq
Petroleum Company) in 1925. Between the wars the gradual
awareness of the importance of Middle Eastern oil began to
influence the attitudes of Western powers towards the new
shape of the region. In Iraq, for example, the realization that
the former Ottoman vilayet of Mosul probably contained large
reserves of oil spurred Britain to make sure that the district
was incorporated into its new client state, rather than being
given to either Turkey or France. Under the terms of the Sykes–
Picot agreement, Mosul was supposed to have been under
French control. Britain resolved this difficulty by guaranteeing
France a share in the future exploitation of oil there. Oil production in Kirkuk began in 1928–29.

In 1932, Bahrain became the first of the other states in the
region to find oil. This discovery sparked interest in the surrounding region – not just from Britain, France and the Nether-
lands, but also from the United States. Despite strong objections
from Britain, Standard Oil of New Jersey won a concession
from Saudi Arabia in 1933. This was the start of a close relationship between the United States and the kingdom – under the
deserts of which a quarter of the proven oil reserves in the world
are to be found. The economic, political and military ties
between Riyadh and Washington grew stronger as the decades
passed, culminating in the despatch of an American-led international force to the kingdom in 1990 to defend it from possible
attack by the Iraqi army which had occupied Kuwait. By this
time, Arab oil, and the need to secure and guarantee its safe
passage out of the Gulf region, dominated Western concerns
in the Middle East. As the Egyptian analyst Fawzy Mansour
wrote, in Saudi Arabia 'the West had indeed found a most
loyal, unquestioning and unswerving ally'.[2]

In the early days of oil production in the Gulf, the foreign
firms capitalized on the naivety of the ruling families in drawing up concession deals. As a result, the agreements 'with the
producing countries reflected the unequal balance not only of
financial but of political strength, with British power supporting, in the last resort, the position of the companies; the concessions under which they operated gave them control of

exploration, production, refining and export, over wide areas and for long periods, subject to payment of limited royalties to the host governments and the provision of limited quantities of oil for their use.'³

All the cards were in the hands of the major oil companies. In the view of Yusif Sayigh, a leading Arab economist and oil expert, 'the combined weight of all these components of power gave the companies the added power to intimidate and later effectively to influence the governments of the oil-producing countries. This situation remained largely unchallenged till the mid-1950s, or over thirty years after the first agreement had been signed with an Arab country.'⁴

In the 1950s, demands in the Arab world for a bigger share of the fruits of oil exploitation intensified, coinciding with the burgeoning of the pan-Arabist nationalist movement. 'Arab Oil for the Arabs', was the slogan. But the major companies were reluctant to give ground. According to Yusif Sayigh, 'in the early phase, the style was essentially one of reasoning or arguing with the companies to take greater account of the strong desire to have a larger say in the control and management of production and pricing, and of the pressing financial needs of the producing countries and their right, as real owners of the resource, to receive more revenue than they were in the practice of receiving.'⁵

A more assertive style was adopted by the oil states after the formation of the Organization of Petroleum Exporting States (OPEC) in September 1960. The first OPEC meeting was held in Baghdad, and the Iraqis led the challenge to the supremacy of the major oil companies. In December 1961 the Baghdad government reclaimed more than 99.5 per cent of the concession area of the Iraq Petroleum Company. But the Baghdad government paid a heavy price for its policy towards the foreign companies. The 1960s was an era of confrontation between the Iraqi government and the companies. The latter kept production low throughout this period, depriving the country of a sizeable share of its potential income. It is a grudge against the West which is still borne by the Iraqis. The Iraq Petroleum Company was eventually nationalized in June 1972. The

Algerian oil and Libyan oil industries were also nationalized around this period.[6]

Iraq, Algeria and Libya, countries in which strong anti-Western moods prevailed, were the most bold and aggressive in their dealings with foreign oil companies. Other Arab producers, like Saudi Arabia and Kuwait, followed more gingerly in their footsteps, choosing to acquire steadily increasing concession rights rather than going for outright nationalization. The final results were the same and by the end of the 1970s all the Arab oil producers had at least majority control over their industries.

The producing countries may have reached satisfactory agreements with the oil companies in the early 1970s but the new arrangements did not come in time to prevent deep resentment developing in Arab minds. The struggle put up by oil companies (backed solidly by governments and public opinion in the West) to defend their concessions has been regarded ever since as proof of the extent to which the Western industrialized world exploited cynically and ruthlessly the precious natural resources in (and belonging to) the Middle East.

The 1970s represented both 'the most significant decade in the history of Arab oil',[7] and the start of an era when oil complicated still further the relationship between the Arabs and the West. The change came about as a direct result of the Arab–Israeli war in October 1973. Yusif Sayigh has pointed out that until this moment there was little consideration given in either the advanced industrial world or the Third World to complexities of the oil exploitation and marketing process. To the world at large, 'oil was gasoline to feed cars with, fuel-oil to operate central-heating systems, or kerosene for primuses to cook on in the poorer households.'[8]

From 1973 onwards governments and the public in the West began to focus increasing attention on Middle Eastern oil and on the rich Arabs who controlled it. The reason for their concern was the decision of Arab oil producers, meeting in Kuwait on 17 October 1973, 'to cut back on production by 5 per cent a month until Israel evacuated all occupied territories; at another meeting on 4 November these cutbacks were enlarged to 25 per

cent. In addition to the general cutbacks, there was a selective
embargo against Western supporters of Israel and a concerted
price rise of 70 per cent instituted by all Arab countries.'[9]

The use of the oil weapon in the 1973 war came against the
background of euphoria at the spectacular early Arab successes
in that conflict. President Sadat of Egypt denied reports that
he had asked the Saudis and other Gulf producers to back the
frontline states with the use of the oil weapon. The Egyptian
leader said he travelled to Saudi Arabia in August 1973 to tell
King Feisal of his intention to launch, with Syria, a war against
Israel. In his memoirs, President Sadat claims to have said to
the Saudi king: 'As for your role, I leave that to you. Do what
you can and see fit.'[10] However, an independent account of
this meeting says that 'Sadat went no further than discussing
contingency planning, without revealing how imminent war
was. But he succeeded in exacting firmer – but unspecified –
pledges from Feisal of support through the use of Saudi oil
resources and increased financial aid, if and when the battle
were to commence. Similar assurances were obtained from
Qatar and Kuwait.'[11]

The Saudis' action shocked the West but failed to bring the
United States and Europe to its knees. The tactic enabled the
Arabs to enjoy, all of a sudden, 'a brief moment of elation.
All, including Palestinian self-determination, seemed possible.
Great and sudden wealth spawned all sorts of dreams about
development, about military power, about the resurrection of
the Arab world.'[12] But the brief moment passed. Anger in the
West at what was regarded as Arab impudence was translated
into swift action. Measures were taken to find new reserves of
oil outside the Gulf, to develop alternative sources of energy
and to encourage conservation. The result was that for the
overwhelming majority of Arabs nothing had changed. Yusif
Sayigh's view is that the joint Arab action was carried out 'with
insufficient stamina'.[13] The intention had been both to express
displeasure at the way the West had rallied behind Israel in
the war and to mobilize international pressure, through the
United States, to force the Israelis to withdraw from occupied
Arab land. But the West stood firm, angrily and indignantly

insisting that it would not submit to pressure. Public opinion railed against the Arabs – the image of the 'filthy rich oil sheikh' lodged itself in the Western mind – and the industrialized nations displayed almost aggressive determination to lessen their long-term dependence on Middle Eastern oil. On the demand that the West should take steps to secure a Middle East settlement, the United States – and in particular President Nixon's pro-Israeli Secretary of State Henry Kissinger – insisted that Washington would not even consider encouraging the withdrawal of Israel from occupied land while the embargo was still in force. The joint Arab resolve crumbled in March 1974. King Feisal insisted that the initiative to end the embargo should come from Presidents Sadat and Assad; a request to this effect was made and accepted at an Arab summit in Algiers in February 1974.

The tactic was thus abandoned before it had any opportunity of achieving its aim, and the period of collective Arab euphoria was followed closely by another era of despair for the millions living in the 'green'. In the opinion of Albert Hourani 'military weakness, the growth of separate interests and of economic dependence all led to a disintegration of whatever common front had seemed to exist until the war of 1973.'[14] The Egyptian sociologist Saad Eddin Ibrahim described this period in the following way: 'The quadrupling of oil prices, meant at the time as a pressure tactic on the West to expedite an honourable resolution of the Arab–Israeli conflict, triggered instead the birth of a new Arab order. The march of socio-political events during the remainder of the 1970s compounded a crisis of legitimacy in this emerging order. Petrodollars spoke louder than revolutionary ideologies. Pragmatism gained precedence over idealism.'[15]

It turned out that unity had been yet another beguiling mirage; and despite attempts by Sadat and other leaders to portray the war as a military victory, the only real winners among the Arabs were those who had wielded the oil weapon. They benefited from staggering increases in oil revenues which, in turn, bought them political power. The oil states found that their continued prosperity depended on cooperation rather than confrontation with their intended targets in the West. The new Arab order meant that the 'yellow' was inclined increasingly to follow an independent track, looking more towards London, Paris and Washington than Cairo, Damascus and Baghdad. 'What led the Arab system downhill was, ironically, the war of 1973,' Jamil Matar, a Cairo-based political scientist said. 'This opened for the first time in the Arab world the cleavage between rich and poor. Before 1973 you could not say there were very rich Arabs and very poor Arabs. Some Arabs were rich, but nothing like the way it was after the 1970s.'[16] The pattern of inter-Arab relationships established after the 1973 war, fused with the West's increasing political and economic involvement with the Gulf states, influenced Arab–Western attitudes in the decades which followed.

The change in attitudes and relationships forced the Arab people to come to terms with the fact that – to quote the play on words in Arabic coined at the time – *tharwa* (wealth) had taken on more importance than *thaura* (revolution). The problem which has left the region sharply divided ever since stems from the fact that the overwhelming majority of Arabs have found themselves stranded empty-handed between any prospect of revolutionary change on the one side, and any hope of benefiting from oil wealth on the other.

The effects of this new phenomenon were clearly visible in the economic problems faced by Egypt in the years after the 1973 war. President Sadat's unique recipe for coping with these problems led eventually to a further cleavage in the Arab world.

Egypt's difficulties stemmed from the fact that, despite the enormous rise in revenue from the sale of Middle East oil, only a small amount of the new wealth 'percolated to Egypt, first in the form of loans and grants from Arab governments, then in the form of remittances from hundreds of thousands of Egyptians who temporarily migrated to work in the oil-rich Arab countries. These transfers and remittances (between US$3 and 4 billion a year) created an atmosphere of euphoria among the Egyptian people.' But this was borrowed prosperity without foundation, and 'Sadat began to get into deep trouble with his budget, his balance of payments, his creditors, and the legitimate demands of the masses whose standard of living was increasingly undermined by the period of "restoration" and *infitah* [open door economic policy to attract foreign investment] which followed the 1973 war. The oil-money loans and grants miraculously dried up, or were made conditional upon agreement with the IMF.'[17] The accumulation of economic difficulties led to serious food riots in January 1977. Crowds rampaged through Cairo, attacking restaurants, casinos and nightclubs – symbols of wealth and the favourite haunts of both the Egyptian elite and the newly rich Arabs of the Gulf.

Faced either with seeking further short-term remedies for the catastrophic economic problems at home or with attracting Western aid and investment by making peace with Israel, President Sadat decided to gamble on the latter option, whatever the political cost. Muhammed Sid Ahmed said he interpreted Sadat's action 'less in terms of wanting to go to Israel than feeling, in a way, betrayed by the Gulf Arabs. It was thanks to his war that they got rich. But then he had to cope with the hunger riots. Why should he be in solidarity with them when they were not in solidarity with him? So he decided he would obtain his own cards and play on his own. This created a position where Egypt played the cards of the West. And this has not changed. What President Mubarak has done is to restore a certain equilibrium – not to appear to the Arabs as being part of the West at their expense. But not abrogating anything that Sadat did.'[18]

In the view of Jamil Matar, President Sadat was well aware of the political isolation in the Arab world which he and his country would face by seeking peace with Israel. 'Sadat did not want any pressures from the Arabs, even though some of them, like Saudi Arabia, were his allies. The Saudis would have given him money, but with a condition attached – not to go fast in the peace process with Israel. He did not want even that condition. So he began to cut his links with the Arabs. The process culminated in the 1976 summit in which he said frankly: "I don't want any involvement in Arab affairs." This finally led to his own isolation in 1979–80.'[19]

The momentous and astonishing events of this period – Presi-

dent Sadat's visit to Jerusalem in November 1977, the talks in
Camp David in the United States the following year and the
signing of the Egypt–Israel peace treaty on 26 March 1979 –
were greeted with overwhelming satisfaction and joy in the
West. The Egyptian leader, it was said, had finally broken the
mould of Middle Eastern bigotry and shown himself to be a
man of imagination and courage. Most Arabs, by contrast, were
outraged and depressed.

From a Western viewpoint, Sadat's actions were bound to
be applauded because they brought the largest and most influential Arab country firmly into the camp of the United States,
Europe and Israel, shoring up the West's influence (at a time
of continuing superpower rivalry) and helping to ensure security in a region which was essential for the supply of oil to the
industrialized world. Hope was expressed, too, that other Arab
states would see the wisdom of Egypt's decision and follow its
example. Camp David and the peace treaty were, in every
sense, a good thing. Few voices in the West could be heard
either expressing reservations about the treaty or trying to
understand and interpret the generally negative attitude
towards it of the majority of Arabs. As a result of this, the
West's views about Camp David and the treaty have solidified.

For Arabs – especially those outside Egypt – Sadat was
regarded as dancing cynically to the tune of the United States
and the West for his own motives and, more seriously, of
destroying 'the formal Arab consensus'.[20] Technical measures
adopted by the Arab consensus in reaction to the Egyptian
moves, like Cairo's twelve-year suspension from the Arab
League and the temporary removal of the League's headquarters to Tunis, could do nothing to heal the psychological
damage to the collective Arab mind. Practical harm, too, was
caused by President Sadat's actions. The opening of the dialogue with the Jewish state and the increasing identification
with the consumerism of the West fuelled the Islamic fundamentalist movement in Egypt which continues to threaten the
stability of the country. Stability has been threatened also by
the failure of the promise of the peace treaty to bring prosperity
to the mass of Egyptians. On the contrary, ordinary Egyptians

have been treated to further 'provocative flaunting of worldly goods' by the rich elite. In general, in discussion with Egyptians from across the political and sociological spectra, one senses strongly that the formal normalisation of relations with Israel has not been accepted by the public.

Outside Egypt, the Lebanese and the Palestinians (along with many Israelis) have pointed out on more occasions than one that the Israeli invasion of Lebanon in 1982 would probably never have happened if the Jewish state had not signed a peace treaty with Egypt. In the event, Israel felt confident committing its armed forces to the north, knowing that its southern flank was secure. Thousands of Arabs were killed, injured or uprooted from their homes by the 1982 war in Lebanon.

The Palestinians also point out that the sections within the Camp David agreements regarding autonomy in the Israeli-occupied West Bank and Gaza Strip were concluded without consultation with the Arabs concerned. Muhammed Sid Ahmed, an opponent of the peace treaty at the time, has continued to argue for a reappraisal of it, partly because of the way it led to the betrayal both of the Palestinians and of the Arabs as a whole. He believes that 'Egypt had no business committing itself to Israel on the Palestinian issue. Egypt could deal concerning Sinai, because that was its problem. But it had no business committing the Palestinians to autonomy. Even if they never get more than this in the end, it is not up to Egypt to commit itself as an Arab state in order to project the image that it [the treaty with Israel] was a comprehensive Middle East arrangement and not just an Egyptian one. So to cover itself, Egypt cornered the Palestinians. They have got nothing more since, and it was a precedent to that extent. This was a very serious mistake made by Egypt; but it was not the most important one. I would say the most important one is this: Israel departs on the assumption that a peace arrangement with Egypt is peace – that all the rest is irrelevant. As long as Egypt is not a threat to peace, then peace is achieved. So Egypt betrayed the rest of the Arab world as far as that is concerned. Getting itself out was leaving others in the cold, unable either to achieve peace or war.'[21]

Debates along these or other lines over the wisdom of President Sadat's actions continue in Egypt and elsewhere in the Arab world – bringing to light side-effects and nuances of the Camp David affair which are generally ignored in popular Western assessments of the period. Similar debates began towards the end of 1993 after Arabs saw television pictures of the PLO Chairman, Yassar Arafat, shaking hands with the Israeli Prime Minister, Yitzhak Rabin, following the signing of an autonomy agreement for the occupied territories.

Most Arabs living outside the Gulf region found themselves at the end of the 1970s forced to accept roles as spectators watching the wealth pile up in the Gulf. Resentment brewed in the large and overcrowded cities around the Middle East. In the words of Mohamed Heikal, 'a prize of unimaginable proportions had been handed to desert people who lacked the history or the culture to absorb it, while Egypt, the centre of Arab experience and culture, received only small change. The masses who had struggled for independence and Arab control of oil production were left out ... City-states created more through colonial carelessness than Arab history began to regard themselves as real countries.'[22]

Within a few years, Abu Dhabi (later to be the nucleus of the United Arab Emirates), Kuwait and other sheikhdoms became not just 'real countries', but extremely rich ones – registered in the top bracket of states with high per capita income. Between 1970 and 1980, major Arab producers raised their oil revenues from less than US$5 billion a year, to US$100 billion, a 2000 per cent increase.[23]

Heikal's view that the cities of the Gulf were created through 'colonial carelessness' will be challenged by many Arab analysts. Fawzy Mansour, for example, has attacked the former colonial powers and the United States for having deliberately moulded many of the Gulf countries so that the interests and sympathies of the ruling elites were directed as much, if not more, towards the West as towards the rest of the Arab world. Saudi Arabia, while never having been dominated by a foreign power nor having had a ruling hierarchy shaped or imposed from outside, came under strong American influence in the

1930s. Other Gulf states were bound to Britain by a string of treaties which were signed in the last half of the nineteenth and the early years of the twentieth centuries. Mansour has specifically blamed Britain for suppressing 'the traditional Arab trading activities which had for so long sustained the Arabian ports connecting the Far East and India with the Mediterranean and the West'. The result was 'the shift of the political centre of gravity from the ports and trading towns to the tribal heartland, and the rise to prominence of the markedly tribal formations which became the basis of the political divisions (or partitions) which emerged in the wake of World War One'. A further result was that 'instead of the more or less primitive cycles of alternation of power between tribal elites, based on that judicious mixture of vigorous leadership and democratic consent characteristic of the desert political system, a rigid hereditary system was imposed.' In this way, Mansour continued his thesis, 'absolutist power replaced tribal democracy; conflicts over frontiers which had no historical basis became both rife and insoluble; conditions of citizenship in this or that state or statelet became arbitrary; and instead of the general sentiment of belonging to one people, even though divided into various tribes, artificial local patriotism was created and fostered.'[24] Local patriotism became more pronounced as the riches gained by the sale of oil grew, leading to the squandering of money as states in the region vied to outshine each other in the creation of lavish new cities in the desert. The era of the 'yellow' had opened.

To visit the oil-producing states is to enter a strange, multiracial world. It is possible to stay several days in one of these countries and have no contact whatsoever with an indigenous Arab. Most of the jobs which involve day-to-day contact with the public – at the airport, at the hotel check-in desk, at restaurants and the like – are performed by foreigners; none of the manual work is carried out by Gulf Arabs. Kuwait, before the Iraqi invasion of 1990, was 'prosperous and relatively stable; to its wealthy and indolent upper classes it was home, while its imported masses, the mainly Asian guestworkers, saw it as a temporary haven and a source of high wages'.[25] Before and during the 1991 Gulf war, most foreign workers left; others, including around 500,000 Palestinians, were expelled when the hostilities ended. But Kuwaitis were not queueing up to apply for their jobs. 'No Kuwaiti will get his hands dirty,' a factory owner said in May 1992. 'Nothing has changed.' A civil engineer in the same period reported that of his twenty employees, only six did the work. 'If the rest come in at all they sit around and drink coffee,' he said.[26] One might wonder how the Gulf states survive in this atmosphere of indolence. To find the answer you have to step only a few metres behind the façade of fashionable shops, five-star hotels and shining high-rise office blocks. Here, where the tall buildings cast shadows over narrow and dirty backstreets you find the engine-room of the Gulf states. It is a world of spicy aromas, hessian sacks of basmati rice and yellow and brown beans, bright saris, bales of Indian silk lined up in small shopwindows, Pakistani tailors and the large black cow-horn bicycles with brand names like 'Phoenix' and 'Flying Pigeon'. Oil generates the money in the Gulf but the Indian subcontinent supplies much of the labour which, behind the scenes, provides the foundation on which the economic prosperity survives.

Nader Fergany, a political scientist in Cairo, ascribes the negative attitude of the Gulf Arabs towards labour to the failure of the social incentive system throughout Middle East, in rich areas as much as in poor ones, 'to reward honest, productive work'. According to Fergany, in the Gulf, the problem is compounded by the presence of a large foreign workforce which is attracted to the region by the relatively high wages on offer. 'In a country like Kuwait, for example, or many Gulf countries, we have a mosaic of expatriate labour and local population; but it ends up with people – nationals and expatriates – having very low social productivity.'[27]

Airports and ports in the Gulf are frequently packed with foreign workers, from Europe, the United States, the Asian subcontinent and beyond, queueing at immigration desks or waiting in departure lounges surrounded by the spoils of their stay in the region. But many of the travellers are Arabs – a high proportion of them peasants from the overpopulated

or poor countries like Egypt and Yemen. Commenting on the
phenomenon of the Arab workforce on the move in the last
quarter of the twentieth century Saad Eddin Ibrahim observed
that a steady movement of Arabs around the region had been
'a common occurrence for centuries (from the eighth to the
beginning of the twentieth). Cultural affinities of language,
religion, and lifestyles facilitated such movement and subsequent adjustment in a new residence; and the absence of
rigid national state borders made it all possible. However, with
the exception of brief large-scale migrations, namely in the
early Arab–Islamic conquest of the seventh and eighth centuries, human movement remained small though frequent.'[28]
The oil boom of the 1970s changed the pattern. The desire of
the newly rich countries to build modern states complete with
infrastructure and service industries, to diversify their economies away from dependence on oil and to develop defence
capabilities made the import of labour in an under-populated
corner of the region a necessity. Of the major oil producers
only Iraq and Algeria had populations large enough to meet
the demand for labour. Before the 1973 Middle East war, total
inter-Arab migration stood at 680,000; in 1980 the figure had
reached an estimated three million.[29]

Those countries providing the labour benefited greatly from
the mobility of the Arab workforce. In Egypt, for example, the
migration of millions of workers to the Gulf and elsewhere had
the effect both of easing the strain on the labour market at
home and boosting the domestic economy through the arrival
of workers' remittances. In 1987, the Foreign Minister of Egypt
Dr Boutrous Boutrous Ghali (who later became Secretary General of the United Nations) spoke about the problems faced by
a country in which 50 million people were living on just 5 per
cent of the land – in Cairo, along the Nile valley and in the
delta. Dr Boutrous Ghali admitted that Egypt had failed in all
efforts to control the population explosion – with the total
number of Egyptians expected to reach at least 70 million by
the end of the century. 'We have tried to encourage birth control,' he said, 'but without success. I believe that the only solution now is to to try first of all to get people out of Cairo and

then out of the Nile valley. After that, I would say, we have
to encourage emigration. Otherwise we will face a unique problem at the end of the century.'[30]

Millions of Egyptians have responded to government encouragement and economic necessity by finding work abroad. But
the picture is not as simple as it seems. The movement of so
many people has naturally caused social disruption in the
labour-supplying countries; and workers in the host states have
frequently had to tolerate poor living conditions and the
humiliation of being treated as inferior citizens there. This is
because the Gulf states have been at pains to prevent migrant
workers – Arabs at least as much non-Arabs – becoming integrated into their societies.

Also, because the migrant workers become part of a low-
productivity, parasitic economic system, their return home has
tended to be doubly damaging to the domestic economies. The
first and obvious effect is the halting of remittances. As well as
this there have often been difficulties experienced by returnees
in re-integrating themselves into the economic life of their
home countries. Jamil Matar has noticed a restlessness on the
part of Egyptians who have worked abroad, many of whom
have been pitched straight from remote villages into the dazz-
ling twenty-first-century world of the Gulf. 'When they were
in the Gulf they were frustrated at the bad treatment there.
They also lived badly. When they found they had made money
they escaped from the bad treatment. They said: To hell with
the Gulf. We're going back to our own country. When they
got back here they were often not content to return to their
villages. So they stayed in the cities, and their money began to
be spent. At which point they started thinking about going
back to the Gulf – forgetting the bad treatment there, and so
on.'[31] Fawzy Mansour has pointed out another related factor.
During their stay in the Gulf migrant workers have usually
earned enough money to be able to buy electrical and elec-
tronic goods, and to develop a taste for such consumer dur-
ables. This taste does not desert them when they are back on
home soil. Merchants in their home country are equally keen
to meet the demand for video recorders, deep-freezers and

other items of this kind. All these goods have to be brought from abroad, adding to the country's import bill.

Some of the workers returning from the Gulf have invested their money in land, small factories and businesses in rural areas. But many thousands more have contributed little towards the productive sector of the economy, the earnings from which are needed to meet the rising import bill. 'Whatever is left of the migrant worker's savings usually goes to finance some sort of parasitic or marginal activity in which he attempts to set himself up as an independent operator, since he had learnt little in the way of directly productive activities in the oil-rich country and has now come to consider himself liberated from the toil which drove him to migrate from his own country in the first place.'[32]

For a full decade after the oil-price boom of the mid-1970s the demand for foreign labour in the Gulf states was so great that Egyptians and other Arabs could feel confident of finding liberation there from their toil at home. Between winter 1985 and spring 1986 oil prices, which had been stable at around US$28 a barrel, fell to $9. When OPEC ministers met in September 1986 they succeeded in checking and reversing the slide in prices by agreeing on restraint in oil production. Prices settled at around US$18 a barrel.[33] The slump was brief, but it was long enough to cause a severe shock to Arab oil producers. The sudden fluctuation served as a warning that the days of guaranteed high income and unrestricted spending might not last for ever. In the years which followed the price collapse, Saudi Arabia and the other Gulf countries began talking for the first time about the need to tighten their belts.

If Gulf rulers started feeling anxious when their spending power diminished, most of the blame lay at their own feet. In all the Gulf countries, 'the state owns the oil revenues and the ruler or ruling family virtually owns the state. The form may differ from one state to another, but the end result is the same.'[34] According to my own sources in the Gulf states, ruling families tend to take between 40 and 50 per cent of oil revenues for themselves. The rest goes to the state. Regardless of how many foreign advisers the rulers of the sheikhdoms may employ, the ultimate power to spend or not to spend rests with them and their families. There are no detailed budgets, and no checks and balances on spending. 'The ruling families not only cream off the oil revenues,' one Arab economist who has detailed knowledge of conditions in the Gulf said, 'they also take a commission on the big contracts with overseas firms.'

The reality is that the decade after 1973 saw an orgy of spending and overspending – with Western companies queueing up for lucrative contracts and shamelessly overcharging whenever they could get away with it. Fortunes were spent, and fortunes made – not least by import agents in the Gulf states who, with the right connections with the ruling clan if they were not part of the family holding power, found they could accumulate wealth with minimal effort. Even in the mid-1980s, when the days of bumper fortunes had passed, an American arms dealer is said to have paid US$12 million to agents in the United Arab Emirates to secure a major deal because 'that was the going rate for commissions at the time.'[35] As far as the Gulf states were concerned each was acting out of its own self-interest and desire to impress its neighbours. The result was chronic duplication of effort and wasting of money.

In the early 1960s, my father recalled being on board a fourteen-seat de Havilland Dove aircraft operated by Gulf Aviation. The plane was approaching one of the small sheikhdoms and the British pilot was having trouble spotting the flattened strip of sand marked by oil drums which served as the runway. The pilot asked my father to come into the cramped cockpit and help look for the landing site. Proper airports were scarce. Less than thirty years later, Gulf states were facing the problem of having too many airports. At a Gulf conference on aviation held in Bahrain, delegates discussed ways of attracting traffic and business to the fifteen fully equipped international airports in the Gulf. Capacity far outstripped demand because of the desire of each emirate (or each city, in the case of the United Arab Emirates), no matter how small, to have its own international facilities. If the individual rulers had been advised or had listened to advice they would have realized that they were wasting their money. (Western contractors and suppliers certainly would not have been those offering guidance of this kind.) But the decision to spend money on building airports or on the countless other wasted prestige projects was based on inter-tribe (and, therefore, inter-state) rivalry and one-upmanship rather than the principles of economic management. The piecemeal development of states in the region continued despite the creation in 1980 of a Gulf Cooperation Council (GCC) linking Saudi Arabia, Kuwait, Bahrain, Qatar, the United Arab Emirates and Oman. A look at the expansion of aviation in the oil era provides some useful pointers towards the failure of inter-Gulf cooperation and the problems this has caused.

'We should work together. No single state can stand on its own,' a Bahraini speaker said in a moment of candour at the aviation conference mentioned above. 'Regrettably, we in the Gulf are speaking different languages when it comes to promoting the region. Each wants the business for its own country.' The existence of the GCC has not succeeded in bringing the four international airlines serving the six member states under one umbrella, nor of eliminating fierce rivalry among them. Gulf Air, a consortium of four states which is based in Bahrain, was involved in the late 1980s and early 1990s in fierce competition with Emirates – an airline based in Dubai. The picture is complicated further by the fact that Dubai is a member of the United Arab Emirates, while Abu Dhabi, the dominant emirate in the UAE, is a shareholder in Gulf Air. Enmity between Bahrain and Dubai was such that Emirates was not invited to the 1991 regional conference hosted by the former state. When I questioned publicly how such a gathering could ignore the existence of Dubai, the reaction was one of horror – that anyone should have had the nerve to raise in public this delicate, embarrassing and, therefore, unmentionable subject. Some delegates said they expected me to be put on the first plane out of Bahrain. The expressions of shock and apprehension stemmed from the fact that criticism of the blatant failings of the GCC within the Gulf is frowned upon. In December 1991, a meeting of Gulf professors and politicians in Kuwait took the highly unusual step of airing such negative sentiments in public. 'We hear the same words again and again,' Meshari al-Osaimi, the head of the Kuwaiti lawyers' association said. 'We do not see anything . . . except meetings and a lot of kissing. I personally do not expect anything out of Gulf council meetings.' A professor from Bahrain, Abdel-Latif al-Mahmoud, said there could be no progress within the GCC while the systems of government remained unchanged.[36] When Professor Mahmoud flew back home to Bahrain in the evening of the 13 December he was arrested at Muharraq airport. He was later released, but was stripped of his job at Bahrain University and banned from travelling abroad.[37]

Some inter-Gulf disputes are potentially much more serious than rivalries over prestige. The most dangerous of all was the confrontation between Kuwait and Iraq in 1990–91, although Iraq is not formally counted as a 'Gulf' state. Even within the GCC, which was set up specifically in response to the perceived danger of the Iraq–Iran war spilling over into the Gulf, there are serious disputes. Armed forces from two member-states, Saudi Arabia and Qatar, clashed in 1992 in a border dispute; at the same time, the Qataris and the Bahrainis were maintaining a military stand-off over a small cluster of islands in an area which could be rich in oil and gas. Also in 1992, Saudi Arabia sent warning letters to seven international oil companies which were drilling in an area on the Yemen border claimed by both countries. The dispute dates back to the 1930s: under an agreement signed at Taif in Yemen in 1934, compromise was reached on a joint frontier comprising only about 15 per cent of the total common border. The remainder was the subject of agreements variously between the British and the former Ottoman authorities on one side, and Saudi Arabia and Yemen on the other. The US administration successfully persuaded the Saudis not to pursue their claim by any means other than negotiation. But an understanding on this matter has never been reached between Saudi Arabia and Yemen.

Arabs outside the Gulf have watched these regional squabbles and the wasteful spending schemes with undisguised disgust. Also, the hypocrisy of the lavish and profligate lifestyles enjoyed in Western capitals by some prominent Gulf Arabs, who claim when they are in their home countries to be abiding by the strictest interpretations of Islam, does not go unnoticed by ordinary people in the region. The sight of drunken Saudi men staggering out of imitation British-style pubs in the international hotels in Bahrain and speeding off in expensive cars back across the causeway to their home country where alcohol is prohibited, does nothing to help the Arab guestworker in the backrooms develop respect either for the Gulf states or for the Western powers which support and defend them. As the Syrian poet Nizar Qabbani wrote in 'Footnotes to the Book of the Setback', after the defeat of the Arabs in the June 1967 war:

> Our desert oil could have become
> Daggers of flame and fire.
> We're a disgrace to our noble ancestors:
> We let our oil flow through the toes of whores.[38]

'These Gulf princes spend half their time in Europe fucking prostitutes,' a Syrian student in Damascus commented with disgust in 1991, a few months after the ending of the Gulf war and the defeat of Iraq by the Western-led coalition. 'They do this all day, and yet the West welcomes them and treats them with respect.' Bitter remarks of this kind can be heard frequently among non-Gulf Arabs. Another persistent theme in the same vein relates to the failure of the rich Arabs to give financial support to the poor. Of all the Gulf states Kuwait stands out as the one which, since 1962, has contributed more, relative to its gross domestic product, than any other to development schemes within the Arab world and beyond. Kuwait was the initiator of Arab aid schemes, establishing both its own and pan-Arab development funds in the emirate. Only after 1973, more than ten years after Kuwait began to set the example, did other Gulf states become major aid donors. In a region where oil revenue has usually been spent lavishly in the producing states or invested in the West, Kuwait has a record of generosity to other Arab and other developing countries. Libya has been producing a similar quantity of oil to Kuwait since the mid-1960s; the populations of the two states are also roughly the same. But, in the words of a leading Arab economist, 'Libya has hardly given any aid to anyone.'

The London-based daily *Al-Quds al-Arabi* developed the theme of the general Arab reluctance to invest in the region in an editorial in 1992. It pointed out that 'less than 10 per cent of all Arab oil money and revenue is placed in Arab investment schemes, while the rest is circulated through Western banks and financial institutions in Europe and the United States. The second Gulf war revealed that the size of Arab investments in the West had reached US$760 billion, most of which came from the oil states. At the same time the collective total of Arab debts stood at US$205 billion – with Egypt owing US$50 billion, Algeria US$30 billion, Jordan US$8 billion, and so on.' The editorial went on to criticize the arguments put forward by the Gulf states to justify their investment policy – that instability in the Arab world would put their money at risk if it were deposited there. The paper pointed out that in the collapse of the Bank of Credit and Commerce International (BCCI) in July 1991, Abu Dhabi lost an estimated US$15 billion which had been invested in the West – a figure close to the total investment by the Gulf states in the Arab world. The editorial also argued that by investing in Arab states the Gulf sheikhdoms would encourage the kind of stability which they claimed was absent in the region.

The Gulf war of 1991 reinforced still further the accumulation of resentment felt by the countries of the 'green' towards those of the 'yellow'. It also brought into focus in Arab eyes the apparently unquestioning support given to the latter by the West. (Once again, resentment was directed at the Gulf oil producers, rather than at the others, like Iraq, Libya and Algeria – apparently because of the close political and economic links between the former states and the West.) For those Arab countries which are not rich, the oil wealth of the Gulf is an emotive subject. In discussion of it, reason can be distorted. An Egyptian commentator wrote in May 1992 that because the wealth of the Gulf was unearned, 'it was considered by the other Arabs as almost illegitimate, almost indecent; and this was the main reason why public opinion in countries like Jordan, Yemen, Sudan, Mauritania and many others sympathized with the Iraqi invasion of Kuwait.'[39] In the view of a student in Damascus, 'the Gulf war was not just a war between the Arabs and the West. It was also a war about equality, the "haves" and the "have-nots." What Saddam Hussein said struck a chord here and throughout the Arab world.'[40] A wealthy Jordanian businessman, on the same topic, commenting while Iraqi troops were still in Kuwait, said that 'only a fool would not support Saddam Hussein. I do not mean him personally, but what he is trying to do. Kuwait, Saudi Arabia and, to a lesser extent, the other Gulf states have been greedy and ungenerous . . . In money terms they have given a lot, but as with Saudi Arabia's donations to the PLO and others there have always been strings attached. That is not real generosity.' A former Jordanian army officer spoke of Kuwait and Saudi Arabia having 'behaved very badly; they do not share their wealth'.[41] Dr Yezid Sayigh, a Palestinian academic at Oxford University, believes that the attitudes displayed by the Gulf states have contributed to the malaise in the Arab world in the 1990s, what he calls 'the sense of Arab insecurity at both regime and grass-roots levels . . . The Gulf emirates may not have been responsible for this dismal state of affairs, but they are at best seen as indifferent to it and [as such] as sharing some indirect responsibility. At worst they are seen as cynical: willing to benefit from Arab labour and strategic protection, but unwilling to utilize their immense financial clout as a means either of promoting economic recovery and development throughout the region or of pressing Arab and Western allies alike for real solutions to regional conflicts.'[42] Writing a few months later, Khalil Barhoum, a senior lecturer at Stanford University in the United States, said the Gulf conflict had 'squarely placed the West, especially the United States, on the side of the Arab rulers who have persistently resisted political change and have shown no inclination towards sharing their vast wealth with less fortunate Arabs'.[43] A more bitter comment came from a writer in the daily *Al-Ahram* newspaper in Cairo who accused the

Kuwaitis of wanting to get oil exports going again after the war to enable them 'to hire Filipinos to serve them and Americans and Englishmen to protect them'.[44]

Mustafa Hamarneh, a Jordanian historian, speaking about Arab reactions to the defeat of Iraq, said people in the region were disgusted at the way in which the Gulf regimes showed themselves to be in the pockets of the West. 'Clearly when you look at [Operation] Desert Storm, these planes flew from Arab lands, the fuel was Arab fuel, and Arab money paid for it. People look at the Saudis as – yes – lackeys of the West. They even describe them as agents of the West, on their payroll. And historically pro-Western regimes have been the most corrupt in the Arab world. Not necessarily the most vicious in terms of their population, but the most corrupt. This is because of the structure itself. There is room for commissions through arms deals and all kinds of stuff. The mechanisms of the market economy in these societies immediately led to the emergence of groups who aligned themselves with the ruling establishment. They both exploited the scene and both got rich.'[45]

As the twenty-first century approaches, the Arab world is seriously divided along 'yellow–green' lines. Differences in attitude have become as important as disparity in wealth. Osama el-Ghazali Harb, director of Al-Ahram Center for Political and Strategic Studies in Cairo, has gone so far as to doubt whether the indigenous inhabitants of the Gulf 'have any true Arab feelings, especially after the [1990–91] Gulf crisis. The suspicion is that they prefer to have direct relations with their friends in the United States and England rather than those in our area. Of course, they have their Arab feelings; but their feelings of interest are more with the outside world. I think Saddam Hussein has caused a lot of confusion in their minds – about their identity as Muslims and Arabs as against their special relationship with the West. I believe that every one of them thinks that the only powers in the world able to protect them against any threat are the English and the Americans.'[46]

Proof of the Gulf states's strong leaning on military matters towards the West and away from the Arab world came in the months after the 1991 war. In June of that year Saudi Arabia and the United States agreed to expand the existing broad area of mutual military cooperation. This was a sensitive matter for precisely the reasons that Harb mentioned. Saudi Arabia prides itself as the protector of the two most sacred cities in Islam: Mecca and Medina. During the Gulf crisis the Saudis were sensitive to the criticism directed at them – from Iraq, in particular, but also in popular expressions of disapproval from other countries around the Arab and Islamic world and from Islamic fundamentalists within the kingdom – for allowing Western troops to 'desecrate' sacred soil. The pressures of the moment gave the Saudis the courage to ignore such comments. After the war, it was a different matter. In a move designed to minimize criticism the Americans and the Saudis 'settled on an obscure fifteen-year-old military training pact as a legal framework to expand strategic cooperation. Kuwait and Bahrain, meanwhile, had no qualms in signing full-scale military agreements with Washington.'[47]

The strengthening of military ties between the Gulf and the West was put in even sharper focus by the failure of attempts to organize a regional force to safeguard security. At a meeting in the Syrian capital in March 1991, the six member-states of the GCC, together with Egypt and Syria, signed what became known as the Damascus Declaration. Both Egypt and Syria had sent troops to join the anti-Iraq coalition. From the Western perspective the presence of troops from these two countries was crucial to give a veneer of Arab legitimacy to the stationing of foreign troops on Saudi soil. The Damascus pact envisaged, among other things, the continued deployment of Egyptian and Syrian troops in the Gulf as the backbone of a new regional force. The costs would be met by the oil-producing countries. In the weeks following the signing of the agreement nothing happened. Then, without explanation, the Egyptian and Syrian contingents were brought home.

Muhammed Sid Ahmed interpreted the failure of the Damascus agreement as an inevitable consequence of strains in the 'yellow–green' relationship that had surfaced before the Gulf conflict. In 1989 King Hussein of Jordan played the leading part in the creation of an Arab Cooperation Council (ACC) which brought together Iraq, Jordan, Egypt and Yemen. The formation of the ACC was seen as an attempt to counterbalance the GCC – the 'green' against the 'yellow'. 'The thinking of the ACC,' Muhammed Sid Ahmed said, 'was this: there in the Gulf are all those rich states with no use for their wealth. Here we all are in debt. A rearrangement is needed.' The idea, born out of resentment at the perceived miserliness of the rich states, was to put pressure on the Gulf countries by threatening them with a new pact which contained both Egypt and Iraq, two of the most powerful states in the region. But the plan collapsed after Iraq invaded Kuwait. 'Here you had the "green" physically attacking the "yellow". Egypt could not play it as rough as that. Egypt could play it as long as it was respectfully played – some sort of intimidation, some sort of convincing the others in the Gulf that they should play the game differently. But clear-cut aggression was impossible for Egypt, given its commitments with the Americans, with the West, with Israel. So it moved out of the "green" alignment.'

This realignment was temporary. The Damascus agreement required Egypt and Syria – two countries from the 'green' – to become involved with the 'yellow'. According to Muhammed Sid Ahmed 'the six states in the Gulf would not countenance clear-cut cooperation with regimes, whatever their stand today, which came out of military coups. They would have robots as armies, but not Arab military men. They would have the Americans as their army, but not Arabs. What has happened after the Gulf war is that inter-Arab conflicts have taken precedence over conflicts between the Arabs and anyone else.'[48] The Gulf regimes were afraid of their own officers being influenced by those from other Arab countries; they feared, too, in case the permanent deployment of forces from outside the Gulf would be regarded by Iran as a threat to regional stability, thus increasing tension in the area.

Another option for the Gulf states, as they continued to worry about security in the region, might have been to develop further their own armies. The main argument against this has been that the indigenous populations are small – there are not enough men to form a strong and effective fighting force. Yezid Sayigh has argued, though, that the Gulf states have made difficulties for themselves by their consistent refusal 'to integrate Arab expatriate workers and professionals into local societies. Such a process would have strengthened national security and provided the basis for stronger military defence prior to the eruption of the Gulf crisis. In part, this would have removed the constant suspicion that guest communities harboured a potential "fifth column", and in part it would have enlarged the general population base and the skilled manpower pool.'[49]

The sympathy and support expressed by the Palestinians and the majority of Arab people (as distinct from regimes) for Iraq during the Gulf crisis served to increase the paranoia of the Gulf states. Hundreds of thousands of Palestinians, Yemenis, Sudanese and others were deported during and after the crisis. 'All those who stood behind Saddam Hussein must go,' declared the Saudi daily newspaper *Okaz* in the days after the war ended. 'Our people have the right to take all these to account, to smash their skulls after they toyed with our fate.' At the aviation conference in Bahrain in October 1991, the Kuwaiti Director General of Civil Aviation, Sheikh Jaber Mubarak al-Sabah, was asked what measures his country would be taking to encourage the return of passenger traffic after the Gulf war. 'Frankly speaking as the government of Kuwait,' he replied, 'we are not going to encourage any visitors.'

At the same time, while the majority of Arabs continued to bemoan what they regarded as the lack of financial generosity on the part of the Gulf states, the oil-rich countries cut their existing financial payments to the PLO, to Jordan and to anyone regarded as having adopted a pro-Saddam Hussein stance during the Gulf conflict. A senior government minister commented: 'What has been proven is that handouts of money do not make friends. We gave tens of millions of dollars to King Hussein and to [Yasser] Arafat, and they turned against us. The feeling here now is that there will be no more handouts.'[50]

As the months passed, some of the tension between the 'yellow' and the 'green' began to ease. But the basic divide looks set to remain into the twenty-first century, with the Gulf states relying heavily on political support and military protection from the West. Western powers in turn will go on encouraging the development of the Gulf into a fortress to protect the interests of the industrialized world – which means making sure that there is never a threat to the safe passage of oil from the region. 'The Gulf states's confidence in their own capabilities has been reinforced,' an editorial in the *Khaleej Times* – a daily newspaper in the United Arab Emirates – declared on the first anniversary of the 1991 Gulf war. This was a statement of self-delusion – another mirage.

While the West looks like being on hand for the foreseeable future to provide the 'capabilities' needed by the Gulf, there are possible problems ahead. In the early 1990s, within Saudi Arabia as within the region in general, there was a growing disillusionment with Western-based secularism and a rising interest in a return to the fundamental tenets of Islam. The pressures were felt even in Saudi Arabia. In 1992, as King Fahd was announcing limited moves towards devolving power to a Shura [consultation] council and to regional bodies – as well as widening the consultation process on the succession of the monarch – the government was coming under pressure from religious leaders. In the August of that year, a protest document of more than forty-five pages was circulated in defiance of the authorities. What made the document particularly significant was that it was signed by dozens of prominent religious figures from the core of the Wahhabi establishment – not by fanatical Islamic fundamentalists. The document demanded more authority for the *ulema'* (religious scholars) in the country's legal system, it denounced commerce and banking in the kingdom (on the grounds that they operated for profit – a concept proscribed by Islam), it challenged the government's oil policies and its policies of giving aid to countries which do not abide by Islamic law, it criticized the country's high spending on defence and it denounced corruption. Balancing these kinds of demands with pressures from liberals for greater and faster democratic reforms and with the continued need to maintain good relations with the West will be the main challenge of Gulf regimes in the years ahead.

For most Arabs, developments in the Gulf will remain far beyond the domain of their daily concerns. For them oil brought hope and then disappointment. It is likely that the majority of people in the region share the view of Mahjoub Omar, an Egyptian political commentator, that the oil era, like the struggle against Israel will be just a small phase in the broad sweep of history. 'Oil', said Mahjoub Omar, 'is just a nonsense in history. In a hundred years it will all be gone.' To illustrate his point Omar chose a local metaphor; he likened the oil era to a visit to the Cairo International Fair in the Nasr district, an outlying area of the city built in what was until comparatively recently open desert. 'First you walk a lot to get there. Then you sit down and drink Saudi coffee. You have reached "yesterday". Then you walk some more until you reach "today", with all the computers and machinery in the fair. Then you carry on walking a bit until you find desert, the real desert of the Nasr district. And that is "tomorrow".'

When 'tomorrow' comes there will be no more luxury construction schemes and no more surplus money to pay all the foreign workers. This will be a moment of reckoning – showing whether or not oil revenue has been invested wisely to enable the region to enjoy still the material benefits brought by the oil era. Whatever happens, the Gulf Arabs will, most likely, rediscover some of their traditional ways of life; the peasant in Egypt will have no choice but to work the fields; and the poor in Cairo and other cities will have to continue to fend for themselves as best they can.

CHAPTER SEVEN

Families at War

Professor Nazek Yared packed some papers into her briefcase and locked her office at the end of another day of teaching at Beirut University College. She had stayed on after classes to keep an appointment with me. Nazek Yared then drove, as she does each day, from the campus in the predominantly Muslim western half of the Lebanese capital to her home in an exclusively Christian mountain region north of the city. Nazek Yared, a writer and academic, is different from most of her Christian compatriots both in moving comfortably within Muslim-dominated society and in stressing the Arab character of her Lebanese nationality. She is Professor of Arabic Literature and writes novels and other books in the Arabic language. Lebanese Christians generally feel more comfortable with French than with Arabic literature and like to distance themselves from the Arab (and overwhelmingly Islamic) world. Nazek Yared's stance causes her problems; but she is prepared to confront them. 'I think most Lebanese Christians do not consider themselves Arabs,' she said. 'I do not blame them. Muslims equate Arabism with Islam, even though there were Christian Arabs before Islam. On the other hand, the Muslims always treat the Christians as traitors – because they are Christians, and so (they argue) not Arabs. Any Christian like me who considers herself or himself Arab is caught in between. The Muslims refuse to consider me an Arab because I am a Christian, and the Christians refuse to admit that I am an Arab because I am a Christian.'[1]

Nazek Yared's children no longer face such dilemmas relating to their identities. All three, like tens of thousands of young Lebanese (Christians comprising a large percentage of the total) before them, have emigrated, creating a deep sadness in their family homes.

The experience of people like Nazek Yared in Lebanon illustrates characteristics of the Arab world in painfully sharp focus. More than any other country, Lebanon has been torn apart by a combination of strong attachments to religious groups and disruption to traditional family life. In no other country in the region has the weakening of clan loyalties in favour of allegiance to the state been such a long and painful experience.

The civil war which racked Lebanon from 1975 to 1990 was fought ostensibly in the name of religion. But calling the war a Muslim–Christian conflict was to attach a label of convenience which belied the true causes. Many mosques and churches were damaged or destroyed in the fighting; but it was not a conflict in which places of worship were generally targets. Rather, the civil war was a battle between groups in Lebanon competing for political influence. Each group, while paying lip-service to the concept of Lebanese sovereignty which was foisted on the region by the French and British colonial powers after the First World War, continued to maintain its traditional ties of allegiance to extended families or clans sharing a particular religious faith. The view of Kamal Salibi, Professor of History at the American University of Beirut, is that the various religious communities in Lebanon during the century were 'essentially tribes, or in any case behaved like tribes, and the game that came to be played between them was a tribal game. At an overt level, the game was a contest between different concepts of nationality for the country [with Christians wanting Lebanon to remain aloof from Arabism, and Muslims insisting that it must be an integral part of the Arab and Islamic world]. At the covert level, tribal rivalries and jealousies were mainly involved. As long as this devious game was played only among the Lebanese, it could pass for day-to-day Lebanese politics, and the Lebanese state headed by the Maronites could somehow control it. There always remained a lurking danger, however, that the game could run out of control.'[2]

It did so, in large part, because 'tribes' either sought the assistance of foreign powers or found themselves being manipulated by them into nurturing regional or international ambitions. Leaders of the Maronite Catholic community in the early 1980s, for example, were successful in seeking political and military help from Israel. The Israelis, in turn, hoped to use the Maronites to install a strong and friendly government in Beirut which would eliminate the threat posed to the Jewish state by the Palestinians and other armed groups on Lebanese soil. The Israeli plan backfired. Amid growing opposition inside Israel to the military involvement in Lebanon, it gradually became clear that a strong Maronite-dominated government with which Israel could deal would not emerge in Beirut. Nor would the continued Israeli presence on Lebanese soil stop the factional fighting there. So Israel abandoned the Maronites, and no other group came to their assistance. From that moment, Christian (and more particularly Maronite) power went into decline. Inter-Christian warfare towards the end of the decade weakened still further the status of Christians in Lebanon and left them defeated and dispirited with the choice of accepting political reforms, which saw their formerly dominant share of power reduced considerably, or leaving the country.

The civil war in Lebanon ended when the various communities realized the futility of the conflict being conducted in their name by the heavily armed militias. After fifteen years of bloodshed, leading to heavy loss of life, along with widespread suffering caused by economic and social upheaval, it became obvious that there would be no clear winner. Tribal rallying calls no longer drew a resounding response from a tired and disillusioned public. Syria, with the blessing of the Arab and international communities, took upon itself the task of dismantling (by force when necessary) the military wings of the Lebanese tribes, of establishing a new central government, and of making sure that Lebanon thereafter would have its roots firmly based in the Arab (and Islamic) nation.

Tribal conflicts in the Middle East may have ended with the conclusion of the war in Lebanon. But the emotional power of the clan remains strong and is still expressed frequently (in Lebanon and elsewhere) in religious terms. 'I would murder my daughter rather than see her marry a Muslim,' a Western-educated Maronite in Syria told me. Throughout the Middle East, in a variety of regimes, clan power is dominant within the formal state structure. In the sheikhdoms of the Gulf, the overwhelming majority of top positions inside and outside government go to members of the ruling families. In Iraq, the most prestigious and influential jobs have frequently been assigned by President Saddam Hussein to members of his clan from the town of Tikrit. Since the late 1960s the Ba'athist regimes in Syria have been dominated by members of the minority Alawite community which is based around the port city of Latakia. The Lebanese-born American academic Fouad Ajami has written of the early day of Ba'ath rule in Syria, asserting that 'all they cared about was the securing of public jobs for their relatives. Salah Jadid, the quintessential conspirator, the Alawite officer who shunned the spotlight and was at one time the real power in Syrian politics, had every person in his family over eighteen years of age on the public payroll. Clans battled for advantage and conspired to eliminate one another. The state remained an extension of that tribal mentality.'[3] Attachment to clans and pride in ancestral history and tradition – tendencies abandoned by broadly secular and ethnically fluid societies in the West many decades ago – remain strong in the Arab world.

The nucleus of the clan-based society in the Middle East is still the extended family, although circumstances have connived to weaken it in some communities. In particular, there are wide variations between urban and rural societies, with disruption to traditional patterns being much more marked in the former than in the latter. In general, however, despite various upheavals and changes 'the Arab family may be described as patriarchal, pyramidically hierarchical, and extended. It constitutes an economic and social organization in all three patterns of living (bedouin, rural and urban). The behaviour of an individual member becomes that of the family as a whole . . . In the traditional Arab family the father holds the authority and the responsibility. The wife joins his kinship group (patri-local) and the children carry his surname . . . It is stratified on the basis of sex (females are subordinate to males) and age (the young are subordinate to the old).'[4]

The traditional family structure has had to withstand a number of pressures throughout the twentieth century, not least those caused by the emigration of Arabs out of the region in search of work. Most of these migrants went to Western countries; many returned, bringing Western ideas with them. The region also became exposed to Western values by the arrival of communities from Europe and America, and by exposure to foreign films, television and advertising. All these influences were strongest in the last quarter of the century. Saad Eddin Ibrahim, a sociologist in Cairo, pointed to political reasons for the ability of Arab society in the 1950s and 1960s to resist Western influence on society. 'The region was engulfed by the Arab nationalist movement. While that was a secular movement, it was also anti-imperialist, anti-Western; so the issue of undermining the authentic and indigenous values by Western influence was not really the salient problem. In the 1950s and 1960s we were engaged in battles with the West – in confrontations with imperialism, colonialism, Zionism, reactionary regimes. There was the Baghdad pact, the Suez Crisis in 1956, the 1967 Arab–Israeli crisis, the liberation of Algeria, the liberation of the Gulf.'

Saad Eddin Ibrahim added that the following two decades, the 1970s and 1980s, brought a major assault on traditional values, with widespread migration of Arab labour within the Middle East. 'This was the era when we had the oil boom, which in the West is called the oil crisis – an interesting reverse in terms of reference: what the Arab world considers a boom, the West considers a crisis. But that aside, the period was one in which many of the traditional values began to suffer as a result of mass migration, of the flow of money and revenues resulting from consumerism, of the arrival of Western goods and ideas, of mass media, and of mass travelling on a large scale. So many of the conventional values of the family, as well as people's relations with each other, their respect for elders, for institutions and for sacred symbols, began to be shaken.'

This trend, in the view of Saad Eddin Ibrahim, was halted and reversed in the 1990s as a result both of the economic recession in the region and the world at large, and of the general psychological malaise which afflicted the Arab world. 'The fate of the family is related to these developments. The family becomes the refuge of last resort when things are uncertain or bleak. This is not unique to Muslims. Family and family values are like religion, a refuge of last resort.' Despite the erosion of family values in the 1970s and 1980s, those values have not been forgotten. 'The family unit in the West became weak several decades ago – or up to a century ago – whereas here the family remained a basic unit of social structure until probably twenty years ago, before the mass movements of oil and consumerism, the appearance of the nuclear family and so on. The idea of the close-knit extended family is still in people's memory. Part of the aim of the current Islamic movement in the region is to re-assert family values.'[5]

Saad Eddin Ibrahim believes that the century is ending with Western and Arab attitudes to family life as far apart as ever – with society recovering from a brief flirtation with Western values. But Sari Nasir, Professor of Sociology at the University of Jordan, sees the corroding influence of the West continuing. Sari Nasir studied and has taught extensively in the United States. He believes that a century of contact between the Middle East and the West has altered traditional Arab values for the worse. 'The family structure has changed immensely. You find there has been a definite change from the extended family to the nuclear family. There is still some sense of the extended family, but I think that it is fading. I can notice it being here in Arab world. I can see how it is passing away. And I think this is one of the negative things that the Arab world has acquired from the West. It is primarily the West which has influenced many of the prevalent values in this part of the world – especially the British and French who dominated parts of it. You find that people who studied in the West or visited it were quite influenced by the "modern" way of life.'

But why should these developments be regarded as 'negative'?

'Because I feel that as a result of this drift that we are witnessing in the Arab world, many social problems are emanating. For example, take juvenile delinquency – that is something that the Arab world never experienced before. Take homelessness, drug addiction, prostitution. You find so many problems emanating from this. At the time of the extended family you did not find such problems. So in that sense I feel that the trend is negative. We intellectuals are very concerned at the way the region is drifting – to see the kind of problems that you have in the West and think that one day that is what we will end up with.'

Sari Nasir takes the view of traditionalists in the region that the price being paid for urbanization and modernity in Arab countries is too great. He is fearful also of what he calls a 'cultural invasion' from the West having a negative impact on the Arab world. 'You find cultural borrowing, such as jeans, fast-food and casual relationships. For instance, you find that the taboo in relationships between the sexes is breaking down. You find more and more that people from the Arab world want to emigrate to America. I feel that this is part of the image, this cultural invasion, that seems to portray the West – especially the United States – as a haven and a heaven, a place of opportunity, a place of happiness where the young, especially, will be able to fulfil their ambitions. And, of course, I have seen many of these people being very, very disappointed at what they have experienced in the United States. They tell me there is a great difference between the ideal and the real thing.'

Sari Naser, and those who share his views, would not argue for turning back the clock and restoring the status quo of the nineteenth century. But the reservations which they feel about current developments point to a broader unease about the future which is reflected in most aspects of life in the region. The Arabs – even after a century of contact with the West – have not found a comfortable balance in their relationship with Europe and the United States in terms of how much they should open themselves up to the influence of outside values.

These difficulties, in turn, point to the inability of the Arabs to find a coherent and indigenous formula for life in the next century.

The bombardment of images from the West does not make the search for this formula any easier. Television opens a big window on Western life – or more precisely on a sanitized or romanticized version of life in Europe or the United States – for Arabs as much as for any other underdeveloped area of the world. Turn on a television set in any Arab country and you stand a high chance of finding yourself watching a Western film, soap opera or quiz show. Once again, Sari Nasir is unhappy about this. 'You are getting two kinds of education: one traditional, one modern. Regardless of what the book says at school, or what the teacher says at school, you go home and are exposed to the latest craze in dancing, American things. Any Western programme seems to pronounce Western values. Also if you analyse the local programmes you find that they are emulating Western programmes. When you look at the values built into the programmes you find that they are going towards the nuclear family, towards the Western view.'

Like Saad Eddin Ibrahim, Sari Nasir believes that the Islamic movement in the Arab world is working towards reasserting gradually family values – even though he thinks that counter-pressures will still be felt for some time to come. 'What is of concern to me and others is the sense that we feel we ought to learn from the West, not emulate it, not to drift and lose control. It seems to me we are at an advantage in the Arab world, looking at the West, at a society which is going in a particular direction and seeing what is happening to it. We should work out what kind of values to maintain to avoid falling into the pits that these people have found themselves in. But this is a tall order, trying to educate people to see the dangers.'6

Another academic who has long experience of living in the West shares the view that the cultural and ethical values of the United States and Europe will fail ultimately to usurp those of Islam. Muhammad Aziz Shukri is Professor of Law at Damascus University. His wife holds American nationality; his son

was born in the United States. Despite pressures and difficulties
which he has experienced living back in Syria, Shukri cites
traditional family life, based on the principles of Islam, as a
major reason for staying on in his home country. 'I began to
feel unhappy here in the 1960s. I would be lying to you if I
said that we did not pass through some difficult times. Between
1967 and 1969 there were some real dictatorship regimes. I
would be lying also if I said I did not consider applying for my
Green Card [to be able to live and work in the United States].
But at the last moment I decided against it. It does not mean
I am extremely happy. At times I feel depressed with many
little things – the limited income, the particular climate, whatever. But in order to have tranquillity, strong family ties, the
humane touch that we have in this part of the world, the caring
for each other – you have to pay for it. In 1989 I spent a whole
year lecturing at Harvard and considered moving to the States.
But I studied the society there and came to the conclusion: no
way, no way.'

What exactly is so special about family life in the Middle East
that makes it so different from that in the West?

'In this part of the world your family is your social security.
The father spends every penny he earns on the education,
health and welfare of his kids. In return, when they grow up
they take over responsibility. Secondly, our religion teaches us
to be intimate within the family, within the tribe or clan, and
within society. It is a combination of interests and ideology
which makes me closer to my brother than any American to
his brother. We have been brought up this way. Maybe this is
one of the reasons why we [the Arabs] are a bit backward.
But I feel this backwardness is an asset. Because look at the
Americans. They have reached the moon, and yet they still
lack the humane touch. I can not accept the abuses in America
– drugs, violence, sexual abuse, family abuses, a man beating
his wife. We Arabs are accused of being unfair to our women.
But what I saw on television in the United States increased my
grey hair. Here if you hear that a friend, not to speak of a
brother, is in need you do everything possible to help. But the
fact is that in America everyone is concerned about himself.

Of course I am not criticizing. That is the way they were
brought up. And had it not been for that they would not have
reached the moon. But frankly speaking, I do not care about
reaching the moon. I want to live happily on earth. The structure here is not as solid as it used to be. We are less attached
to each other than our fathers and our grandfathers. But the
roots are still there, and we are teaching our youngsters not to
try to imitate the West, but to go back to their roots.'[7]

Roots of traditional life in rural areas have been largely
unaffected by the era of mass migration to the oil states of
the Gulf and by the influence of the West through films and
television. Within middle-class urban society there have been
staggering changes in outward appearances – with a great
increase in the awareness of and interest in international
fashions and trends. But it would be a mistake, I believe, to be
deceived completely by outward appearances. The casting aside
of traditional dress in favour of American-style jeans need not
mean that there has been a corresponding change in mental
attitude, erasing suddenly a whole cultural inheritance. Similarly, the growing trend among girls and young women in
many Arab countries of wearing headscarves does not necessarily indicate sudden mass support for Islamic fundamentalism, although Western observers often interpret it this way.

In the attitudes of Arab men towards women, as well as in
the status of women in Middle Eastern society, one finds roots
of tradition which have been shaken only a little by other
changes in society. This is one more area where a huge gulf
exists between the Arab world and the West. Despite all the
contact between the two regions, the spread of education in
the Middle East, changes in the law, and the gradual acceptance
of the presence of women in universities and in the workplace,
the region remains one dominated by men and male values.
Any appearances to the contrary are misleading. In Syria, for
example, there is a high proportion of women both among the
professors at the University of Damascus and among members
of parliament. A friend was talking about the role of women
in society, saying how common it had become since the 1960s
to see women going out to work. To emphasize the point he

indicated an office in a ministry building across the street where we could see five women (all wearing white headscarves) and one man. It is true that wherever you go in the Arab world, with the exception of some of the most conservative corners of the Gulf, you will find women at the workplace – particularly in the fields of education and medicine, but also in government departments and the service industries. But examples of women holding top jobs in these areas are rare. In Saudi Arabia and the Gulf states, most working women are foreigners from other Arab countries or outside the region. A survey published in 1986 indicated that women comprised only 4 per cent of the paid workforce in Saudi Arabia, where traditions of strict male/female segregation and discrimination against girls in education have kept down the number of women in work. But the popular view in the West of veiled Arab women (no matter how well educated) imprisoned in their homes by their husbands and brothers is accurate only in some Gulf states where a tiny proportion of the region's population lives. Only in one country, Saudi Arabia, are women forbidden from driving. Nevertheless, while women are free to earn a living, in Damascus and elsewhere in the Arab world, legislation enshrines the male duty to be the main breadwinner for the family, and illustrates popular perceptions of male and female roles. For example, military service is compulsory for young men in Syria when they leave school. But an only son of a family is exempted army duty because he might get killed, leaving his relations without a breadwinner. For similar reasons, two brothers are not required to do military service at the same time. If a woman is divorced or widowed and has one son, he does not go into the army – the reason here being that he is the only male who will be able to carry on the family name.

Male dominance of Arab society and the way that attitudes in the Middle East differ from those in the West can often be seen in mixed marriages. I know many examples of Arab men meeting and then marrying European or American women while studying or working in the West. In the Western environment the Arab has seemed liberal in his views, allowing the woman the degree of freedom to which she was accustomed.

Once couples move their homes to the Middle East, the picture
frequently changes, with restraints placed on the women and
their freedom of action curbed in an effort to bring their
behaviour into line with the customs of the local society. A
Western woman's position under these circumstances can be
doubly difficult because she may feel trapped by her husband's
extended family, without a clan of her own to support, protect
or comfort her.

Such experiences, percolating back into Western society,
serve only to reinforce prejudice, enhancing the most clichéd
and racist stereotype of the Arab – which in its most extreme
form is that of the barbaric Muslim husband with his coterie
of veiled wives. This image is far from the truth; while male
attitudes towards women in the Arab world are generally more
chauvinistic than those in the West, just as in other parts of
the world, one finds a range of views. Also, because of financial
constraints and changing attitudes in society, polygamy is
becoming less and less common. 'It is still not unusual to find
men with more than one wife in the Gulf states,' an Arab
academic working in the region said. 'But even there, polygamy is not as common as before. Elsewhere it is a rare
exception – so much so that it attracts attention when a man
takes a second wife.'

The fantasy about Arab men is compounded by an assumption that the slavery of women is in some way enshrined in
Islam – a religion regarded widely in the West as being backward and repressive. The interpretation of Islamic doctrine in
some countries, like Saudi Arabia, imposes restrictions on the
freedom of women. But as often as not, aspects of life in the
Middle East which have been seized on by the West to enhance
the stereotype of the Arabs and which are assumed to be essential ingredients of the religion turn out to be based on local
customs and tradition. Islam, in common with other religions,
incorporated traditions from the region in which it was born.
In their introduction to a major study of women in Islam, Nikki
Keddie and Lois Beck point out that 'the basic patterns of male
domination, the virginity-fidelity-son-producing ethos, a
sexual double standard, and so on, existed in the Middle East

and other parts of the world long before Islam was born. Even veiling is not original to Islam: the earliest iconographic depiction of it dates from Palmyra in the first century A D, and it was practised in the Byzantine Empire and adjacent areas before Islam, although it is not known to what degree. As Muslim converts and Arabs extended this Near Eastern custom, they interpreted certain Koranic passages as referring to veiling, and Islam spread the custom further in territory, and possibly also in class, than before.'[8]

Far from subjugating women, the new religion aimed at improving their social position because 'under the customary tribal law existing in Arabia at the advent of Islam, women as a general rule had no legal status. They were sold into marriage by their guardians for a price paid to the guardian, the husband could terminate the union at will, and women had little or no property or succession rights. The tribal law was radically modified by various concrete provisions of the Koran.' Marriage became a contract between man and wife, rather than man and guardian, and women were accorded rights of inheritance. On specific matters relating to the rights of women mentioned by the Koran there was no problem in ensuring implementation. Difficulties arose in interpretation of more general principles, and in these cases 'the tendency was to interpret the Koranic provisions in the light of the prevailing standards of the tribal law . . . Islamic law continued to reflect the patriarchal and patrilineal nature of a society based upon the male agnatic tie. Within the scheme of family law which developed in this way, woman, whether as daughter, wife, or mother, occupied an inferior position.'[9] This unequal relationship between men and women continues because, unlike in the West, the basic patterns of society have remained unchanged.

The difference between theoretical principles and practical application of laws relating to women in the Middle East is as relevant in the latter half of the twentieth century as it was in the seventh and eight centuries, furnishing further proof of the degree to which society is still dominated by men and male values. In Saudi Arabia and the Gulf states, little has been done to change laws regarding the personal status of women.

Elsewhere, changes were introduced advocating equality between the sexes. In Syria, for example, family laws were revised in 1953. There was a similar move in Egypt in 1956, and in Iraq in 1959. Tunisia is regarded as a leader in this area. Sweeping legal reforms introduced in 1956 made Tunisia one of the most progressive Arab countries in addressing the needs of women. A newly introduced Code of Personal Status, among other things, raised the minimum marriage age of girls to seventeen, made polygamy illegal, abolished forced marriages and decreed that husband and wife should be punished equally for committing adultery. While the code was welcomed by the women's movement in the Arab world, campaigners pointed to 'glaring drawbacks'. These included the provisions that no marriage could take place between a Muslim woman and a non-Muslim man and that women would continue to receive only half of the inheritance of men. More importantly, when the effects of the legislation were reviewed three decades later the conclusion was that, 'as in many other Arab countries, in Tunisia there is a wide gap between the law and its implementation. Often people stick to their traditions (which include unfavourable aspects vis-à-vis women's liberation). Women are often not aware of their rights, and those who are, are subjected to social pressure and interpretations which are opposed to the ultimate rights of women.'[10] A Tunisian woman writer in 1988 made an observation about her own country which could be applied to most others in the region. 'Women today,' she wrote, 'have to face two problems that hinder their progress: first, is the conflict between granting equality and the necessity to compromise with traditions; second, the struggle against socio-cultural prejudices resulting from the menial tasks to which women are relegated and which serve to weaken their position.'[11]

Traditions in the Arab world run much deeper than in the West. Arabs have a strong attachment to the past – as much as anything else because they have failed to discover an ideology which both meets their daily aspirations and allows them to cope with the rapid changes introduced from the West in the twentieth century. The struggle faced by campaigners for women's rights in the Middle East – even if sweeping changes have been made to legislation – is bound to be tougher than that faced by campaigners in the more liberal and forward-looking atmosphere of Europe or the United States.

Another problem faced by women's rights activists in the Arab world throughout the century has been the difficulty of making an impact beyond the minority educated classes. This handicap explains the limited amount of progress that the movement can claim in the closing years of the century after what looked like a promising start. As early as 1914 no fewer than fourteen magazines in Arabic specializing in women's affairs had appeared. All were founded and edited by women. At this stage in the century 'the major demands of women were the right to education for all and also the reform of family law. They [women] also started to scrutinize the Islamic origins of the veil. The women's movement remained upper class mainly because these issues were primarily of concern to this class.'[12] From the educated classes, too, women eventually began knocking on the doors of top state institutions. In Egypt in the mid-1950s, for example, laws were liberalized giving women rights including maternity leave. In 1957, two women were voted into parliament and five years later the Egyptian government appointed a woman Cabinet minister for the first time.

Once again, though, it is dangerous to make generalizations from a few specific cases. For the overwhelming majority of women in the Arab world, life continues to be led firmly in the shadow of men. In 1986 Rena Mus'aad, a Lebanese Christian involved in women's affairs, gave this assessment of some of the difficulties confronting females in the Middle East. 'One of the problems that some women face is their lack of income – economic independence. Women have always been described in relation to men, either as wives, mothers, daughters. She leaves her father's house to go to her husband's. Very few women remain single and it is a rare phenomenon when they live apart from their families. This kind of tightly knit Middle Eastern family protects the woman and oppresses her at the same time.'[13]

This observation underlines the point that despite superficial
changes in legislation and the willingness of women to demand
greater rights, male attitudes have changed little, even in the
upper classes. Men from all classes in the Arab world proudly
adopt the title Abu (father of) their first-born son. My first
child was a girl; when the second also turned out to be a girl
the reaction among my Arab friends and acquaintances was
one of polite indifference, if it was not expressed openly in
terms of: bad luck, better luck next time. My third child was
a son; his arrival was greeted by exuberant expressions of con-
gratulation. Now, the implication was, you can relax and hold
your head up high. An American doctor working among Palestinians near Sidon in Lebanon in 1983 noted that 'the birth of
a daughter could still bring about an audible moan of disappointment in the delivery room.'[14] The same doctor also
described a male colleague's method of treating a problem with
a female patient which could be psychosomatic, like abdominal
pain. In such a case 'he always noted on the chart whether
she was married or not. The implication, of course, was that if
she wasn't married, she was more likely to be a "hysterical
case"; marriage solved these problems.'[15] Diagnoses of this kind
are still found among some old-fashioned medics in the West
– but they are much more common in Arab countries.

Personal attitudes of Arab men to women are harder to gauge
and quantify. The Syrian poet, Nizar Qabbani, for whom
women have been a major source of inspiration, explained
the reason for his obsession with this particular subject in the
following lyrical terms: 'Woman was never the dream of the
Arab man. She was his hostage and his saddle – a farm on
which he was a feudal master from the old days. If women
were an Arab's dream, Arab society would be a garden, with
a moon, and a fountain; and there would be no need for me
or for poetry books because all men would be poets talking
with women in the language of the dove, feeding her with
the leaves of violets and adorning her wrist with bracelets of
sunshine. But Arab man does not deal in the language of
dreams and cannot be a poet in his relationship with women.
His tribal and feudal roots constrain him to deal with women as

he deals with land, seeds and animal husbandry. I feel sometimes that the relationship between the Arab man and the Arab
woman comes under the category of land ownership with all
the regulations about tax, duties and such like.'[16]

Arab men, in general, still expect to be domineering in their
relationships with women. 'What I cannot stand in Arab men,'
I was told by a Lebanese Christian woman who is married to
a European, 'is their refusal to show any emotional vulnerability. It was always a case of bragging about how many
women they had conquered (implying that you were just
another along the line), what flash cars they drove, what prestigious jobs they had – that kind of thing. They could not bring
themselves to say they needed you. There was still this idea
that they wanted a beautiful woman on a pedestal, not a real
woman with feelings and flaws.' Similar complaints are heard
in the West, but in the Arab world the attitude is more extreme.
Throughout the Middle East, the relationship between men
and women is traditionally viewed by men in terms of possession, whether women are treated like cattle or put on a
pedestal.

Attitudes of this kind are reflected and, perhaps, encouraged
by films and the broadcast media, and by popular songs in the
Arab world. Unlike the West, where popular songs can cover
a range of issues – love from all possible perspectives, political
and social protest, and so on – in the Arab world the subject
is invariably romantic love. Nada Awar wrote a study of two
songs which are popular among all social classes throughout
the Arab world: 'Int'al-Hubb' (You are the love) and 'Habaitak
biSaif' (I loved you in summer). They were recorded by two
of the best-loved female performers in the region, Umm Kul-
thoum, an Egyptian singer who had become a legend throughout the Middle East even before her death in 1975; and Fairouz,
a Lebanese performer whose recordings are played in every
Arab country. 'Both songs', Nada Awar wrote, 'depict an
ancient well of traditional female submission and surrender
to male lovers who are only heart-breakers. The heroines are
helpless and dependent. Their stories are old-fashioned tales of
tears and lament for the superman of their dreams, who never

really acknowledges or reciprocates their love. Ironically, both songs "beautify" the image of submissive women by emphasizing determination and loyalty to an essentially melancholic, unjust and unequal relationship.' 'Int'al-Hubb', she continued, 'portrays a master–slave relationship in which the heroine insists on playing the role of the everlasting martyr. The song seems to reinforce traditions of women's passivity to love, whereas men, on the other hand, are blessed with their freedom. The hero is welcomed into the heart of the heroine, even though he is lavishly enjoying other women, when she says: "So many hearts are flying around you wishing to reach happiness and gain your satisfaction, but I am the one whose heart belongs to you, you make me happy, you deprive me as you wish . . ."'[17]

In the written and broadcasting media, women are frequently portrayed as playing a passive role in society. A study of mass-circulation women's magazines in the Arab world showed that among the most common portrayals were 'the sacrificing, self-effacing wife, the loving mother; the skilful housewife; the oppressed, helpless woman; the beautiful woman who is concerned only with her appearance; the woman who, outwardly liberated, is inwardly deprived and whose self-awareness is limited; the woman who concerns herself with social work and service, but out of a desire for stardom; and the woman who is devoted to satisfying her husband and social norms. Very rarely is the discussion of these topics rooted in the real situation of the Arab woman or the realities she faces. On the whole, articles are translated or adapted so as to be relevant only to a very limited category of Arab women – those who are extremely wealthy.' The survey quoted a study of the broadcast media in Egypt – the main centre for the production of films, soap operas and other programmes which draw mass audiences throughout the region – revealing an emphasis on 'aspects of a woman's life as a wife, as a mother, or as a female. They stress concerns with fashion and beauty, childcare and how to treat one's husband . . . Women's programmes tend to deal with only one segment of the female population: the young, average-educated middle class or the

extremely well-off or wealthy who live in the cities. They tend
to ignore adolescent, pre-nuptial girls, as well as middle-aged
women, and do not adequately cover issues of concern to the
working woman or the woman with higher education. There is
a total neglect of women in rural areas, where 75 per cent of the
Egyptian population lives, women whose day-to-day concerns
are quite different from those of urban women.' The survey concluded that media in the Middle East treat 'the Arab woman as
a pretty doll, concerned with trivialities and flattery'.[18]

Women in the West might argue that a number of the topics
covered by these Arab magazines are mirrored in those found
on sale in Europe and the United States. This is true. But in the
Middle East there is little choice; widely available periodicals
dealing with more serious aspects of women's lives are rare,
and are aimed at readers from the rich elite. In one edition of
Samra, a thick, glossy magazine for women published in
Kuwait, readers could find articles about violence in marriage,
divorce, and female frustrations at inequality in the Arab world.
But of the sixty-seven pages of prestige colour advertising,
twenty-six were for expensive (mostly French) perfumes, ten
for make-up and other beauty products, eight for gold jewellery
and watches, six for shops selling European couture clothes
and five for de luxe cars. While the magazine was prepared to
tackle thorny subjects in its articles, its style and the advertisements it contained reinforced the traditional view that
women's main concern should be to make themselves as alluring as possible to men.

An examination of women in television drama in Egypt
reached a conclusion about the limited roles of women on
screen similar to that reached in the report on periodicals, and
reveals a contrast with the variety of female roles depicted in
Western television. 'In terms of age and marital status,' it said,
'female characters are depicted as young, usually in their twenties, physically attractive, overdressed and over made-up, and
are identified mainly by their affiliation to the men in their
lives. Whereas male characters are in their thirties, identified
by their professional or occupational status, and only second-
arily by their relationship to women.'[19]

Again, appearances can be deceptive, and a brief visit to a bustling Arab capital might leave one with an impression that women have asserted themselves to a far greater extent than is evident from the surveys just quoted. For example, it is a fact that hundreds of thousands of Arab women go to university and acquire professional jobs. But, even in Christian areas of Lebanon where attitudes are closer to the West than anywhere else in the Arab world, it is rare for girls or students to live away from home – let alone with a man without being married – a habit which is common in the West. It is still true, also, that a girl who acquires a high level of education or who goes out to work will often jeopardize her chances of a good match.

Marriage remains the single most important goal for women in the Arab world – and for their families – not so much for legal advantage as for social prestige. In this respect there is a wide gulf between Arab and Western attitudes. 'No matter how well qualified you are,' a woman teacher in Jordan said, 'unless you are married – and preferably have borne a male child – you are nothing. There is pressure from your parents. It is a matter of family honour. If parents have produced a daughter, and done everything for her, and she has not married, then they are considered to be failures.'

These pressures can inhibit a woman's professional career. 'In the marriage market the working girl is still judged by many as loose, immoral and, in certain cases, promiscuous, in contrast to those girls who are secluded in their homes and thereby considered paragons of virtue and chastity. Given these circumstances, it is not surprising that very few young women continue their schooling beyond age fifteen, however late they may actually marry.' Girls at university or at work can expect, too, to come under 'the continual scrutiny of their family in every move they make outside the home. It is precisely because of this strict control that marriage comes into perspective for the single woman as an avenue of greater freedom.'[20] Also, once she has married and produced children, her status within the family increases. Old women command enormous respect and wield considerable power within the home. 'Older women are much more powerful than older men in some respects,' a young Syrian who had just returned from study in the United States told me. 'If a twenty- or thirty-year-old man is asked by his mother to do something, he will obey without hesitation, while he might hesitate with his father. There is a sense that she has sacrificed her life for her offspring, and now she expects her reward. What happens in her youth is not as important as what happens later on. Memories are fine, but they have nothing to do the present. Among Western women, being young is the ultimate thing. As she gets older she wants a face-lift. Here, the older you get, the more respect you command. If I came to this world as a woman from outer space I would choose to live in the West when I was young, and here in the East when I was old.'

A high percentage of Middle Eastern marriages are still arranged by the respective parents – though not all, as is commonly thought in the West. The arrangement process can vary considerably depending on circumstances. An Iraqi friend told me how, during the Iran–Iraq war, families would send video-recordings of weddings to their sons in the army. The sons would then study the recordings, choose which of the single girls at the wedding party took their fancy, and ask their mothers and sisters to make inquiries about their availability for marriage.

Aside from variations between the Arab world and the West in traditions of courtship, there is also a big difference in the importance attached to female virginity before marriage. A Lebanese lady who lived for many years in Europe and the United States expressed the difference thus: 'In the West you may be afraid to admit you are a virgin after you are eighteen or nineteen. In the Arab world, you are terrified of admitting that you have lost your virginity.' The whole question of promiscuity and virginity is linked to the broader and still immensely important concept of family honour. In essence, any sexual indiscretion committed by a female (if discovered) causes dishonour to her father's family, and more specifically to her father himself and to her brothers. This applies as much when the girl has left the family home and is married as it does when she is single. In the wake of sexual indiscretions becoming public it is not unusual to hear of crimes of honour being committed by the girl's father or brother. If, for example, it is discovered by the male members of a family that one of their daughters has had a sexual liaison outside marriage, they might take it upon themselves to kill the man with whom she was involved; and the authorities can be expected to deal leniently with such crimes. As in other matters relating to family life, traditional attitudes are much more entrenched in rural areas of the Arab world than they are in urban and middle-class society.

Even in middle-class circles the kind of open boyfriend/girlfriend relationships which are normal in the West are very rare. There are few places where couples can meet without being observed, even if the girl is allowed out on her own, except at university or at work. It is common practice for a girl to be chaperoned in some way. In a hotel lobby in Damascus early one evening, I noticed a smartly dressed young man sitting anxiously, fingering his moustache and watching the main entrance. He smiled as three elegant girls, who looked like sisters, came in. After nervous handshakes, the young man led the group away towards the hotel coffee shop, the shortest of the three girls by his side; the other two followed at a discreet distance. With this elaborate ritual, the couple's 'date' had begun.

The concept of honour is bound up with basic attitudes in the outlook of Arabs, and represents yet another major difference between Middle Eastern and Western thinking. Wa'il Kheir, a Lebanese university lecturer on subjects related to humanities, makes a distinction between a 'shame' culture in the Arab world and a 'guilt' culture in the West. 'Western culture, based on the Christian factor – there is no doubt about that – is built on one's own questioning of oneself rather than of the surroundings. If you understand the guilt culture then you realize why people in the West feel the need to help the starving in Somalia, or protest against the Vietnam war, and so on. The shame culture, on the other hand, is different. You never question your conscience, you just have to conform with society. For example, the Arabs are not shocked, or say less

shocked than Westerners, at the killing by Palestinians of col-
laborators with the Israelis in the occupied territories; whereas
Jews are shocked by something like the killings at Sabra and
Shatila and make demonstrations about it. In the shame culture
it does not really matter what you do or what you feel.
The most important thing is that you should not violate the
standard behaviour of the community. Honour is tied up
with shame. The moment dishonour becomes known, you
have to do something about it. It is a question of what
you can get away with without violating normal behaviour.
Conscience is less important. The same goes for corruption
in business. No one questions how you make your money.
As long as you are well-off, so what? As long as you can
get away with it, the ethical question is not the most important one: the most important thing is not to violate the social
standard.'[21]

These differing attitudes in society colour the way that Arabs
– and in particular Arab men – view the status of women in
the West. Arabs see Western women, whether in real life, in
films or in books, flouting the codes of honour by which Middle
Eastern society is ordered. The West, with its easy mixing of
the sexes, seems to offer a paradise of opportunity. 'I need
such a girl,' a character, aged seventeen, in a novel by Naguib
Mahfouz says, as he thinks about a fifteen-year-old Cairene he
has just seen, 'to accompany me to the cinema, to play and
talk with me. There'd be no harm in kissing and embracing
her. My barren life has no pretty face to attract me. I have had
enough of the boys' friendships at school and the Shubra Club.
I want a girl. I want this girl! In Europe and America boys and
girls grow up together, as we see in films. This is true life. But
this girl, no sooner did she set her eyes on us than she fled
from us as though we were monsters who would devour her.'[22]
Another Egyptian writer, Nawal el-Sadawi, describing her first
visit to Europe, noticed immediately the difference in Arab
and Western attitudes to male–female relationships when she
went on the Paris Metro and was faced with a scene which
would be unimaginable in any Arab city. 'In the seat facing me
in the train, a girl and boy embraced each other, engrossed in

a long kiss – although the train was packed nobody looked at them. I tried to take my eyes off them.'[23]

Another common conclusion among Arab men is that women in the West are, to put the matter crudely, loose and available for male conquest. In the Arab world, with all its constraints and inhibitions on the mingling of the sexes, there is a high degree of sexuality in the way that young men and women eye one another. Women cast glances discreetly and bashfully and men not so discreetly – to the extent that they can often be seen lusting openly with their eyes. (In the Mahfouz novel quoted above, the same character sees again the girl he desires, 'his eyes ravaging her'. Blushing, 'she lowered her eyes in confusion.'[24] In a novel by Nawal el-Sadawi, a female character, wedged among a crowd on a bus, becomes the centre of attention when confronted by a ticket inspector. 'Men's eyes took possession of her body the way they appropriated those of prostitutes.'[25]) One can detect among Arab men, too, a suggestion, based both on their own expressions of lust and on the implied assumption that young women are all eager to have sex – why else would they need to be chaperoned and scrutinized so carefully? – that any private and secluded meeting between a male and female would in all likelihood lead to sexual contact. When Arab men consider Western girls they make the same assumption about the female craving for sex, with the key difference that the females in question are seen to be living in an environment with different and much more relaxed codes of conduct. By implication, the argument goes, Western girls must be willing and free to have sex.

Needless to say, this is a broad generalization of Arab male attitudes, and does not apply to all – especially educated and widely travelled – Middle Eastern men. But the Middle Eastern stereotype of Western women is reflected even in Arab writing of quality. For example, in a short story, a respected Syrian author, Abd es-Salam al-'Ujayli, has a European girl console her former Arab lover in the French capital, saying: '. . . Paris, my dear, is full of beautiful girls. Many of them, no doubt, are like me with blue eyes and blonde hair, and with lithe bodies that please you. It is quite feasible that you will meet one of them who turns out to be a German from Hanover, from my home town. If you like the look of one of them, all you have to do is follow her, as you followed me once, from the museum, to the Metro to the café. And if you see her accidentally spilling some coffee on her dress from the cup she is holding, point it out to her, then approach her, offering yourself first as a guide, then a friend, then a lover.'[26]

The Arabs find Western explicitness in matters of sex and violence in the media hard to understand. This is not to say that sex and violence are not part of life in the Arab world. The difference is one of attitude to keeping such matters out of sight. Thus the horror expressed earlier in the chapter by Muhammad Aziz Shukri at what he had seen on television in the United States. Women in the Arab world enjoy the protection of the family; at the same time, the family can constrain a woman's ambition and camouflage injustices committed against her. In the West, by contrast, women are caught between the benefits of freedom on the one hand and fear of isolation and attack on the other. Arabs often assert, correctly in my view, that a woman on her own in a public place is safer from serious acts of violence or sexual assault in Arab cities than she would be in Europe or the United States – she would, however, be the focus of far more public attention and, possibly, verbal abuse in the Middle East than in the West.

Discussion of Western women and the perception in the Arab world of their morals brings one back to the subject of the veil. Just as women in Damascus and other cities continue to cover their heads with scarves to demonstrate their modesty and purity as they have done for decades, so the last years of the twentieth century have seen a gradual, but limited, move back to the wearing of veils – symbols, in the minds of campaigners for women's rights, of female subordination in society. A study of women in Algeria conducted in the 1970s, many years before the rise to prominence of the Islamic movement, spoke of pressure being exerted on city women to prove that they were true Muslims. This pressure was reinforced by 'a rural exodus that brought to the cities numerous traditional peasants who were shocked by the opulence and relative freedom of the bourgeois

way of life. An unveiled and hence "immodest" young woman
became the object of continual verbal and other attacks, especially in the capital city, and many preferred to return to traditional dress and appearances to avoid being molested in the
streets. The model of the Western woman, who was the ideal
of these young bourgeois women, was categorically refused by
other classes of women; the Algerian woman was considered
incapable of behaving "decently" if she became "liberated".'[27]

The reappearance of traditional dress in Algeria was significant in the context of the country's history in the second half
of the twentieth century. Women fought alongside men in the
long and costly war of liberation that brought to an end more
than a century of French rule. Jamila Buheired, a woman
fighter with the National Liberation Front was captured, tortured and condemned to death by the French. She was
regarded as a heroine throughout the Arab world and was the
subject of many poems written in the 1950s. The assumption,
once the battle for independence was won, was that equality
of the sexes would become an integral part of life in the new
Algeria. The country's constitution enshrined these ideals. But
the spectacular gains for women's rights won during the long
period of armed struggle soon evaporated. The egalitarian principles contained in the constitution 'were not followed by serious laws or actions . . . as the governments of Ben Bella and,
even more, Boumedienne catered to the beliefs of their petty-
bourgeois male supporters and propagandized for the return
of women to the home and to old ways. The existence of huge
unemployment in post-independence Algeria (paralleled on a
somewhat smaller scale elsewhere in the Maghreb and the
Middle East) made many men hostile to the idea of women as
competitors for jobs and open to the easy arguments of "back
to the home", rather than to more radical or socialist attempts
at solution.'[28]

Developments in Algeria and other Arab countries in the
1980s and early 1990s have pointed to the possibility of further
reversals in the campaign for women's rights – coinciding with
the Islamic revival in the region. Over the years, women have
won the right to vote in most Arab countries where elections

are held (Kuwait is a notable exception); but it must be doubtful whether the female entry into politics in the Arab world would withstand a sustained onslaught from Islamic radicals. As yet, the erosion of ground gained by women is limited in comparison with what has been achieved in all but the most conservative Gulf states, and in some rural areas elsewhere in the Middle East. Women have secured the right to study, work, drive a car, enter public life and so on. Women's campaigners are watching carefully to see how their hard-won status might be challenged. In Algeria, for example, the success of the Islamic Salvation Front (FIS) in the first round of general elections in December 1991 caused anxiety in women's movements in all corners of the Middle East. The second round of voting was cancelled by the Algiers government because the FIS looked certain to win. The Islamic party said, before the elections were cancelled, that on coming to power it would make major changes to the constitution. These would include the introduction of provisions preventing women working outside the home, and making sexual relations outside marriage punishable by death.[29] In the Islamic world, there is an assumption among believers that religion, and the laws associated with it, should regulate a person's private life as much as it does the life of the country. In the West, on the contrary, the introduction of legislation regulating actions inside the home – like the law in the United Kingdom protecting a wife from rape by her husband – was met initially with stiff opposition from those who felt that individual privacy was being undermined.

Algeria is not the only country where Islamic groups have been successful in attracting votes. General elections in Lebanon in 1992 brought significant gains for both Shiite and Sunni Muslim fundamentalists, even though their influence on life in the country continued to be less noticeable than in some other Middle Eastern states. But while Lebanon remained the most Western-oriented Arab country, Lebanese women, by 1992, had made little progress in making their voice heard in politics. Nayla Mu'awad, the widow of a former president, received more votes than any other candidate in the general elections of that year. But there was no other development to

encourage women to think that male domination of political
life could be challenged. Only three female deputies were
elected to the 120-seat assembly; and in the capital, Beirut,
none of the candidates was a woman. The entry of Arab women
into the male-dominated world of politics has been slow but,
in this respect, the Middle East is not so different from the
West. In the United Kingdom and other Western countries
where female emancipation is much more firmly rooted than
in the Middle East, men still greatly outnumber women in
public life.

In politics and in all other fields, campaigners for women's
rights are likely to face increasing problems if the Islamic trend
in the Middle East continues. The Egyptian writer Nawal el-
Sadawi is also one of the leading proponents in the Middle
East of female rights, and is President of the Arab Women's
Solidarity Association. She described the effect of the Islamic
movement as being 'negative, quite negative' on the struggle
for sexual equality, accusing religious fundamentalists of trying
to drag society 'back more or less to a slave system with increasing discrimination against women'. While Nawal el-Sadawi has
been threatened by Islamic fundamentalists for her liberal
views on women's issues and other matters (she lives under
police guard in Cairo), she has also been criticized and
imprisoned by the Egyptian authorities for her writing. 'We,
as progressive writers, women and men, are like a sandwich
between the regimes which do not approve of our criticism
and the religious, fanatic fundamentalist groups who consider
us against religion.'[30]

Illiteracy is widespread in the Arab world. But the written
word is regarded by the various regimes to be just as powerful
(and therefore potentially dangerous) as the word spoken at a
political rally. Arab writers – especially women – have to be
aware, therefore, of the degree to which their works will be
scrutinized by the authorities as they struggle to represent the
soul and conscience of their homeland. The Iraqi poet, Nazek
al-Mala'ika, spoke in an interview in 1974 about her writing:
'A basic fear of death, an innate freedom I lacked, wounds I
suffered as a result of the woman's humiliating state in the

Arab world, consecutive national setbacks and political defeats: these are the elements that have painted my poetry with sorrow.'[31]

Much of the poetry of Nazek al-Mala'ika and other Arab writers was published in Beirut. During the years of anarchy in Lebanon as tribes battled for military and political supremacy, Beirut thrived as a centre where words could be spoken, written and published without fear. Writers and intellectuals who faced restrictions or persecution in their own countries were free to express themselves in Lebanon. The saying was that Arab books were written in Egypt, published in Lebanon and read in Iraq. But the ending of the tribal conflict among the Lebanese, along with the increasing influence of conservative Islamic thinking have combined to restrict even further the freedom of Arab writers.

The restrictions placed on writers are part of a wider problem. As much as popular magazines and newspapers fail to tackle serious issues affecting women in Arab society, so publications in general are careful to avoid detailed and balanced discussion of sensitive issues of any kind. Publishers and editors try to avoid subjects which threaten the status quo. As a result, traditions in the Arab world remain largely unchallenged and free speech continues to be denied to the majority of people in the region.

CHAPTER EIGHT

To War with Words

From 1980 until 1992 only two years passed in which Iraq was not at war. A short break followed the eight-year-long conflict with Iran before President Saddam Hussein ordered the invasion and occupation of Kuwait, precipitating a conflict with a formidable international force led by the United States of America. Hundreds of thousands of Iraqis died in the two wars which, by any impartial standard, were disastrous and costly failures from Baghdad's perspective. The conduct of the two wars was accompanied by a torrent of words uttered and published by the Iraqi leader and his military and civil lieutenants. Millions of words gushed out of the official mouthpieces in Baghdad justifying military action, denouncing Iraq's direct enemies and their allies, and making extravagant (and frequently fictitious) claims of success on the battlefield.

The Arab world has been called by one writer an 'expressive verbal society';[1] everyone has a lot to say, words are part of the bread of daily life. 'Yes, this is true,' an Arab intellectual said when I discussed the matter with him. 'We Arabs have a lot to say, but we do not necessarily mean what we say. This is something you have to understand in the West.' Flamboyant speeches from presidents and kings, and all in authority below them, are part of the daily diet in the Arab world. But, in the view of the same intellectual, 'the speeches frequently do not balance with reality – with how much the individuals can deliver. The words have no connection with actual power. You see this, too, with academics and professors. They make grandiose speeches. In a way it is a form of boasting. But the words

cover the fact that professionals or intellectuals really have little
of substance to say. Leaders talk to their people; but they are
not accountable for their words. No one remembers. Words
take on a life of their own in abstract.'

This is true at every level of life in the Arab world – even in
everyday dealings with shopkeepers or others offering service.
More often than not a question about whether something is
available or some particular service can be provided will be
answered in the affirmative – even when it may be quite obvious that this is an impossibility. Partly it is a case of never
wanting to lose face by saying no, and partly a desire to please
by saying what you think your audience wants to hear.

In Iraq, in its two wars, words were required to perform an
impossible task: to create a colourful panoply to cover the dismal failings in the planning and execution of ill-judged military
campaigns. In the conflict with Iran, words were used to elevate
President Saddam Hussein from the status of temporal leader
to one perceived to be emerging out of the mists of the glorious
traditions of Arab history and folklore. A whole new world of
fantasy was created. The Iraqi leader became the heroic knight
who would revive ancient glories by inflicting a decisive defeat
on the Persians, evoking memories of the Arab victory over
Persia at the battle of Qadisiya in 637. If such grand compari-
sons were the embellishment on the panoply, the base of the
structure was a dense layer of military communiques giving,
sometimes, an extraordinary amount of detail, but obscuring
any clear view of the progress (or more often than not, lack of
progress) of the military campaign. Midway through the first
Gulf war, on 31 October 1984, communique No.1636 told the
Iraqi people that 'an enemy patrol was driven back and 62
rifles, 20 light rocket launchers and 7 machine-guns were captured. There was firing on enemy positions in the northern
sector killing 7; firing in the sectors each of Basra and Misan;
and an unsuccessful enemy air raid on the ports of Bakr and
Amiq – the planes were intercepted and forced to flee by Iraqi
air defences.'

Similar claims, to have fought off enemy air attacks, were
made during the second Gulf conflict in 1991. The invasion of

Kuwait in August 1990 and the subsequent refusal to bow to
international demands that the Iraqi army be withdrawn were
justified in various ways – but invariably with rich and copious
outpourings of words. At one point, the invasion was said to
have been an heroic but logical move to correct injustices of
colonial history by returning Kuwait to the bosom of Iraq. Later
Saddam Hussein adopted Islamic slogans and described the 'liberation' of Kuwait as the first step in a military campaign which
would end with the Israelis being driven out of Jerusalem. He
told his people to prepare for the 'mother of all battles'; he
warned the Western coalition allies that his army would 'water
the desert with American blood' and that American soldiers
would return home in coffins. But the threats were no more
real than the bombastic claims made by President Gamel Abdel
Nasser in the days before the outbreak of the 1967 Middle East
war. The words of the Iraqi President, as much as those of
Nasser before him, disguised the inadequacy of the preparation
for the conflict ahead.

The Iraqi adventure in Kuwait and the threat it posed to the
security of the flow of oil through the Gulf prompted the West,
for a relatively brief period, to take greater interest in Iraq and
the machinations of the Arab world than it has normally done
during the century. The rhetoric coming out of Baghdad
prompted reactions of incomprehension and ridicule. Such
purple language is alien to the Western ear. In the Arab world
the outpouring of words from Iraq led, in the end, to a sense
of embarrassment and shame. But this was because Saddam
Hussein failed to match his promises with action; the thrust of
his rhetoric, like Nasser's before him, had been believed on the
Arab street. It had raised excessive expectations.

The use of rich and rhetorical language in oratory and in
political tracts is part of the tradition of the Middle East of the
twentieth century as much as of previous ones. A manifesto
produced by Arab nationalists in Cairo at the start of the First
World War provides an example: 'O sons of Qahtan! O
descendants of Adnan! Are you asleep? How can you remain
deep in your slumbers when the voices of the nations around
you have deafened everyone? Do you not hear the commotion

all around you? Do you not know that you live in a period
when he who sleeps dies, and he who dies is gone for ever?
When will you open your eyes and see the glitter of the
bayonets which are directed at you, and the lightning of
their swords which are drawn over your heads? . . .
You have become humiliated slaves of the usurping
tyrant . . .'[2]

The speeches of Saddam Hussein and the hours of official
commentaries on Baghdad radio, as well as in state-controlled
newspapers and magazines, were products of this same inheritance. Whoever the speaker may be, and whoever the enemy,
the language is remarkably similar. If the names were changed,
the language used in the following extract from an Iraqi opposition radio broadcast could have been heard on any station,
whether official or clandestine. 'In a desperate attempt to suppress the rebelling masses, particularly the struggling pioneers
from the Iraqi armed forces,' the broadcast in October 1991
said, 'the cowardly and criminal authorities recently carried
out an execution campaign against those forces. Fifteen officers
were executed in Baghdad on charges of collaboration with
the blessed uprising . . . In another development, new groups
recently have been established to confront the Aflaqite military
intelligence patrols and prevent them from carrying out their
dirty mission of detaining the struggling youngsters opposed
to the US-defeated regime of the enemy of the people of
Islam . . .'[3] On and on, the torrent continues, back and forth
across the airwaves of the Middle East and on the pages of the
region's newspapers and magazines which are characterized
more by bland conformity to the dictates and whims of the
particular regime than to freedom of expression and the pursuit
of truth.

Some of the most venomous verbal tirades have accompanied conflicts or even disputes between rival Arab regimes.
In November 1991 continued Libyan criticism of Egypt's role
in helping the Western-led coalition defeat Iraq clearly irritated
the Cairo government to the point at which it decided to retali-
ate. The columnist Anis Mansour sounded off in the semi-
official daily *Al-Ahram*: 'By God I really do not understand

President Qadafi. I do not credit him with having an opinion on war or peace. I do not know how he could have an opinion on war when he has never tried it – or on peace because he has never known it. What does President Qadafi want, as he denounces all Arabs as traitors. From Anwar Sadat, to Hafez al-Assad to Arafat. Sadat, because in war he conquered the path to peace; Assad, because he wants to liberate the Golan Heights; and Arafat, because he wants the lands of Palestine back. What is the crime in that? Qadafi has never fought nor given a penny to those who do fight. President Qadafi is the most miserly of Arab leaders, he has not given a single piastre to anyone . . . People should know about Libya. The money gushes up from under their feet there. For this reason they think with their feet, and their thoughts are grains of soil that should be swept up, one by one . . .'[4]

On occasions, whether wrapped in flowery rhetoric or barbed criticism, even what appear to be the most obvious of truths are denied. In Iraq, the epithet, 'mother of all battles', which was invented to herald victory over the Allied coalition, remained part of the official vocabulary long after Saddam Hussein's army had been crushed. The war was described unequivocally as a 'victory', thus stretching the elasticity of Arab rhetoric to breaking point. Baghdad radio reported in October 1991 a visit of Saddam Hussein to a military base. According to the broadcast 'a large number of officers and personnel of other ranks gathered around his excellency expressing happiness over the visit and demonstrating the sentiments of love and loyalty felt by the soldiers towards their victorious leader.'[5] Neither the troops greeting the President nor anyone hearing the broadcast could possibly have believed that Saddam Hussein was a 'victorious leader'. Words were being used here, once again, to camouflage the continued inability of Arab regimes to examine and come to terms with past mistakes. One Arab academic expressed the opinion that the Arabic language 'was not so much a means of expression but an end in itself: a great writer was not measured by the worth of what he said but by his mastery of the language. The language – its nuances, its rhythm – was an instrument of entertainment rather than a medium for transmitting thought and information. Unless liberated from the spell of the language, the Arab would remain a captive of a sterile system of thought.'[6]

In the view of many liberal intellectuals, the retreat into language as a substitute for facing up to mistakes of the past is a trait which will hamper attempts to build regional unity sufficiently to enable the Arab world to deal with the West on an equal footing. Muhammed Sid Ahmed believes that momentous decisions taken in the region in the past – like declarations of war or the signing of the Camp David agreements with Israel – need to be re-examined. 'If we want, as Arabs, to get together in the future, we will not be able to do so if we leave open questions about the past. These prevent us from going forward. Issues which are deep questions of debate in the Arab world should be settled one way or the other. The files should be opened.'[7]

Such an exercise will be difficult to accomplish because, for the most part, words in the Arab world are not free: rather, they are prisoners or tools of the regimes. 'Freedom is a plant alien to our part of the world,' an Arab writer commented. 'Whenever implanted, it dies . . . We used to blame the colonialists. Then some of us colonized others and the plant of freedom died over and over again.'[8] The words were written in 1980 after the murder of a Lebanese magazine publisher, Salim al-Lawzi, who had returned to Beirut from his base in London. The assumption was that he had been killed for criticizing the Syrian military presence in Lebanon. But this has never been proven, and others have suggested that one of the internal factions in Lebanon may have arranged his murder.

Whatever the exact motives for the killing of Salim al-Lawzi, the event seemed to show that Beirut – up to the late 1970s regarded as the last centre of uncensored expression in the Arab world – was falling victim to the forces which stifle free speech in the rest of the capitals in the region. In the last decades of this century yet more writers, intellectuals and publishers, like Lawzi before them, have chosen exile in London, Paris, Washington, or some other foreign city in preference to leading psychologically fettered lives in their home countries. By the 1990s, London had become an important Arab publishing centre, with the most respected Arabic-language newspapers being produced there and printed simultaneously in Europe and the Middle East. An Arabic-language satellite television service was also established in London. But even these new outlets based in Europe could not escape totally the restraints of the region. Several newspapers and magazines, along with the satellite television channel, are owned by Saudi Arabia. 'The Saudi plunge into media ownership,' one Iraqi writer living in Europe said, 'has had both advantages and disadvantages. It is true that they are providing money to enable professional products to be put out. If you look at the newspapers that they own – yes, there is interesting and credible news coverage and you will find articles by liberal Arab and Western writers. But appearances are deceptive. In a very intelligent way the Saudis are blocking any meaningful news about developments in the Gulf.' The implications are obvious: on any matter, whether developments in the Gulf or anything else, what is regarded as undesirable by Saudi Arabia has little chance of reaching a mass readership or audience in the Middle East.

A Syrian intellectual in Damascus made a similar observation. 'To get a play or series shown on the Saudi or Gulf television stations you will have a much better chance if you insert a religious element. So, for instance, you might have an Egyptian talking to his wife, and as the writer you insert a line saying: I am saving money for the *hajj* [the pilgrimage to Mecca]. You do this just to please the Saudis. Secular views are not allowed, so you do not express them – otherwise the Gulf states will not buy your programmes. Countries like Syria or Libya or Yemen do not have the money to finance anything in competition.'

The restraints of which television producers with an eye on the Gulf market have to be aware are considerable. The following are some of the restrictions, according to a report in the *Index on Censorship*: 'Unmarried couples acting the part of a married couple are not allowed to sit on the same bed together;

unmarried actors are not allowed to be shown sitting in the same room together with the door closed; . . . women are not allowed to be shown singing or dancing . . . it is forbidden to show a crime being committed . . . the name of God may not be taken in vain; no statues or figures may be shown that represent the human or animal form as these are graven images and hence forbidden by Islam.'[9]

Aside from restrictions like these, regimes in the Gulf and elsewhere make a habit of 'buying' both magazines and journalists. For example, before the 1990–91 Gulf crisis the magazine *Al-Tadhamun* was financed by Iraq. According to an Egyptian journalist, 'we knew that anyone writing in that magazine was writing for the Iraqis and getting good money. They would write an article and get paid as though it was an advertisement for the country – they would get paid at advertising rates. After the Gulf crisis, Kuwaiti and Saudi papers paid big money for articles praising the Gulf regimes and denouncing the Iraqis.' There are brave voices denouncing such malpractice, but their impact is minimal when matched against big money and the need to keep a job in difficult economic and social circumstances. 'When Arab intellectuals become like belly-dancers,' one writer complained, 'having to wiggle their loins for a living, gyrating ever more enthusiastically when the money starts flying from the audience; when 150 million Arabs (that is what the censuses say) become 150 million frozen fish. That is when we have to concede that donkeys have the intellectual edge over the mode of thinking of some Arabs! This is not an article to denigrate the Arabs (who needs more denigration?) Nor is it an attempt to justify. Every people has its dirty linen. But the atmosphere in the Arab world has become like the water of the Gulf: so polluted with spilt oil that we need a miracle to clean it up . . .'[10]

In the Arab world, language is traditionally an instrument in the hands of the powerful. The poet Nizar Qabbani chose a range of metaphors in his poem on the subject, 'Morphine':

> The word is a bouncing ball
> The ruler throws from his balcony.

The people run after the ball,
Their tongues hanging out like hungry dogs.
The word in the Arab World
Is a nifty marionette
Who speaks seven languages
And wears a red cap.
He sells paradise and gaudy bangles,
Sells wide-eyed children
White rabbits and doves.
The word is an overworked whore:
The writer has slept with her,
The journalist has slept with her,
The imam of the mosque has slept with her.
Since the seventh century
The word has been a shot of morphine.
Rulers calm their people with speeches.
The word in my country is a woman
Who's solicited men
Since the Book became law.[11]

While at times the aim of Arab leaders might be to use words to create an hypnotic effect, at other moments their purpose is to block out or obfuscate information. This practice is not unknown in the West, especially at times of conflict. During the Gulf war of 1991 and in the Falklands conflict a decade earlier, the British government imposed stringent restrictions on access to information. But in general official attempts to hide or camouflage information are challenged in liberal Western societies where the role of investigative reporting has become firmly established. This is not the case in the Arab world. As one of the sayings there goes: 'Not everything that is known can be told.' The televised questioning of senior figures in public life, which is a common occurrence in the United States and elsewhere in the West, is not a practice that one could imagine being adopted in the Arab world. I happened to be in the Gulf in 1991 while a senior American judge was defending himself in front of a Senate committee in Washington against charges of sexual harassment. The hearings were being shown live around the world on the Cable News Network (CNN). 'What are the Americans doing?' an Arab government official asked. 'If someone here was accused of sexual harassment we would say: so what? We would not put the whole thing on television.' The official's comment reflects the scorn expressed commonly by Arab men at the degree to which their counter-parts in the West have bowed to feminist pressures. More than this, however, it shows how in Middle Eastern society there is a clear understanding that the private actions of people of high rank are not the business of the general public and are certainly not subjects for public debate. In Arab countries, with the poss-ible exception of Lebanon, knowledge and the degree to which information is channelled to the public are the prerogatives of the privileged elite.

One negative effect of this attitude is the way that it encour-ages the spread of rumours. As Mohamed Heikal has observed, 'in the absence of reliable information, any good story becomes an accepted fact' and this contributes to the malaise and lack of cohesion in the Arab world. The mushrooming of news and infor-mation outlets in the region in the second half of the century made the task of finding reliable information even harder and more con-fusing. Heikal believes that 'in the 1950s and 1960s the Arab media had a sense of direction guided by the idea of Arab nationalism, which gave it the power to influence the masses. By the 1980s, each Arab government was steering the media in its own country, creating a chaos of conflicting aims. Using the media to convey or defend pan-Arab values had never been easy, but a lack of united vision made it impossible.' The Arabic language broadcasts of the BBC, Voice of America and Radio Monte Carlo became the main sources of reliable information.[12]

The seepage of Western news broadcasts and other pro-grammes by satellite into the Arab world is seen by some people in the region as a mixed blessing, and not necessarily one which will lead to better Arab–Western harmony and understanding. Arab regimes, for example, may try to impose restrictions on public access to programmes containing criticism of their par-ticular countries, or espousing ideas regarded as seditious. Even within the Arab viewing public, there is not unanimous

satisfaction at the growing Western influence in the media of
the region. The West may assume that for the Arabs to have
free access to its channels of information and entertainment
could only be welcomed by the inhabitants of the region. An
Egyptian political commentator, Mahjoub Omar is one of those
who differs from this view. 'What we get from the West is
propaganda. Of course, we all follow the West through its
media. Without dubbing the dialogue into Arabic, Arab television stations are putting out their programmes with subtitles.
So we find that Western culture is permeating our bedrooms.
And when we talk about the trend towards a commodity-
consumer society, we blame the West. I personally blame as
well the Westernized elite in Arab states. Look at our streets
here. Suddenly you find Kentucky Chicken, Wimpy, super-
market, cafeteria, coiffeur. These are all Western words,
Western terms. They are all connected with a high way of living
which the simple people cannot afford. Try thinking about how
a poor Arab seeing this picture of wealth thinks about what is
going on in the world.' Mahjoub Omar believes also that when
Arabs see how Western television stations cover events in the
Middle East the gap of sympathy and understanding between
the two regions is widened further. As an example he mentioned the coverage of the closing moments of the 1991 Gulf
war, and the celebratory gloating in the West over Iraq's
humiliation on the battlefield. In particular, he mentioned a
sequence of pictures, beamed all around the world by satellite,
which showed a defeated Iraqi kissing the feet of an American
soldier. Mahjoub Omar's opinion is that such images have
inflicted incalculable damage on Arab–Western relations. 'The
people in the West do not know how we feel. Mr Bush [the
American President at the time of the war] tried to inject an
element of religious thought into his language during the Gulf
crisis. But he was making a mistake, he was not fooling us. His
CNN presented us with an Iraqi Muslim Arab soldier kissing
the boots of an American soldier. This picture will not' –
Mahjoub Omar, a Coptic Christian, shouted out the word – 'be
forgotten. No one will forgive them for that. The Arabs have
seen in this picture the image of the new oppressor.'[13]

Mahjoub Omar's remarks echoed and reinforced the sentiments of a leading Arab nationalist from an earlier period of the century, Sati' al-Husri. He spoke of a fierce struggle that had lasted for many centuries between East and West, resulting in a 'spiritual estrangement between the two cultures'.[14]

This estrangement has taken many forms and has been fostered in different ways by the two societies. At the end of the twentieth century one of the most stark disparities in attitudes relates to the freedom of expression. Karim Alrawi, an Egyptian playwright and author, has an intimate knowledge of both cultures. His father is Arab and his mother is English; he received a formal Muslim education in Egypt and later experienced schooling in the West. As an adult, he became a published writer in both languages.

Karim Alrawi lives in Cairo, one of the main literary centres in the Arab world. He told me about the difficulties of getting a book published in the Egyptian capital. 'The official position is that there is no censorship in Egypt, and the Minister of Culture has gone on the record saying that. But this just is not true. What happened was that in 1985 a law was passed which permitted the Islamic Research Council at Al-Azhar, Cairo's Islamic University, to check all books which dealt with religious subjects to decide if any of them were blasphemous; in which case Al-Azhar could ask the government to have these books banned. What has happened since then is that Al-Azhar has increased its own brief to cover more and more of what is published, to the point that books on linguistics have been banned, novels have been banned, and so on. All sorts of works that really have very little to do with religion have been banned because Al-Azhar has decided that it does not accept the points of view expressed in them. So in that way censorship has increased – it has been privatized.'

Plays and songs fall into a different category. All scripts and lyrics have to be submitted to the state censor. 'Officially,' Alrawi said, 'the censors are only allowed to ban work which is a threat to national security; but to get the censor actually to define what is national security is very problematic. I have had several plays banned, and when I have gone to the censor to challenge his banning order I have asked for a list of what is allowed, and have been told that none exists. In the 1960s such a booklet was available. President Sadat, in the 1970s, abolished it as part of his liberalization programme. But he did not abolish the censor, which basically meant that he was allowing the censor to use his initiative more. This meant that more plays were banned because the writer could not come back and argue. Nasser, although he was a dictator, was also very liberal when it came to cultural matters and quite often when writers would appeal to him, he would overrule the censor. This has not been the case with the last two presidents.'

Given the Western stereotype of repressive Islamic regimes, one might expect all mention of sex to be banned from Arab theatre. While this is not the case, the degree of freedom cannot be compared with that in the West in the second half of the twentieth century. According to Alrawi, homosexuality is an even more problematic issue. 'This is a subject that causes a lot of controversy. As a writer you can treat homosexuality in the theatre as long as you make fun of it and as long as gay men are portrayed as effeminate. It is not allowed if the subject is treated with any seriousness. If a gay character is serious, if homosexuality is treated as something one could call normal, then that is not accepted.'

Alrawi believes that the combination of the various constraints is killing off Arab theatre. 'Drama is conflict. No conflict, no drama. Many critics now say that plays are no longer being written. Scripts are being produced, but they have no structure, no build-up, no climax. It is an observation that is being made in a number of Arab countries. Critics believe that the era of the play lasted from 1950 to the early 1970s. I think this is true, because it is very difficult to write plays under current circumstances.'

Even when an Arab writer succeeds in publishing his work, he or she can face problems in reaching a wide readership in the region. The restrictions placed by the Saudi and Gulf authorities on subject matter in the visual media apply equally to written material. The authorities will not allow the import of books or other publications dealing with what they regard as controversial or contentious issues of politics or religion, or with sex. Women writers must also overcome male prejudice, which suggests that it is inappropriate for women to write about sex or stir up controversy over women's role in society.

Ultimately, of course, the authorities have the power simply to ban a book. The Lebanese author, Emilie Nasrallah has written of the problems which she faced with a novel called *Al-Rahena* (Bondage) which tells the story 'of a girl who is promised to a man even before she is born; the man is a landlord and the parents are working on his land. The girl grows up not knowing that her fate is set, that she is "bonded" in this way. When she becomes aware of this she starts struggling against this pre-set destiny arranged by her parents with the landlord – her future husband-to-be. The novel is banned in many Arab countries . . .'[15]

One of the great mysteries of the Arab world is the amount of attention that regimes place on monitoring the publication and distribution of books – given that that the levels of illiteracy and poverty are so high in the region. An Arab friend who travels often around the Middle East told me how he carefully selects the right book to take to a particular country before he sets out in order to avoid getting into trouble at the airport. On one occasion he was accosted by officials at Damascus airport who found an Arabic novel in his luggage. Only when the authorities were convinced that the author was a Syrian, accepted by the regime, was he allowed to enter the country. It seems strange that Arab authorities should pay such fastidious attention to the printed word given that, according to Karim Alrawi, 'books will get read by a limited circle of people and debated by people in that circle. It is very cliquey and tends to be peripheral to what is really happening. And yet, at the same time, the various regimes tend to treat writers and their products with an exaggerated importance. It is very difficult to work out a rationale for it. Some people will give a semi-mystical explanation and say it is because in days long gone every tribe had its poet and the poet's job was to praise the tribe and its leader; and that poets who did not do that were driven out of the tribe. But I think that is really stretching it a quite a bit.

Maybe it is just that the printed word is considered dangerous, even in a country with high illiteracy.'

Superficial observations reveal that it is rare to see Arabs reading anything other than newspapers or magazines in public places. Where Westerners, at airports or on trains, will become engrossed in reading paperback books, as often as not of a genre that is described as the 'airport' novel – a work which may be well written, but never too serious in subject matter – no such genre exists in Arab culture. Karim Alrawi says this is because 'to be a really popular novelist you need to have a large enough readership. That is why there is not a Len Deighton in Arabic; there are not enough Len Deighton readers. Most people who read novels are well educated, certainly middle class, and therefore have different aspirations and perceptions of what a novel should be about. That is not to say that there is not a lot of trash that is written – there is – not all Arabic literature is high art. It just means that the aspiration of even the bad novelist is somehow to say something serious and to have an impact; because ultimately the pool of readers that they can reach are middle class and well educated.'

Another Egyptian author, Sonn'allah Ibrahim, expressed similar views – telling me how the Arab writer 'is expected to deal directly, in artistic form of course, with social and political situations. People expect to read a kind of comment. And as much as you can deal with such problems, you are accepted or welcomed by the small set of readers.' As for the absence of the popular, low-brow, 'airport' novel, Ibrahim points to 'the low degree of the development of Arab society. Society itself is not so modernized. The works of Le Carré or Deighton are the products of a society that is highly technological. Readers have had a wide range of experiences, and they learn to move fast with the book. There is a jumping narrative that forces to you to think hard – to wonder what is going to happen. We would have a person coming to the door, knocking and then explaining the whole situation. It is connected to our limited social experience. You in the West would not need this explanation, because you have a wider background.'[16]

*   *   *

In time, social differences between the Arab world and the
West may narrow, but this would still leave a wide disparity
in the nature of the languages of the two regions. Languages
in the West have evolved and adapted themselves to social and
technological changes, shedding whenever necessary relics of
former ages, and allowing themselves to be bent and fashioned
according to daily needs. Arabic does not have that flexibility.
There are several different branches to the Arabic language
family. At the centre lies the classical language, in which the
Koran was revealed to the Prophet Muhammed. Because it is
the language of the sacred book, it has survived without alter-
ation since the seventh century. Next in the scale of purity
comes modern classical Arabic. This is the formal language of
news bulletins, books and newspapers, and is understood
throughout the region. Then, there are scores of regional dialects, encompassing numerous variations of the same language.
Egyptian dialect is probably the most widely understood
because most Arab films and television dramas are produced
in Cairo. It is fair to say, therefore, that the majority of Arabs
speak or understand four versions of their own language: formal classical, modern literary, a regional dialect, and the Egyptian dialect. ('If I speak my own dialect to a Moroccan,' an Iraqi
told me, 'we will not get anywhere. So I speak Egyptian Arabic,
and that is fine.') The differences between dialects are so great
that some leaders of the pan-Arab nationalist movement earlier
in the century, including Sati' al-Husri, regarded the colloquial
language as a factor working against regional unity and argued
that its use should be discouraged.

Despite all the local variations, Arabs look to the classical
language as one of the precious jewels of their inheritance, and
one that has to be handled carefully. This presents problems
from time to time for modern writers like Karim Alrawi. 'Arabic
is both a sacred language and one of everyday discourse. To
use a language which is sacred is to risk constantly blaspheming
or offending religious authorities. I think that that accounts to
a large degree for the big difference between the classical and
colloquial languages. Having written both in both English and
Arabic, what struck me when I started to write plays in Arabic

was the different way I had to relate to the language. What I found with English was that I had a degree of freedom to make up words, phrases, and expressions. It was taken for granted that a writer could do this. I realized that writing in Arabic you could not really do that; you were constrained by the language. Also, English is full of words borrowed from other languages. In classical Arabic this is not the case. Old words take on new meanings, and so what happens is that you find words with layers of meaning. This is great for poetry and probably explains to a large degree why Arabic poetry is so difficult to translate into any other language. But it means also, as a writer, that you constantly risk profaning the language of God.'

As in many other parts of the world, there are groups within Arab countries campaigning for the elimination of foreign words from modern Arabic. Such groups have become increasingly vociferous with the spread in influence of the conservative Islamic movement. A demand frequently made by these campaigners is for all subjects at Arab colleges and universities, including science, to be taught in Arabic. They argue that classical Arabic is rich enough to be adaptable to meet all linguistic needs. Ibrahim Bayoumi Madkour, the Chairman of the Arabic Language Academy in Cairo, argued in 1992 that 'you cannot have a complete picture unless a science is taught in the language of the country. Each person should know his Arabic language perfectly. He should also know at least one European language well to allow for cultural exchange; but teaching in universities must be changed to Arabic.'[17]

Even if Arabic language campaigners achieved their goal in the universities, it is unlikely that the battle would be won on the street level, where such words as 'bus', 'taksi' (taxi) and 'telfun' (telephone) have become ingrained in everyday speech.

Protectionist attitudes to the Arabic language often go hand in hand with a desire to eliminate Western influence from the culture as a whole. Since the rule of Muhammed Ali in Egypt in the nineteenth century, many thousands of books from Europe and elsewhere have been translated into Arabic. For

many Arabs, writers as well as readers, works in translation
provide the only available insights into other cultures. But the
problem is that a particular translation is not always an accurate
reflection of either the substance or the spirit of the original.
Karim Alrawi, in an issue of *Index on Censorship*, analysed an
Arabic translation of *Mountain Language*, a play by Harold
Pinter. Alrawi argued that the treatment of the play in Arabic
had turned it from a hard-hitting and disturbing work into 'a
comedy of manners'. The translator 'turns Scene Three, which
is so disturbing in the original, into a scene of polite conversation. "That fucking woman" becomes "that improper
woman". "Lady Duck Muck" becomes "the respected lady".
The critical speech marking the character's final acquiescence:
"Can I fuck him? If I fuck him will everything be all right?"
is changed to "Will this Mr Dokes lay with me? If he does, is
everything all right?" In the translation, the active subject of
this sentence is Mr Dokes. The Young Woman is passive. She
is not made to embrace her oppression.' More important still,
Alrawi argues, is the way in which the spirit of the play has
been changed. '*Mountain Language* is a play of great relevance
to the Middle East, which is made up of so many minority
communities. It is a play that raises questions about the structures of power and authority in our societies and its relationship
to language. This is precisely what the translation avoids dealing with. The use of self-censorship by translators is another
means of spreading the load of censorship and making it more
difficult to recognize it as such.'[18]

In such an atmosphere of unease about language, nervous-
ness about censorship and concern about the sanctity of Arabic,
it is hardly surprising that a clear picture of events within the
Arab world does not emerge. 'One of the wonders of the Arab
world,' the Egyptian writer and analyst of Islamic affairs, Fahmi
Huweidi commented, 'is that when you leave it you have the
opportunity to become better acquainted with it, more
informed about it and more involved in the course of events.
At least this is how I felt as I followed the Algerian elections
[in December 1991] and subsequent events while travelling
between Cairo and London over these past two weeks. It is a

curious irony that has a long history. In brief, I realized that
the volume of information about the Arab world available in
London is much greater than that available in any Arab capital.
Also there is no comparison between the quality of the news
in the Arab press and that in London. I believe that it is important to note that our media not only provided little help in
understanding events in Algeria, but were also frequently misleading.'[19]

The restrictions imposed on the flow of information in the
Middle East have seriously hindered the promotion of the Arab
cause in the West. At times of war or other crises, Arab governments have generally been slow and inefficient in telling their
side of the story – particularly when matched against the
efficiency of the propaganda machines of the West and of Israel.
An Arab's retort to this observation is invariably an accusation
directed against governments and media in the West of being
either influenced by or sympathetic to the Jewish cause. Whatever one's personal view on this, it is certainly true that the
Arab embassies suffer in their attempts to give their version of
events and attitudes in their home countries. Arab diplomats
are frequently frustrated in their task because of the lack of
cooperation from their governments. 'I believe that this is a
serious problem,' Edmund Ghareeb, an adviser to the embassy
of the United Arab Emirates in Washington, said at a seminar
in 1980. 'Part of the problem, I think, stems from the nature
of the system of government that exists in some Arab states.
People, unless you are the responsible official, don't have the
authority to give information.'[20] Ghareeb identified another
factor working against Arab embassies providing a smooth
channel of information to the outside world: the quality of
senior embassy staff. In many Arab countries, he said,
'ambassadorial posts are given either as a punishment or as a
reward, and so this is again a serious problem.'[21]

The need for channels of information from Arab capitals to be
cleared to Europe and the West is acute. In the West, the Arabs
face a wall of popular prejudice, bigotry and racism. So far, their
efforts to present their case successfully, through diplomatic
channels or through written and broadcast media have failed

– despite a hundred years and more of contact at many levels between the two societies. Arabs have failed, for example, to make the West understand the role of rhetoric in Arab life. In the absence of such understanding, the bombastic oratory of leaders like Saddam Hussein easily strengthens Western prejudices. Arabs believe that Western attitudes to them were formed at the time of the Crusades. Since then, through the creation of Israel and beyond, Arabs feel they have been involved in a political and cultural struggle with the West which is founded in prejudice and misunderstanding on the part of Europe and the United States. When Sati' al-Husri wrote about the 'spiritual estrangement' between the cultures of the two regions he went on to comment (his words paraphrased) that 'the [East–West] struggle has given the West an unfavourable view of Orientals in general and of Arabs in particular. This bias is manifested in studies which find Westerners "withdrawing from neutrality" when they write about the Arabs.'[22] Similar observations have been recorded in the subsequent decades – notably by Edward Said in his book *Orientalism* in which he challenged the motives and methods of those in the West who laid the foundation in the nineteenth and early twentieth centuries for subsequent studies of the Middle East. 'My contention,' he wrote, 'is that Orientalism is fundamentally a political doctrine willed over the Orient because the Orient was weaker than the West, which elided the Orient's difference with its weakness ... The Orient existed for the West, or so it seemed to countless Orientalists, whose attitude to what they worked on was either paternalistic or candidly condescending – unless of course, they were antiquarians, in which case the "classical" Orient was a credit to *them* and not to the lamentable modern Orient.'[23] Rabee' Dejani, a Palestinian professional, believes that the West has continued to distort facts about the Arab world throughout the century. 'I would not go so far as to say that among the decision makers in the West today there is no in-depth understanding of the Arab world. There is a great deal of intelligent understanding. But the West looks at us through its own value system, and from its own perceived position of superiority. The way that it interprets very accurately and meticulously collected data is not always correct. Let us please speak candidly. There is a lot of hypocrisy and cynicism in the way that the West views us.'[24]

The popular image of the Arab in the West has changed throughout this century, but has shown an astonishing inability to shed the trappings of condenscension and contempt. In colonial times, the Arab was seen either as a lazy and dirty peasant or a fat sultan in his harem. After the Second World War, when the pan-Arab nationalist movement was popular, President Nasser of Egypt, along with the many millions of Arabs who supported him, became a figure of hate for Europe and the United States, symbolizing a demonic force bent on undermining the West. In the 1960s and 1970s, the Arab was given the mask of the ruthless terrorist or the flowing robes of the greedy oil sheikh. Jack Shaheen, Professor of Communications Studies at Southern Illinois University, wondered during a seminar in 1980 'why this threatening, shifty-eyed, hook-nosed, dirty, sulking Arab image continually appears?' He noted that on American television 'Arab leaders and their associates are seen as men who are either blood-feuding Bedouins or oil blackmailers. They're depicted as sex-starved pimps, cheats and back-stabbers . . . Television series also imply that Arab men are unable to love their own women. It is further implied that Western women are not attracted to Arab men. If we go back to the films of Rudolph Valentino, we see that Arabs were always rejected by Western women. In *The Sheik* and *Son of the Sheik*, the women never really succumbed to Valentino's charm until they found out he was an Englishman, not an Arab.'[25]

The final decade of the century began with popular Western prejudices against Arabs as entrenched as ever. The Iraqi invasion of Kuwait and the subsequent war in the Gulf cemented them further. The popular press in Britain used stereotype and cliché to condemn and belittle the Iraqis and all other Arabs who did not support the Western-led coalition. The mass-circulation *Sun* led the way. When British women and children, who had been trapped in Kuwait by the invasion, were finally given permission to travel overland to Baghdad on their way home, the paper printed an illustrated map, pointing out the dangers that the convoy might face. The map was entitled: 'Brits' 500 Miles of Terror'. As the convoy left Kuwait, the paper suggested, 'a trigger-happy guard might lose his head and try to halt the buses, despite the promised safe passage'. Another *Sun* suggestion was that 'armed gangs would find a slow-moving convoy of unarmed women and children an easy target'. Another stereotype which made appearances throughout the century: the marauding Arab, with no scruples about shooting innocent women and children.

Racism in films and in popular fiction was as evident in the early 1990s as at any time in the century. For example, in *Miami*, a work of pulp fiction published in 1992, an Arab makes a brief appearance. His name, predictably, is Abdul. The reader is given the impression at once that he is both rich and dissolute. 'In the capital cities he frequented, he stuck to the restaurants where they knew him and his money. Otherwise, he was just a greasy nobody.' Two pages later, a female character insinuates, in her thoughts, that Arabs are bisexual and, therefore, that her male companion might be the object of Abdul's attention. 'Lisa looked at Abdul sharply. Okay, Arabs dealt from both ends of the pack, but watch out, sandy gland. Don't play the Saddam Hussein around my boy, or I'll nuke you.'[26] Racism against Arabs today does not arouse the same level of indignation as it does against other ethnic groups.

Another feature of the early 1990s was an upsurge in physical attacks on Arabs in France, Germany and other European countries. The fear of racial assaults, as well of the effects of the severe economic recession of the 1990s, looked likely to force many Arabs to return home, taking with them often a gloomy and frightening picture of life in the West.

The existence of such attitudes, in conjunction with the accusations of double standards in the West's handling of the Kuwait crisis at the opening of the decade, left Arabs feeling that the gulf in perceptions between the two regions would show no signs of narrowing in the immediate years ahead. The Egyptian political commentator Fawzy Mansour, writing several months after the ending of the 1991 Gulf war, concluded that 'Arabs of all ilks, immigrants and "guestworkers", tourists and terrorists, playboys and bankers, gambling oil sheikhs and fundamentalists are given top rank in the latest, revised edition of Western demonology.'[27]

Above all, Arabs are offended by what they see as Western high-handedness and smugness towards the Middle East. 'Arabs are distrustful of the West,' Mahjoub Omar told me, 'partly because of racist behaviour towards them in Europe and America. But generally the Arabs are not xenophobic. The trouble is, they are usually treated as defeated and conquered people. If you read Western literature you see the Arabs referred to as barbarians or conquered people – as if we had no history at all.'[28] A Palestinian refugee in a camp in Jordan voiced similar sentiments. 'The West still regards the Arabs as barbaric and having no culture,' he said. 'It is time their attitude changed and they realized that we do have a culture.'

Cultural traffic in the twentieth century has moved overwhelmingly in one direction – from West to East. Only a tiny minority of the millions of Westerners who have lived and worked in the Middle East have shown interest in learning about the language and culture of the region, despite the prolific output of Western Orientalists. (According to Edward Said, 'around 60,000 books dealing with the Near Orient were written between 1800 and 1950; there is no remotely comparable figure for Oriental books about the West.'[29]) In general, based on my own experience over many years of observing expatriates in the Middle East, foreigners have preferred to live within their own communities, while seeking ways of reinforcing their preconceived views of the Arabs and their customs in their brief encounters with the local population. As a result, the foreigners have left at the end of their stay with their views of the 'Lebs', the 'Gyppos', the 'Gulfies', and the 'bloody A-rabs' as entrenched as ever, and have been in no position to help break down prejudice back in their own countries. At the same time, the popular Arab view of Westerners – as being remote, arrogant and ill-mannered, while lacking in moral and spiritual values – has continued to be reinforced.

Arab writers with experience of both Middle Eastern and

Western cultures, like Karim Alrawi and Nawal el-Sadawi, have been trying to build bridges between the two. Both are liberals and see a need for flexibility on the part of both Arabs and Westerners to try to find areas of common understanding. Each has had works in Arabic translated and published in English. But both are living and writing in a part of the world where, in the final decade of the twentieth century, liberal ideals are being challenged by those in authority, and by influential groups outside ruling circles who are demanding a return to conservative traditions of Islam. Nawal el-Sadawi says that publishing books in the Arab world with any kind of controversial element is getting increasingly difficult. 'I think now that the intellectuals, progressive people on the left and progressive women, are becoming more and more the minority groups; and even the powers in authority are trying to push them aside and marginalize them.'[30] The desire on the part of those in authority, or those seeking it, to control words and information in the Arab world is as strong as ever. Karim Alrawi believes that liberal intellectuals face a difficult time as they campaign for freedom of expression. 'There is a feeling that is growing in the region that we are on the verge of a sea-change, and it is one which most of us would not welcome. There is a growing awareness among many of the intellectuals within Arab society – and specifically within Egypt – of the growing influence and power of the Islamic movement; and there is a growing sense of inevitability that this movement will come to power in one shape or another.'[31]

CHAPTER NINE

Revolution and Refuge

A portrait of the former spiritual leader of Iran, Ayatollah Khomeini, hung on the classroom wall. The young children – Shiite Muslim orphans from many areas of Lebanon – were in the middle of an English lesson when I was shown in. The teacher, a lady in a white headscarf and full-length skirt, was pointing to a drawing of a tennis game in progress, which had been pinned to the blackboard, and asking the children to identify, in English, the various objects in the picture. The children were responding enthusiastically.

The orphanage, in the foothills just south of Beirut, is funded by Iran and is closely associated with the Iranian-backed Lebanese Shiite organization, Hizbollah. This group is best known in the West for its involvement in the kidnapping of Westerners in Lebanon during the 1980s, for suicide car-bomb attacks on Western and Israeli targets and for its stubborn guerrilla campaign against Israel's occupation of a strip of territory in southern Lebanon. These are all activities which fit the common image in Europe and the United States of Islamic fundamentalists – that they are violent and ruthlessly anti-Western. The idea that fundamentalists look after orphans and provide essential services to the needy within the Arab world seems unlikely to gain currency in the West in the foreseeable future. In the minds of people in the West, Islam, and the fundamentalism with which it has largely become synonymous, has taken on a demonic image. There can be little doubt, also, that Western views of the Arab world in the next few decades will be based on the negative view of modern-day Islam. What the Arabs see as hostile Western attitudes and prejudices towards the Islamic world – in Bosnia as much as in the Middle East – seem certain to foster a greater defensiveness among Muslims, who frequently express fears that following the collapse of communism, Islam has been selected by the international community – dominated by the United States – as the new global enemy. The talk is of confrontation, rather than of compromise or dialogue aimed at clearing up mutual misunderstanding.

Misunderstandings begin with Western perceptions of fundamentalism. The Islamic trend in Arab countries reflects the diversity of the region itself; it is not a united movement of fanatical armed militants bent on wreaking vengeance on the West – as it is often portrayed in Europe and the United States. Militant groups exist; but all indications suggest that they are in the minority. The Western vision of fundamentalism has obscured the more significant trend in which ordinary people in their millions have quietly started to reassert religious values in their everyday life, as has happened in other parts of the world. Saad Eddin Ibrahim, an Egyptian sociologist, told me that he is opposed to the use of the word fundamentalism because 'it gives all kinds of connotations to the Westerner. I use the word activism. Because we are not talking about simplistic, crazy, crackpot religious fanatical elements. They are mostly very educated people – students or graduates of medicine, science or engineering which in Egypt are the elite branches of university education. They come from somewhere in the middle class, they are very sane, very sophisticated and well-versed in societal and world affairs. That being the case, the mass media in the West give the average viewer a sensational, alarmist view of Islamic activism. To be sure there is an extremist wing. It's actually a small part of the movement. But because its actions are often dramatic and lethal – like assassinating President Sadat of Egypt or blowing up the US Marine headquarters in Lebanon – they appeal more to the media-makers because this is what makes a good headline. The danger in the medium term is to condition the Western viewer or listener to associate violence, chaos and fanaticism with the word Islam. And that doesn't do either the Muslims or the Westerners much good.'[1]

Saad Eddin Ibrahim's observation about the background of Islamic activists was borne out by meetings with members of the Muslim Brotherhood in Egypt and Jordan. The Brotherhood was founded in Egypt in 1928 by Hassan al-Banna, 'an eloquent and charismatic former schoolteacher'.[2] Al-Banna had been a follower of Rashid Rida, one of the most distinguished Islamic reformers of the early part of the century. According to Rida the question of why Islamic countries appeared to be backward in every aspect of civilization needed to be addressed through Islam: 'The teachings and moral precepts of Islam are such that, if they are properly understood and fully obeyed, they will lead to success in this world as well as the next – and to success in all the forms in which the world understands it, strength, respect, civilization, happiness. If they are not understood and obeyed, weakness, decay, barbarism are the results. This is true not only of individuals but of communities: the Islamic *umma* was the heart of the world's civilization so long as it was truly Islamic.'[3] The Muslim Brotherhood, and other fundamentalist groups, have continued to win followers on the basis of this simple and alluring formula. Hassan al-Banna had particular ideas on how a state should be organized. He believed that 'political parties should be prohibited, the law should be reformed and brought with the bounds of the Shari'a [the body of law based on the Koran and the principles of Islam], administrative posts should be given to those with a religious education. He made it clear too that the Islamic government should maintain a strict control over private morals and education: primary schools should be attached to mosques, religion should be the centre of education and Arabic its medium.'[4]

In Cairo, I contacted Dr Issam el-Arian, a Muslim Brother and a prominent member of the doctors' syndicate. The Brotherhood office was in a narrow market street in a poor district of Cairo. Through a jungle of stalls selling vegetables, live birds, rabbits, clothes and pots and pans, and amid smells of decay, I reached the door to the appropriate building. An elderly, unshaven *bawaab* (doorman) sat on the step outside, oblivious of the flies around him. Despite the gloom inside the doorway one could tell that this once had been an elegant

building. The designer had been proud to have his name associated with the finished product: on a wall in the hallway was
a plaque reading 'M. Olivetti. Architecte 1925'. The subsequent
decades had seen it fall into a state of neglect like many areas
of Cairo and other Arab cities where millions of potential supporters of the Islamic fundamentalist movement struggle to
survive. The marble steps were chipped, the plaster on the
ceiling was flaking, part of the wall had crumbled away to
reveal black electricity cables. Up on the third floor where the
Muslim Brotherhood had taken offices, it was a different world
– clean, modern and efficient. Dr el-Arian, a small, sprightly
man, smartly dressed and fast-talking, was keen to stress the
importance that his movement puts on the use of modern technology – the marriage of up-to-the-minute gadgets with
religious principles rooted in history – as he talked about the
aims of the Brotherhood to establish an Islamic state in Egypt
and throughout the Arab world. 'We are for peaceful change
in society,' he said. 'Mainly our aim is to educate people, to
train people how to live their lives well in relation to religion.
We want them to have good relations with Allah and also to
make use of the new achievements of high technology, of the
new civilization. We want them to learn to use this high technology without feeling that it conflicts with their behaviour
based on their religious views.'

Islamic fundamentalists believe that Islam is sufficiently
broad and universal to offer guidance to Muslims in all circumstances. According to Dr el-Arian, 'Islam provides a way of life
for people. It provides policies for life in all aspects, in education, in war and peace, in foreign affairs, in health matters,
in everything.' Dr el-Arian's voice became more strident when
he denounced what Muslims regard as the hypocritical way
in which the West tends to concentrate on the punishments
enshrined in Islamic law – like the cutting off of hands of those
guilty of theft. 'If you look at the history of Christianity in
Europe in the Middle Ages you find horrible things. So, it is
the same with us: we have a good practice of Islam and also a
bad practice by our former peoples. We are trying to clarify
that practice to achieve a good one. But I am surprised at

Western people. Why are they astonished that Islamic people want to apply Shari'a, the law given by Allah?'[5]

In Amman I met Hamzeh Mansour, a Muslim Brother who has been elected to parliament. He was a man of more than average height, worldly looking, dressed in a grey-striped suit, light-blue shirt and patterned tie. On his head he wore a red and white *keffiyeh*. He told me that the aim of the Brotherhood was to fight the backwardness and sense of inferiority in Arab society. 'Our objective is to make people see better what they can do. The main problem that faces many Arab societies is the lack of trust in themselves, and this lack of trust is the reason why many societies are backward. We are trying to build people's self-confidence.' Hamzeh Mansour said the longer-term aim of the Islamic movement was to bridge the gaps between societies in the region 'by building a national unity, an Arab unity, followed by Islamic unity. We believe that the only way the Arabs can ever unite is under the Islamic flag.'[6]

The most dramatic victory for the Islamic movement in the Middle East in the second half of this century came in early 1979 with the toppling of the Shah of Iran, one of the strongest allies of the West in the region. The event shocked Europe and the United States and contributed to the demonic image of Islam which already existed in many Western minds. The outrage increased when Iranian students ransacked the United States' embassy in Tehran in November 1979, taking fifty-three members of the staff hostage and holding them for two months. Television pictures of the streets of Tehran packed with demonstrators – the women wearing black veils – burning the American flag and chanting anti-Western slogans, like 'Death to the Great Satan', were alarming for viewers in the world at large. So, too, were reports of Revolutionary Guards hunting down Iranian officials who had been associated with the Shah. Despite disparaging remarks in the West suggesting that the leaders of the revolution were no more than rabble-rousers, it was successful, and Iran became an Islamic republic. Here was an example of what appeared to be a frightening new combination: fundamentalist Islam and political power. Even more disturbingly, the revolution to depose a secular, Western-orientated regime and replace it with a system rooted in religion, seemed to be driven by the irrational force of the mob.

The West was wrong to view developments in Iran as new – a measure of the ignorance in the West about the religion practised by hundreds of millions of people around the world, including around 200 million on Europe's doorstep in the Middle East. The marriage of Islam and politics was not new; the two had never successfully been divorced. The Prophet Muhammed was not simply the messenger of God for the community gathered around him in the Arabian peninsula in the seventh century, he was also its military and political leader. His successors continued this tradition through the centuries. Islam was inseparable from all aspects of life.

Christians played an important part in the development of the Arab nationalist movement around the turn of the century, but they could never detach nationalism from the political, social and cultural climate of the region which was and remains dominated by Islam. (The Maronites of Lebanon are an exception in this respect, feeling stronger emotional attachment to Christian Europe than to the Islamic Arab world.) Rami Khouri, a Palestinian Christian writer, says the bond between Arab Christianity and Islam remains strong. 'Our predominant characteristic as Christian Arabs is our Arab culture rather than our Christianity. Our political identity and our national aspirations are Arab.'[7] Ahmed Youssef Ahmed, a political scientist at Cairo University, agrees that Islamic traditions and culture have permeated the national aspirations of the Arabs throughout the twentieth century. 'Generally speaking, Islam is at the heart of Arabism. Of course, Arabism is not the same as Islam because we have Arab Christians who are really good believers in Arabism – like Michel Aflaq, one of the founders of the Ba'ath party. People like him had their own understanding of Islam as an important ingredient of Arabism. But there is a difference between Islam as the heart of this nation and Islam as the political agenda or programme of this nation. This is something new – something which relates to the 1920s when Hassan al-Banna founded the Muslim Brotherhood. Since then, around the Arab world we have been seeing groups of Muslims who feel they must rule by Islam, impose special structures, special rules and so on. And I think we are now living in the peak of this period.'[8]

Even though Islam was a vital ingredient of Arabism, the various newly independent states in the region tended to establish regimes that were more secular than religious in character, looking to the modernity of Europe rather than the Koran or the teachings of the Prophet for inspiration. Even in Algeria, where the independence movement was fought in the name of Islam, a socialist republic was established once the French rulers had left; there was no attempt made to set up an Islamic political party or to impose Islamic ideology. The Islamic movement became a strong force in Algerian politics in the early 1990s only 'after decades of failure by the ruling party'.[9]

Failure becomes the key word: the failure of the post-independence regimes to deliver, to meet the aspirations of the people; the failure to eliminate corruption; the failure to sink petty rivalries and jealousy in the name of Arab unity; the failure to distribute wealth fairly; the failure to stand up to the demands of the West; the failure to challenge Western policies in the region based on double standards; and the failure to confront Israel successfully. The uncompromising hostility of Islamic fundamentalists to the existence of the state of Israel has proved to be one of the strongest cards in its hand. 'Israel is implanted here,' Dr el-Arian said, 'it is a parasite, not an ordinary country.' He added with a chuckle, 'I think if Arab Islamic unity is achieved it will be a sort of horrible thing for the Israelis.'[10] Fundamentalists throughout the Middle East agree on the principle that there should be no dialogue with the Jewish state, and express confidence that Israel will be eliminated when Islamic regimes take hold of the region.

Arab governments, the majority of which are strongly opposed to the spread of Islamic fundamentalism, recognize that the Arab–Israeli conflict is a potentially explosive issue. They acknowledge that if the peace process, brokered by the United States and Russia in the early 1990s, were to fail (or become bogged down for many years), then support for fundamentalist groups would grow. The collapse of the diplomatic moves would give a boost to the confidence and popularity of the Muslim Brotherhood in Egypt, Jordan and Syria; Hamas and Islamic Jihad in Arab-populated areas of Israel and in the occupied territories; and Hizbollah in Lebanon. In a newspaper interview in November 1991, the Syrian ambassador to Egypt stressed the importance of the peace process being completed successfully because 'the alternative is extremism and the growth of the fanatical religious tendency in all Islamic countries ... Arab governments will not be able to counter the violent popular reaction if the process fails.'[11]

Fahmi Huweidi, an Egyptian analyst of Islamic affairs, links the despondency over the Arab–Israeli question and the general malaise in the Arab world to frustration at the failure of regimes to establish a clear identity or absolute independence for the states in the region. 'When we talked about getting our independence we were talking about military matters – expelling the foreigners and looking for economic independence. We expelled the British and the French, but we never achieved our cultural independence. Most of the regimes which came to power after the end of French and British rule represented another picture of occupation. We have not been living as independent people. President Bourguiba of Tunisia, for example, did more for French culture in his country than the French themselves. He increased the teaching of French in schools, and so on. Generally, the regimes failed to convince people that they were defending their independence. So Muslims started looking for their own identity'[12]

Despair and apathy set in among Arab people as they watched helplessly the accumulation of humiliations, failures and defeats. Public opinion in the Arab world has no effective means of expression; democracy is a scarce commodity. It has been argued by some Western commentators and by some Arab Christians that Europe and the United States should not expect to see flourishing democracies in the Middle East because democracy and Islam are incompatible. A Lebanese Christian lawyer told me that the issue focused 'on the concept of freedom of choice – a Western concept which is alien in an Islamic world where emphasis is put on the tightness of the community, with its strong, unchallenged leader. Christianity encourages choice, while Islam stresses duty.' The assumption in the West that Islamic states will be both tyrannical and undemocratic lies at the heart of fears about the spread of fundamentalism in the Middle East. But many Arabs who are advocating such states deny that Islam and democracy are incompatible. Salim al-Awa, an Egyptian lawyer who wants to see a peaceful change to a political system based on Islam in his country, said that the cause of the lack of democracy in the region rested with the Arab regimes. The Arab nation 'fought the British together for seventy years. We gained our independence, but the minute we did so, military governments took over and we were all subjected to another kind of internal colonialism. Now we are fighting together to gain our freedom once again and to govern our countries according to the rules of democracy. Forming an Islamic state means holding a popular referendum to accept a constitution written according to the will of the people, and electing freely a parliament where laws would be enacted. When you have free acceptance or rejection of what-ever ideas you are putting forward, everyone in the country will be safeguarded from tyranny on either side. We are offering a model for free choice.'[13] Awa added that the Western vision of Islam as in some way proscribing democracy came from popular perceptions of Saudi Arabia and Iran (even though parliamen-tary elections are held in the latter). Many Muslims insist, though, that the claims of Saudi and Iranian leaders to be ruling their countries strictly along religious lines are false, thus giving the world an incorrect picture of what a true Islamic state would be like.

There seems to be no obvious reason why an Islamic state should not, in principle, be democratic – provided that it did not seek to copy exactly Western systems. In practice, the Arab world is caught in a vicious circle. It is unrealistic to expect states in the region to become fully democratic until their people have had the experience of exercising freedom of choice at all levels of life. This will come about only when the tradition of unchallenged, often ruthless, leadership is destroyed. But this, in turn, is unlikely to happen until leaders have become accountable to the people under a democratic system.

The Arabs are weary of waiting for the day when a new system will come into being, giving them a voice and offering them hope for the future. In their millions, they have simply turned their backs on the discredited secular ideologies and sought solace in religion. Ghassan Abdallah, a Palestinian working at an Arab cultural foundation in Amman, described the return to religion as 'a symptom of the social crisis, of the defeat and impoverishment of the people, of the defeat of other ideologies like pan-Arabism, like communism – even liberalism in a sense. The way is open for these fundamentalists.'[14]

The Islamic movement, for its part, has seen the opportunity to fill the ideological vacuum in the Middle East. By the end of 1992, Islamic fundamentalists in Egypt had started to pose a serious challenge to the ruling establishment in Cairo by taking control of all the professional syndicates. Their success in ballots for the various posts was, perhaps, a reflection more of their energy and organization than of widespread popular support for their cause. They took practical steps, like finding lists of lawyers who had had their syndicate membership withdrawn because they could not pay their dues. In many cases, the Islamic movement paid what was owed in membership fees and organized transport to the polling stations. In an environment of numbing public apathy and despondency, their enthusiasm was striking; in a society where official wheels move at grindingly slow speeds, the Islamic movement showed the Egyptian public that religious activists could get things done.

A good example of the Islamic movement at work came in Cairo after the earthquake which struck the city in November 1992. Some of the worst damage was caused in the slum district of Sayeda Zeinab, packed with ancient buildings which were already flaking and crumbling. Within hours, teams from the doctors' syndicate, organized by the Muslim Brotherhood, had provided tents, food and other essentials for the homeless families. The first government action in the area, a few days later, was to remove most of the tents, and to transport the families – under protest – to unfinished apartment blocks far away in another district of Cairo. Eight days after the earthquake had struck, some families were still living in tents in corners of Sayeda Zeinab. They had received no help from the government, despite promises made by senior officials on radio and television, and the arrival of aid from abroad. In the poverty and squalor of districts like Sayeda Zeinab, where what seems like decades of rubbish has moulded itself in solid waves against the walls in muddy back alleys, the appeal of the Islamic movement is obvious.

At the same time as the Muslim Brotherhood were helping the victims of the earthquake and carrying on their daily pro-grammes of aid and assistance to the underprivileged people of Egypt, militant Islamic groups were continuing their armed campaign against the security forces, the property of prominent Coptic Christians, and foreign tourists. On the face of it, two wings of the Islamic movement were using different tactics, with the single aim of undermining the Egyptian regime and replacing it with an Islamic government.

The difficulty faced by Arabs outside the fundamentalist movement, as much as by foreigners, is to see exactly where the distinction lies between the Islamic activists and the armed militants. All share the common aim of wanting to set up an Islamic state throughout the Middle East. Tactics to achieve this goal have changed over the years. After the 1952 revolution in Egypt which ended the monarchy and eventually brought President Nasser to power the Muslim Brotherhood became alarmed at the regime's plans for land reform and other modernizing measures. These plans ran counter to the Brother-hood's desire to establish a state based on the Shari'a. In October 1954, 'Munim Abdul Rauf, a militant Brother, attempted to assassinate Nasser at a public rally in Alexandria. He failed. He and five other Brothers were executed, and more than four thousand Brotherhood activists jailed. Several thou-sand Brothers went into self-imposed exile in Syria, Saudi Arabia, Jordan and Lebanon.'[15] In 1975, President Sadat announced a general amnesty and allowed the Brotherhood to operate as a counter to Nasserist and left-wing opponents of his regime – although he stopped short of removing it from the list of illegal organizations. Sadat cultivated a public image as a pious and devout Muslim. Egyptian television showed film each week of the President attending Friday prayers. But the public were not convinced of his sincerity. 'The television showed him praying,' an Egyptian academic told me, 'but it also showed him acting like a Westerner, kissing Rosalyn Carter at the bottom of the steps of the plane, when the US President visited Cairo. Devout Muslims do not kiss women in public like that.' By the end of the 1970s the Islamic movement was disillusioned with the policies of the regime and was openly expressing dissent. Sadat had pushed Egypt in a direction which conflicted sharply with the interests of the Islamic groups: he had established close economic and political ties with the West and, more seriously from the Muslim fundamentalists' point of view, had made peace with Israel. In October 1981, four soldiers (members of Al-Jihad, a militant wing of the fundamentalist movement) assassinated President Sadat.

Al-Jihad, Al-Gemaa al-Islamiya and other militant groups are offshoots of the Muslim Brotherhood. At his flat in Cairo I asked Karim Alrawi what he thought about the distinction between the various factions in the Islamic movement. Like many Arabs he is sceptical about the claim made by Dr el-Arian and other prominent Muslim Brothers that they have no connection with the armed groups. Alrawi believes that when Muslim Brotherhood leaders in Egypt were rounded up by President Nasser's security forces 'the prison experience caused factions within the organization to split, and to form the other more militant groups which now espouse a military option to achieve power. The Muslim Brotherhood claims there is a difference between them and these other groups, but I think that the difference is cosmetic – as much as anything because the Brotherhood have shown in the past that they are not afraid of using violence to achieve their aims. I think all that has happened is that they are a little wiser than they were before and they tend to be better at manipulating the other groups to do their dirty work for them.'

Alrawi was full of gloom when he talked about the ability of Arab regimes to counter the success of the Islamic movement. In his view the Egyptian government, for one, was 'faced with a serious problem in that it does not have an ideology and Muslim groups do have an ideology which is appealing to many people because it draws on the vocabulary that many people understand. It makes them think that by using it they can understand what is happening in the world – why they are poorer, why they are weaker, why things seem to be going wrong. By using the vocabulary they can blame, say, the West as being the new Crusaders and they can feel vindicated, they can feel that they are good people. They are Muslims and, in the end, God will make them triumphant.'[16]

The simplicity of the message preached by the fundamentalists wins most support today, as it did in the 1920s and 1930s, from the underprivileged and the idealistic young. As Albert Hourani pointed out, the later decades of this century have seen a large migration of Arabs from the countryside to the city. 'Cut off from the ties of kinship and neighbourliness which made life possible in the villages,' he wrote, 'they were living in a society in which the external signs were strange to them; the sense of alienation could be counterbalanced by that of belonging to a universal community of Islam, in which certain moral values were implicit, and this provided a language in terms of which they could express their grievances and aspirations.'[17]

The most convincing explanation that I have heard of the way these groups in society are drawn into supporting the Islamic movement came, ironically, from a prominent Egyptian Copt, Milad Hanna. He talked specifically about the case of Egypt 'which is not healthy economically – the low income groups are suffering to their teeth from inflation. A family earns 200-to-300 Egyptian pounds a month – that is less than 100 US dollars. How can they live? It is very difficult. Cairo is highly populated, it is very difficult to catch a bus or to buy things. It is very difficult to find a good flat at a reasonable rent. People are very over-crowded, and unemployment is very high. The youth is lost.'

Graduates may wait five or six years for employment – if they are lucky – and will then earn US$50 a month. Because young people do not have money they have to put off getting married, so 'there is a sexual frustration – morally here we are not allowed to have boy/girl friends. People can only have sex in marriage. Girls are tending to get married as late as twenty-seven or twenty-eight, young men at thirty-five or thirty-six – when they have enough money for a flat. The gap between rich and poor is widening. Imagine I was a young person of twenty-five, and someone came along and said: Why don't you go the mosque? And I go and I listen. Do you want to get married? Yes, please, I would love to get married. All right, I will speak to the emir – the ruling person in the countryside and villages. And the emir will say: Yes, we will get you married, we will ask a girl to marry you. We will get you a room with a carpet and something to sleep on. And some pocket money. Now you can join our group. How could I refuse?'[18]

Jamil Matar, a political scientist, was another Egyptian who told me how he felt that the disillusioned young people in the Arab world had become an easy target for fundamentalist groups. 'Young graduates without jobs do not know what to do. There is no unifying idea among the young men – no secular idea. There is no one saying: Let's build Egypt, for example. Patriotism. Let's go back to patriotism. But it is not there any more. Nationalism, of course, is not there any more. It is not one of the ideologies of the regime. So what do you have? You have young people believing in nothing. So when the Muslims come to them, it is easy.'[19]

While Islamic activists are recruiting, another less vocal trend within the Islamic movement is also working for change in society. Like the activists, this group wants to see a greater Islamic influence on the public and private lives of people in Arab countries. But it wants the changes to be both peaceful and democratic, and to be based on new Islamic legislation suited to the needs of the contemporary world. Proponents of this liberal interpretation of Islam find themselves increasingly attacked by fundamentalists. The attacks can be both verbal and physical. As mentioned in Chapter 5, an Egyptian author, Farag Foda, was murdered in June 1992 for criticizing the aims and methods of the fundamentalists. Another prominent and vocal critic, Saeed Ashmawi, is still alive – but lives under twenty-four-hour police guard since having received threats against his life. Ashmawi is a senior judge and the author of several scholarly books on Islam and Islamic law. His friends say that he has particularly angered the fundamentalists by challenging them from within – as a devout and respected Muslim, arguing on theological grounds. A plain-clothes body-guard accompanied me in the lift up to his apartment. Inside, the rooms were dark – the shutters closed against the outside world and its threats. A Beethoven sonata was playing on the radio. Judge Ashmawi, a small, stooped man, sat in the arm-chair in the corner of his living room which has become his protective cage for most hours of the day and night. Because of the need to have a police guard with him wherever he goes, Ashmawi has lost all enthusiasm for going out. 'I have no private life any more,' he said. 'I am dedicating my life to my work.' On a table in front of his armchair stood an illuminated globe and a portable television. As he talked, his left hand rested on a telephone to the side of him – his life-line. Judge Ashmawi, speaking slowly and thoughtfully, accused the fun-damentalists of 'using religion to get power. They are bluffing the people. They have no programme. They have no new juris-prudence. There is an atmosphere of terrorism in Egypt; they are terrorising all the Egyptians. Especially after the assassina-tion of Farag Foda. They are appointing themselves as the only Muslims. And they're telling me – a good Muslim – that I am not a Muslim because I am not joining them. Liberals like myself – we are for renewing Islam; we are offering new juris-prudence. We are entirely against any totalitarian regime.'

Judge Ashmawi is determined both to continue his Islamic scholarship and to go on speaking his mind. He knows that he has chosen a dangerous course. 'If there is an Islamic state in Egypt,' he said, 'people like me will either be assassinated half an hour or an hour after they seize power, or will be put on trial to be executed, murdered through a trial, as enemies of Islam.'[20]

The challenge thrown down by the Islamic movement is being felt by regimes throughout the Arab world. Ahmed Yous-sef Ahmed sees the region as having entered 'a new era of development, one witnessing a new pattern of conflict between the ruling elites which came to power in the mid-1950s and early 1960s, and the new political forces. One of the most important new political forces is, of course, the Islamic one.'

The new political force, in all its various forms, constitutes a challenge to the status quo in the palaces of the Arab world. It is ironic that the threat to the regimes, to a large extent, is of their own making. During the 1970s, Arab governments not only allowed the Islamic movement to develop, but they also nurtured it as a counter to nationalist, leftist and other opposition groups. The Israeli authorities adopted a similar policy in the occupied Gaza Strip in an attempt to weaken support for the Palestine Liberation Organization. Two decades later, these governments are paying a high price for their earlier policies. Coping with the challenge of Islam has become a high priority for Arab regimes (and the Israeli authorities) in the closing decade of the century.

Arab leaders have responded to the threat to their survival in different ways. The Syrian authorities eliminated the danger from the Sunni Muslim fundamentalists, who were conducting a terror and assassination campaign in protest at the secularization of public life, by operating an iron-fist policy in the early 1980s. By contrast, King Hussein of Jordan successfully defused a possible confrontation by allowing the Muslim Brotherhood to stand in parliamentary elections in November 1989. In the same year, the government in Sudan was unable to stop the fundamentalists coming to power on the back of a military coup. In Algeria, the spectacular success of the Islamic Salvation Front in the first round of the general elections in December 1991 prompted the authorities to cancel the second round and to declare war on the fundamentalists. But most countries, including Egypt, continued to waver, cracking down at one moment while at another trying to eliminate the possible threat to the regime by making increasingly large concessions to Islamic militants. Evidence of this could be seen in Egypt in the opening years of the 1990s where it was noticeable that Islamic fundamentalist preachers and scholars were being given an increasing amount of access to the state-controlled television and radio. It was equally obvious that liberal Islamicists, like Saeed Ashmawi, were being denied access to the airwaves. At the same time, the Muslim Brotherhood remained officially a proscribed organization, which meant that while it had been allowed to carry on most activities since its leaders were released from prison by President Sadat, it still could not contest parliamentary elections. Up to the early 1990s, more than forty court appeals from the Brotherhood to be granted official legality had been turned down. Fahmi Huweidi called the Egyptian authorities' attitude shortsighted. 'Here we have a group of Islamic activists who are known as moderate and want to participate in the democratic game. Yet the activists as a whole are accused by the establishment of being extremist fundamentalist terrorists. Young people are saying: You are talking about democracy; so where is it? If you won't let us have it we will work through illegal channels. In other words, those youths are being pushed by government policy to work in underground organizations. It is a dangerous course. But if you close the front door, people will just come in the window or the back door.'[21]

Milad Hanna believed the Egyptian government was 'selling fundamentalism in the hope that if they can do this the fundamentalists won't overthrow them. But they don't need to overthrow the government, because they can Islamicize the institutions – the police, the army, the ruling party.'[22]

The political success of Islamic movements, as shown earlier, is very often a by-product of the social services provided to the community. These services are organized by the Muslim Brotherhood and Islamic welfare societies which in turn are financed, for the most part, by donations from wealthy individuals and institutions in the Gulf and elsewhere. Some of the people involved are former members of the Muslim Brotherhood who took refuge in Saudi Arabia in the 1950s and have become successful businessmen. The Saudi government and individuals from the business community have provided financial backing for the Islamic movement in Algeria and in other Arab countries. Iran gives money and support both to Hizbollah and Hamas, as well as to the fundamentalist government in Sudan.

One of the major problems facing the ruling elites in the Middle East in the last quarter of the twentieth century, as they try to keep tabs on the Islamic movement, is that they have failed either to produce a clear ideology to suit the needs of the area and its people or to find a charismatic leader with regional appeal. No single ruler or regime has provided a model of leadership that has either won respect from the people of the region as a whole or has given Arabs the prominent position that they feel they deserve on the international stage. The crisis facing the Arabs is that they are approaching the twenty-first century without unity and without any clear sense of direction. In the months after the abandoned elections of 1992, Algeria provided a clear illustration of this sense of uncertainty. Having ditched the democratic process mid-way, the authorities in Algiers could offer nothing concrete and positive to steer the country forward. 'What the ruling elite must introduce is something new,' Dr Ahmed Youssef Ahmed said, nine months after the fiasco in Algeria. 'They should be introducing economic development, social justice and a formula for democracy. But I do not think the ruling elite in Algeria or in other parts of the Arab world are able to do so. This is the seriousness of the problem.' Karim Alrawi, looking specifically at Egypt, considered the government 'to be quite impotent, quite incapable of facing up to the real challenge that the Islamic movement has presented. Partly this is because of corruption in the regime. I think there are individuals within the regime whose self-interest is such that they don't want the regime to be strong or to put its house in order, because that would mean stamping out corruption and they would be the losers.'

The question heard often in Arab countries is whether, if Islamic states were established around the region, the new leaders would be any more successful than the old ones in stamping out corruption and in dealing with the economic difficulties and other problems of the modern world. Liberal Arab academics say that when people in the region look at the record of Islamic regimes in existence, they find little from which to take encouragement. In both Sudan and Iran, for example, corruption is as rampant as ever; and neither country has succeeded in raising the standard of living of the poor. Whether the regime is secular or religious, the region still lacks institutions of sufficient stature and integrity to monitor and control those in power.

Liberal Arabs accuse leaders of the Islamic movement of

being deliberately vague about how they would deal with specific problems facing a country. In Algeria in 1991–2, one of the Islamic Salvation Front leaders, Abdel-Qader Hachani, was asked what the Front would do to tackle the problems of housing and unemployment, and the US$26 billion national debt. Hachani replied that 'if there were mutual trust between the leadership and the people, then the government could resolve the crisis, however overwhelming, in a short while'.[23] Mustafa Hamarneh says the fundamentalists fail to the see the importance of 'issues of efficiency and modernity. They concentrate on how pious the institution is. Once you have that objective in mind you do not care about the efficiency of the bureaucracy, or the production of this or that sector. Or the redistribution of wealth according to ideological criteria. For them it is piety that counts.'[24]

Observations about the imprecise nature of fundamentalist policies have been made over many decades. Albert Hourani, writing in the 1960s about the policies advocated by Hassan al-Banna and the first members of the Muslim Brotherhood noted that the Islamicists 'condemned innovations in doctrine and worship, and accepted the rights of reason and public welfare in matters of social morality, but insisted that they should work within the limits imposed by the moral principles of Islam'. Hourani then added the comment that 'it may be doubted whether they made clear how these principles should be applied in modern society.' Also he observed that 'ideas about the regulation of economic life were not so precise' as those relating to social and legal matters.[25]

Some liberal and secular Arabs – not to mention people outside the Middle East – have also questioned the extent to which a religion which was born in the Arabian peninsula can provide the framework and principles for states living in the modern world. But both Islamic activists and many practising Muslims in the Arab world outside the fundamentalist movement reject accusations that Islamic principles are anachronistic in modern society. Ahmed Youssef Ahmed does not think 'that Islam needs any modifications to be applied in the twentieth century. Our problem is that people try to pick up on very minor things that happened in the Arabian peninsula at the time of the Prophet Muhammed and try to say to us that this is Islam. They say Muhammed did not eat at a table, he ate on the ground – so this should be the practice of Islam. Or that you should not drive a car. Lots of things. They try to convince people that this is Islam. But if you read the Koran very well and you study the experience of Muhammed very well you will find that Islam is a democratic model of government. The political regimes in Saudi Arabia and the Gulf are not Islamic ones when judged against the standards of Muhammed and his successors.'[26]

The Islamic movement is, without doubt, concerned at this stage more with broad matters of ideology than with detailed day-to-day policy matters of the kind which occupy the attention of those holding the reins of power. One of the key planks in this ideology is opposition to the West and Western influence in the Middle East. Islamic fundamentalism, with its blend of religious and political motives, has been able to exploit a widespread popular antagonism among ordinary Arabs (outside the Gulf) towards Western political policies in the region. This, as earlier chapters have shown, has never been far below the surface this century, and has frequently broken it. The close relationship between Western governments and some of the most corrupt regimes in the Middle East has served well the fundamentalists' cause. Fundamentalism, as Professor Hamarneh observed, 'is the only organized force as such that can lead the masses to take an anti-Western stance in the way that Nasser and Arab nationalism used to in the past. The rest are all discredited.'

Islamic activists have been helped in their attempts to vilify the West and its supporters in the Arab world by the public expressions in Europe and the United States of attitudes towards Islam. From the days of the Crusades until the present, most Westerners have been unable to expunge a tinge of unease at the image thrown up by mention of the word 'Islam' – a suspicion of something unknown but sinister and feared, a vision, perhaps, of bloodthirsty barbarians preparing to ravage and destroy the refinements of the civilized West. This myth has been fostered in popular novels and films in the closing decades of the century, spawning almost a sub-genre of movies depicting power-crazy and violent Muslim and Arab leaders involved in confrontations with the West. Few attempts are made in films, books, or in any other area of Western public life, to show Islam as a caring and compassionate religion, springing from the same roots as Judaism and Christianity. Much more is spoken about the harsh punishments meted out to adulterers and thieves in Saudi Arabia, where the puritanical Wahhabi doctrine of Islamic legislation is applied.

Arabs see evidence of these attitudes when they visit the West and – as is becoming increasingly common – when they watch American and European films and television programmes beamed by satellite to the Middle East. They read, too, about the rise of racism directed against Arabs and other Muslims in France, Germany and elsewhere. Fahmi Huweidi, when I visited him at his office in Cairo, had a newspaper cutting on his desk quoting a French member of parliament denouncing the establishment in France of a college to teach Islam. 'Are you ready to renew the Crusade experience in the twentieth century?' the French deputy inquired of those involved in the project. 'When we read things like that,' Huweidi said, and see that civilized people think in this way, what do you imagine will be the reaction of the readers? People here say: These are civilized people in Europe and we respect them. But why do they behave against Muslims in a barbaric way?'

Some commentators in the West denounce openly the presence of Muslims in Europe and elsewhere as a threat to security – frequently expressing themselves in strong and emotive language. A writer in the *Wall Street Journal* in January 1992 spoke of the danger of resentment among Arab immigrants in countries like France and Belgium growing to the extent that they 'could create bands of Islamic militants in the heart of Europe'[27].

When I asked the Egyptian commentator Mahjoub Omar for his impression of the Western view of Islam he replied: 'If we are talking about the masses, the West does not know Islam. If we are talking about the elite, some know what it is, but they are deliberately and intentionally distorting it.' At this point he broke off, walked across his office and took down from the bookshelves the autumn 1991 edition of the journal *Foreign Policy*. He quoted from an article entitled 'The World Disorder', which said that 'if the remaining republics fall to infighting in a Balkanized Soviet Union, the twenty-first century could once again find Islam at the gates of Vienna, as immigrants or terrorists, if not as armies. Indeed, massive Islamic immigration into France may already have reversed Charles Martel's victory [against the Arab armies which had conquered north Africa and Spain] at the battle of Tours.'[28]

In the opinion of Karim Alrawi, the West does not wish to promote Islam as a tolerant and liberal religion. 'I find that whenever I am talking about Islam, either in Britain or the United States, I am under attack from two sides: first from the more militant Muslims – and I generally find I can out-argue them quite effectively because the religious evidence, if you like, is against them. But secondly I also get attacked by Europeans and Americans simply for saying I am a Muslim, because they have bought into the idea of what a fundamentalist is like – basically an intolerant bigot, someone who hates women and will not tolerate people from other religions, and basically would like to have everyone put to the sword if they could. That is the view promoted repeatedly by the media. It does seem to me that the West sees that it is in its interest to have another threat, now that communism has ended.'

The popular Western view of Islam is certainly one of a religion preaching intolerance and bigotry – as well as the suppression of women. The image of a faceless female, shrouded in black and kept behind locked doors by a cruel husband has become a cliché. The fact is that only a small percentage of Arab women live in this way – mostly in the Gulf states – although male attitudes towards females in the Middle East are generally more chauvinistic than in the West.

Islam, more than anything else in the Arab world, arouses emotions of suspicion and fear in Western minds. Emotive talk in both the Middle East and the West feeds on itself. 'I am now fully convinced,' Muhammad Aziz Shukri of Damascus

University told me, 'that we Arabs – regardless of religion – are subject to a new Crusade by the West. We are seen as a danger to the Judaic–Christian Westernized civilization.'

Professor Shukri's perception of Arabs 'regardless of religion' being subject to a Crusade is, in part, a reference to the fact that Arab Christians are steeped in the culture and traditions of Islam. In part also, he was referring to the common assumption in the West – which he noticed while living in the United States – that all Arabs are Muslims.

There are some blurred perceptions, too, when the West is viewed from the Arab world, the most common being that Europe and the United States are Christian in the sense that Arab countries may be regarded as Islamic. People in the West generally respect what are loosely called Christian values, but the separation of religion from daily life is clearer than in Islam; there is no identity with Christianity as a unifying political movement.

One group which has suffered as a result of failing to understand the status of religion in the West is the Maronite Christian community in Lebanon. As the Maronites have watched their military and political power shrink they have been dismayed to see the 'Christian' West observe their plight with indifference. Adnan Fawaz, Professor of Political Science at Beirut University College, told me that 'on the whole, the ordinary Christians think that the West has forsaken them, that it has not done enough, that the West is only moved by its own selfish economic criteria and considerations, and that it could have prevented the situation developing in the way it has. Of course, there are some sophisticated Christians who realize that in the West the ideological context is not religion. But here they still go by religious criteria; so, in general, people think that the West has been delinquent.'[29]

The Maronites of Lebanon are the only Arab Christians to have enjoyed a position of political and military power in the Middle East, and are the only group to have sought Western protection. In general, the Christian community, while feeling hurt by the way that Christianity in the West has turned its back on them, are anxious not to be identified with Western political ambitions in the Middle East. These anxieties are connected to their delicate status as Arabs, identifying with the cultural background and supporting the political aims of the region. Also, they can never forget that the first bruising encounter between the West and the Middle East, the Crusades, is an experience which is rooted in Arab memories. 'Arab Muslims,' Gabriel Habib, the General Secretary of the Middle East Council of Churches told me at the end of 1992, as news reports spoke of the persecution of Muslims in Bosnia, 'still have in their minds the old image of the Crusades. What is happening in ex-Yugoslavia is confirming the view of many Muslims in the Middle East that Christianity – together with the West – is trying to eliminate Islam from that part of the world.'[30] Rami Khouri spoke of 'Arab Christians suffering from the fact that in recent and current Western political forces – imperialism, colonialism – as well as in the Crusades of ancient times there is an identification in the minds of some Muslims between Arab Christians and the West. The Christian attitudes coming out of the West tend, in many cases, unfortunately, to parallel the predatory, presumptuous political attitudes of Western powers. There is almost an imperial edge to Western Christianity when it views itself as the source of all morality and right, and wants to go and preach to the rest of the world.'[31]

Difficulties caused by the uneasy relationships between Arab Christians and the West and Arab Christians and Muslims have been compounded by anxieties about the effects of Islamic fundamentalism. When Islam spread through the region in the seventh and eighth centuries, Christians and Jews were accepted as *Ahl el-Kitab* – literally, People of the Book, followers of the two other monotheistic religions in the region. They were accorded the status of *dhimmis*, which meant that they were free to practise their religion, but in return were required to pay higher taxes than Muslims and were denied equality before the law. Because of their second-class position in society, Christians could never play prominent leadership roles. Only after the late nineteenth century did Arab Christians find an important political role for themselves, in developing the nationalist movement and in establishing the secular-oriented states which sprung up after independence in the 1940s and 1950s. From the 1970s onwards, with the collapse of the secular pan-Arab dream and the gradual re-emergence of Islam as a potent and popular political ideology, Christians have become increasingly concerned – not just about their role in society, but also about whether or not they would be tolerated in a region where Islamic fundamentalism was dominant. The attacks on Copts in Egypt have caused Christians to start asking questions about their future. The sale in Cairo of clandestinely copied cassette recordings of fundamentalist preachers denouncing Christians and Jews have increased the anxieties of the Copts. Such developments are making the Copts sceptical about assurances given by the Muslim Brotherhood that they would have nothing to fear if an Islamic state were established in Egypt. 'A lot of people are not very sure,' Leila Tekkla, a member of parliament from the Coptic community said, 'that, if and when the fundamentalists come to power, they will be as good Muslims as they think they are. Under the umbrella of Islam there should not be any difference between Muslims or Copts or Catholics or Shiia or anyone, but I do not know if they are going to implement the spirit of Islam and the principles of Islam as politics, as a political theory.'[32] Similar questions are being asked by Christians throughout the Middle East. In Bethlehem, in the Israeli-occupied West Bank, Christians have watched the power of Hamas grow steadily. Dr Bernard Sabella, a sociologist at Bethlehem University, said Arab Christians wanted to say to the fundamentalists that 'if you are calling for an Islamic state, then I would like to know how I can participate. Where do I stand? Do I fit into the national community or not? I would like, in such a state, to have all the rights belonging to a Christian community. I would like to say my prayers, I would like my bells to ring and I would like my lifestyle to continue. If an Islamic state requires me to change my lifestyle, then there is a problem.'[33]

The Christians of Lebanon are equally unsure about their future, despite public assurances from fundamentalist leaders. The source of their fear is sometimes not hard to see. As I was observing Friday prayers in a Hizbollah mosque in the southern suburbs of Beirut in 1993 a young man urged me to take several copies of a book from a pile that he was carrying and give them to my friends. The books, printed in both English and Arabic, were entitled, *Crucifixion or Crucifiction* – a crude attempt to descredit the basis of Christianity.

The violence perpetrated by militant fundamentalist groups in pursuit of their aim of establishing Islamic states in the Middle East will undoubtedly continue to claim the headlines in the West. But it would be both wrong and dangerous for Europe and the United States to continue to dismiss the Islamic movement in the Arab world as a passing phenomenon attracting a relatively small number of fanatics. The revival of interest in religion is not confined to the poor and underprivileged, who make up more than 50 per cent of their countries anyway. In the winter of 1992, when the Syrian capital was paralysed by a rare snowstorm, mosques were packed as usual by worshippers attending Friday prayers, even in wealthy middle-class neighbourhoods. The religious movement in the Arab world is in large part an expression of popular despair, not least at the West and at the Arab regimes which have either tried to adopt Western ways or have acted as the agents of foreign interests.

The various strands of misunderstanding and distrust have bound themselves into a cord which, it is commonly felt in the Middle East, has tied the hands of ordinary people, while leaving the regimes to act as they please. The net effect, as we have seen, is that the overwhelming majority of Arabs at the end of the twentieth century are more resentful than ever at their inability to control their own destinies. Arabs want to find a way of recovering their self-esteem. Muhammed Sid Ahmed sees no immediate alternative to the growth in influence of the Islamic movement. 'I think that Islamic fundamentalism will be there as long as there is no assurance that politics delivers. It should deliver the feeling that you are master of your fate, that you are not being manipulated.'

CHAPTER TEN

Perceptions of Peace

Approaching the coast by boat it looks at first like an island – a giant molar of limestone and shale dumped into the sea off the southern edge of Spain. For the Arabs this rock, its base attached by a slender thread to the mainland and its peaks often capped by cloud, represented both a powerful monument of victory and a signpost pointing to the new territories of Islamic conquest. The Arabs referred to it as a mountain – jebel – and named it after the commander of the Arab and Berber army that conquered Spain for the Muslims in 711, Tariq ibn Ziyad. It was known as Jebel Tariq, two words that were later shaped by European diction into Gibraltar.

Jebel Tariq was then, as much as Gibraltar is today, an outpost of great strategic value for controlling the narrow strait between the European and African continents. It remained in the hands of the Arabs for more than seven centuries. During this period another giant rock with a steep escarpment found its way into in Arab history. This long low hill with peaks at either end is known as Qarne Hittin – the Horns of Hittin – and is located at the eastern extremity of the Mediterranean, in Galilee, dominating the western approaches to Lake Tiberias. This was the site of a spectacular and decisive victory of the Muslims, led by Salah el-Din, over the Crusaders in 1187. The Crusader footsoldiers, who had been without water for more than a day in fierce July heat, were trapped by the advancing army on the north peak. Many were killed in battle; others fell to their deaths on the hard and barren ground below.

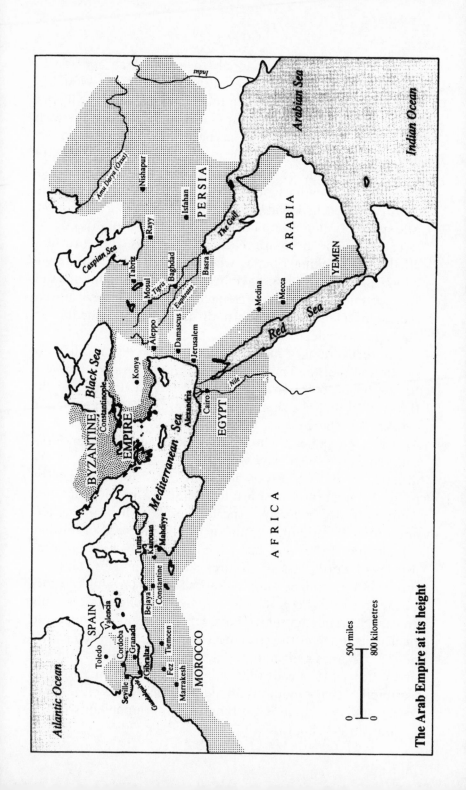

The Arab Empire at its height

Both these natural memorials to heroic Arab and Islamic exploits have, in different ways, been snared by the West. The Arabs were driven out of Spain finally in 1492, and the Iberian peninsula has been part of Europe since then. Since the early eighteenth century Gibraltar has been a colony of Britain – its name having lost in common usage its association with the Arab conquest and occupation and taken on instead a resonance of British military power. The colony, as the twenty-first century approached, had become little more than an anachronistic speck of colonial stubbornness on the map of Europe.

The Horns of Hittin are reached these days from a turning off the road linking Tiberias with Nazareth, two Arab towns which, since May 1948, have been part of the state of Israel. To Arab minds, as previous chapters showed, the Jewish state represents a latter-day Western intrusion into the Middle East – a new Crusade.

The rocks, then, symbolize ultimate Arab defeat. They are symbols also of the barriers between the Arabs and the West. Nazareth and other Arab towns in Israel in the area of the Horns of Hittin are a short drive away from Jewish population centres. Yet the contrast between them is marked: the Arab towns have retained their distinctive look and character. From Gibraltar, on a clear day, you can pick out buildings in the distance, eight miles away, across the strait in Morocco. The port of Tangiers is a short ferry-hop away. But the two continents are, in many respects, worlds apart. The genteel and ordered world of Gibraltar is firmly anchored in Europe, for all that the colony has added to its British roots some aspects of North African cultures and mannerisms. Tangiers, on the other hand, belongs to that sad and depressing category of Arab city, where modern high-rise buildings, cheaply constructed and charmless, have fallen victim to poverty and neglect as much as the structures of colonial and even earlier periods. There is a mood of resignation in Tangiers, as in many other Arab cities outside the Gulf, summed up in an unspoken assumption that conditions are going to get worse rather than better and that there is nothing that the inhabitants of the region can do about it.

By contrast, in the centuries after the conquest of Spain the Arabs felt firmly in control of their destiny. Today they are both tormented and inspired by the memory of this golden age of triumph and self-confidence – when decisive military superiority over their enemies provided the stability and security for the blossoming of sciences and other scholarship. The path of new ideas into Europe passed through Jebel Tariq and Spain. Southern Spain is littered with magnificent remnants of the Arab empire; and the influence of the culture and manners of the races inhabiting the southern shores of the Mediterranean is unmistakable. The West at large is still reluctant to acknowledge the importance of the Islamic era in Spanish history for the development of arts and sciences in Europe. Neither the experience of visitors to the Islamic sites at Grenada, Cordoba and elsewhere, nor all the books written about the subject, have managed to impress upon the common mind in the West the significance of this period of history. To learn about its importance one needs to look no further than commonly available guide books. 'The Moors were more civilized than their Christian contemporaries,' one guide says, adding that the conquerors from the south 'encouraged the efflorescence of the arts and sciences. Through Andalusia, many of their influences were passed on to the more backward Christian nations of the north. Into Spain they imported a cornucopia of new crops – oranges, lemons, rice, sugar, date-palms, figs, cotton and durum wheat – and a wealth of new skills.' The guide book also, correctly, says the Islamic invaders instructed the Europeans in 'mathematics and philosophy, and transmitted the learning of the Greeks.'[1] Why, if the vital link between the Arabs and Europe is spelled out so succinctly, has the message failed to take root in the West? If Europe and the United States understood better their historical debt to the Arabs, the current image of the people of the Middle East in the minds of the West would surely improve.

The problem, I believe, is one of attitudes. The wall of anti-Arab prejudice and bigotry is as solid as ever. In a climate where the Arab is depicted in mass culture in the West in racist or other derogatory terms, convincing people that their

culture is indebted to the Middle East is difficult. It is interesting in this context how the travel guide quoted earlier and
others still prefer to call the conquerors of Spain the Moors –
rather than the Arabs and Berbers. In Western minds, the
archaic word Moor has a romantic connotation which,
perhaps, is associated more comfortably than 'Arab' with the
beautiful architecture of Grenada and Cordoba, and the
outstanding scholastic and scientific achievements of that era.
Such is the contempt for Arab achievements in the minds of
the public at large in the West that they could scarcely be
credited with having produced such masterpieces or having
achieved such high levels of scholarship. Conversely, the
reluctance of the West to acknowledge the importance of the
golden era of Islamic scholarship contributes to the resentment
felt by the Arabs towards Europe and the United States. Arabs
feel the West has no justification in looking at them with
haughtiness and condescension.

Cultural alienation of the West from the Arabs is only part
of the picture. Much more important in shaping the uneasy
relationship between the two parts of the world has been the
tussle for military, political and economic control of the Middle
East. The West-East struggle began with the battles against
the Muslim conquerors of Spain and with the launching of
the Crusades. These were events which set the pattern of
relations in the subsequent centuries. In 732, shortly after
the conquest of Spain, the Arab armies reached Poitiers before
being defeated. This marked the end of their advance into
northern Europe. As one Western writer has pointed out,
while the defeat at Poitiers was 'little noticed in the Muslim
world itself, the battle assumed monumental proportions in
Christian European, especially French, history. It was seen as
the heroic brake applied to the expansion of an alien world
by the West, as a minor skirmish by the Arabs. From the very
beginning there is thus established a difference in the perception and appreciation of the same events by Muslim and
Christian sources.'[2]

History has been a double-edged sword in the hands of
the Arabs and the West ever since then. Differences in

interpretation of events and actions have, at times, coloured attitudes and exacerbated relations between the two. Among examples in the twentieth century was the controversy over the significance of the Arab revolt in the defeat of the Ottoman army. Aside from events that are still open to differing interpretations, there are plenty of instances which give Arabs sound reason to feel aggrieved by Western attitudes and prejudices. The question is whether the Arabs are justified in clinging to recent history to explain their failures in the past one hundred years, as much as they cling to stories of the golden era of centuries past, as a way of escaping from the difficulties of life today. In the twentieth century the Arab world was forced to establish a relationship with the West – the dominant military and colonial power and the source of technology and skills which the Middle East needed for modernization and development. The Arabs found the West eager to sell and provide what they wanted. Despite what were regarded as the dismissive and condescending tone of Western attitudes towards them, the Arabs had (and continue to have) no choice but to deal with the developed powers on terms dictated by London, Washington and other foreign capitals. The West calls the tune; the Arabs dance, and hate themselves for doing it.

The tendency of the Arabs in the twentieth century has been to pile blame exclusively upon the West, and particularly on Britain, France and the other colonial powers, for the woes which afflict the region, and for their inability to control their own destiny. But cursing Sykes, Picot, Balfour, Eden, Bush and Clinton has not helped the Arabs to overcome their difficulties. Rather it has added to the heap of grievances which in turn has contributed to inferiority and defeatism which characterize the Arabs' attitude to the West. The Arabs cannot hope to rediscover collective purpose and vision to enable them to deal squarely with the West in the twenty-first century as long as their grudges against Sykes and the rest constrict their mental outlook. Blindly blaming the West, as President Nasser did in 1967 after the Arabs' humiliating defeat by Israel and as Arabs have done on numerous occasions before and since, is not a substitute for honest analysis of the reasons for failure. A sulky and moody refusal to accept responsibility and to shoulder blame does not constitute a sound formula to take the Arabs forward into the next century. Some Arab intellectuals have had the courage to address this failing. 'What one misses in current Arab and Palestinian culture,' wrote Edward Said, a Palestinian professor at Columbia University in the United States, 'is a moral and intellectual standard by which truth and falsehood can be distinguished, and according to which intellectuals act regardless of profit or patronage. Perhaps the Islamic resurgence with which I am not in sympathy speaks to that lack.'[3]

The search for a formula for the future involves issues which have troubled the Arabs throughout the century, and have contributed to present collective weakness. The debate on political theory continues, centring on the extent to which Islam should form the foundation of public as well as private life. Arguments over whether Islam should be reformed and adapted to take account of modern circumstances, or whether it should be removed from the public sphere in favour of secular systems of politics and law can still be heard. The division of the Middle East by the colonial powers into nation states complicated the picture. The existence of separate nations broke the cohesion, the sense of 'umma' – community – that had existed under the Caliphate. The new states, influenced or manipulated by Western powers, created secular ruling structures. With the creation of national flags and national anthems, the new national borders were sanctified, defeating the aspirations of pan-Arabists, both secular and religious.

As the new states became established, so ruling elites emerged with vested interests in maintaining the status quo. The rulers were invariably autocratic and presided over corrupt and inefficient machines of state. The elites made deals with the outside world (and in particular with Western nations) to ensure their survival in power and to promote their efforts to expand influence within the region. The process of fragmentation in the Arab world has not stopped, and all efforts to stitch together even the semblance of unity have faltered and ultimately failed. Against this background the Arab people feel isolated and impotent, manipulated and deceived both by their own leaders and by outside powers.

Concurrent with the establishment of the new nation state pattern in the Middle East, with its scattered centres of power, came a gradual erosion of the credibility of secular ideology as either the slogan or blue-print for the Middle East of the future. The failures of the newly independent regimes to match the aspirations of their people – the most notable example being the Arabs' collective military humiliation in the 1967 war with Israel – highlighted an important failing in the system imposed on the region by the West and perpetuated by the Arabs themselves. The failing related to the role of religion. While the newly independent states stressed the secular nature of their regimes, they did not proscribe or even discourage private belief in Islam – in contrast, for example, to the fate of Christianity in some communist countries. But imposing secular regimes on countries rooted in Islam was like trying to defy nature. It was ignoring the principle that Islam is inseparable from any aspect of life – even politics. The Western distinction between state and religion can not be made in the Islamic world. A desire to re-establish the natural order by bringing religion back into political life has found expression in the Islamic fundamentalist movement in the latter half of the century.

If ordinary Arabs feel that the manipulation of their lives will end only with a change in the current order, then what are the chances of this happening? In general, the answer must be: not very good. Arab regimes have responded to the challenge to secular ideologies and to their own status both by tightening their grip on power, and by isolating their ruling cliques still further from the mass of the population. Democracy stands little chance of meeting the aspirations of the people, if those aspirations do not serve the interests of the ruling cliques. Equally, the rulers are content that the legacy of tough and autocratic leadership in the Arab world should continue. Furthermore they now have the weaponry and other technology to help them in their task of suppressing internal protest – should they face any. 'We Arabs do not revolt any more,' an Arab academic told me.

We know what will happen. The regimes are prepared to kill thousands if necessary – it has happened in Syria, it has happened in Iraq. And anyway, Arab authorities are much more sophisticated than in the past. They all have several security and defence institutions, several radio and television stations, spread out all over their cities. Once, the radio station, the defence ministry and all the rest were on the one main street. But if you want to stage a coup now, how can you take over everything? It is hopeless.

The West is continuing to play a key part in keeping many of the autocratic Arab regimes in power. It does this by providing political support and by selling arms. Research by a Gulf academic shows that between 1970 and 1990 the Arabs spent US\$ 676 thousand million on arms and other military purchases. If secret and therefore unpublicized sales were taken into account, a rough and conservative estimate would put the figure at around US\$ 1,000 thousand million. This bill, the researcher continued, was the equivalent of half the purchases by NATO countries in the same period, three times the total imports into Israel, Iran, Turkey and Ethiopia, and about the same amount bought by the whole of Africa and South America together.[4]

The overwhelming majority of arms exports to the Arab world have come from the West. I asked a leading Arab economics expert for his views on the logic of large arms purchases. 'Simple,' he replied. 'The West is saying, we will defend you – and by the same token defend our interests – if you buy our arms. And despite what the West says about human rights and so on, it does not matter much what the regimes are like. Provided they play the game.'

As long as there is no incentive for the Arab regimes to change their attitudes it is difficult to see how the prospects for the Arab people feeling that they are masters of their own fate will improve. Initiatives for change have to come from the leaders of Arab society who need to display a level of maturity and courage which has been markedly lacking in most of them so far this century. Leaders have to turn their attention first to the education system within the Arab world, from the lowest level upwards. Young Arabs must to be encouraged to question and analyse the circumstances of their lives and of the world around them. There must be an incentive for becoming educated. Knowledge, rather than wealth or nepotism, needs to become the basis on which to build prestige. This will encourage the development of inquiring minds; in time young Arabs will start questioning the bases of their society – the foundations of the states which have emerged in the post colonial era. Only then will there be a chance that the Arabs as a whole might be able to shed the sense of subservience, both towards their own rulers and towards the more advanced and prosperous world beyond their borders. As long as Arab leaders, often encouraged if not openly supported by the West, are considered by the people to be ruthless, corrupt and self-centred, the continuation of the current popular mood of defeatism and despair seems inevitable.

In this despondent atmosphere Arabs yearn for a return of idealism, for a clear sense of purpose and direction of the kind which enabled their predecessors to conquer Spain and set up a formidable empire, and which kindled passions and galvanized motivation sufficiently to drive the Crusader armies out of the region. By whatever vehicle idealism might return, through the emergence of a charismatic regional leader, perhaps, or through the revival of pan-Arabism, it could not happen, I believe, in isolation from Islam. Despite all the measures taken by ruling elites to stifle dissent, a groundswell of popular feeling expressed in Islamic terms could, in the long term, provide a force for change which leaders could not ignore. Professor Aziz Shukri of Damascus University agrees, and takes the argument further. He is an example of a man in the later part of his life who, after having had a secular outlook for many years, has come to believe that Islam offers the only hope for the Arabs in trying to recover their self-esteem and in discovering a political programme for the future.

Professor Shukri, having spent several years living in the United States, has experience of both Arab and Western societies. For him, even though he is a Sunni Muslim, the Shiite revolution in Iran was a major source of inspiration. 'As a professor of international law – teaching the subject since 1964 – the events in Iran prompted me to find some Islamic roots in what I had been teaching as a Western subject. So thanks to Khomeini, whether I agree with him or not, I have been made to feel I have something that has been hidden.'

The closing years of the twentieth century see Arab regimes and the West facing a choice. They could establish a relationship based both on an understanding that the revival of Islam represents a popular response to popular grievances – a desire to recover self-esteem – and on the acceptance that there is a spiritual and ideological vacuum to be filled. On the other hand, they could face a future based on confrontation, with Arab regimes pitted against their own people and eventually – possibly joining forces with Muslims further afield – in conflict with the West. While Arab regimes are able for the moment, and perhaps for the immediate future, to keep their people in check through increasing use of instruments of repression, they cannot isolate their populations from the atmosphere of Islamic solidarity which binds Muslims in Arab countries with fellow-believers in Bosnia, Turkey, Iran, Afghanistan and elsewhere. Some Arab countries, like Jordan and Egypt, have made varying efforts to accommodate some of the demands of the Islamic movement, while cracking down hard on violent extremists. Others, like Algeria, Tunisia and Syria, have tried to suppress the fundamentalists ruthlessly. Either way, the reaction, uncertain and patchy as it may be, is a sign that the regimes recognize the challenge that faces them.

The experience of Arab–Western relations over the past eighty or ninety years does not leave me with much cause for optimism about the chances of friction between the two regions being eliminated. Just as the century began with Western powers seeking to impose a new order on the Middle East, so is it ending. On 26 June 1993 the United States unleashed a missile attack on Iraq's intelligence headquarters in Baghdad, alleging Iraqi involvement in an apparent attempt to assassinate former President Bush during a visit to Kuwait earlier in the year. The trial in Kuwait of those accused of being involved in the plot had just started when the raid on Baghdad was ordered. The Americans said, in language not unlike that of British and French colonialists in the early part of the century, that the purpose of the attack was to teach the Iraqis a lesson and 'to send a message to those who engage in state-sponsored terrorism'. Among ordinary Arabs outside the Gulf region there was, as there has so often been over the past century, outrage. 'This is Washington breaking even its own rules about courts of law – it did not even wait for the result of the Kuwaiti trial. The Americans, the West, think they can just walk over us.' That reaction from a Lebanese Muslim student reflected a common view among Arabs. The fact is that the United States and the West can walk over the Arab world because, like the French and the British at the beginning of the century, they are the superior military power and have political and economic interests in the region which they want to protect; and today they have the support (won or bought, according to your standpoint) of most of the key regimes in the area. But on this occasion in 1993, the regimes, even those closest to Washington, felt at best uneasy about what had happened. The American action clearly displayed Western double standards. Willingness to take firm action against Iraq for violations against Kuwait, while ignoring Israeli violations of the rights of the Palestinians, had already been noted several times by the Arabs.

There was a louder public outcry in the Arab world in the autumn of 1996 when the United States carried out further military attacks against targets in Iraq – this time to punish the Baghdad regime for venturing into the exclusion zone set up in northern Iraq by the West to protect the Iraqi Kurds after the 1991 Gulf war. President Saddam Hussein had sent his troops to help one Kurdish group, the Kurdish Democratic Party, in its continuing power struggle with the rival Patriotic Union of Kurdistan. The reaction of Arab regimes – with the exception of Kuwait which praised the military action ordered by Washington – was a mixture of concern and condemnation. Among the Arab people, the American strikes were perceived as further evidence of the West's arrogance – an arrogance which had manifested itself on so many occasions in so different ways throughout the century. The Egyptian commentator Nabil Omar, writing in *Al-Ahram*, the government daily in Cairo, summarized how the Arab people viewed the world's only superpower: 'Since it reached the apex of the pyramid in the new world order, the United States has adopted the behaviour of the cowboy and the quarrelsome bully in every international crisis that turns up, rather than the behaviour of a responsible superpower striving for justice and peace. Iraq has not broken any international law, it has not invaded any country, as it did with Kuwait. It was practising its legitimate sovereignty over its territory.'

The perceived injustice of the West's dealings with the Islamic world had been compounded by its unwillingness to take action to help the Muslims of Bosnia ('If what the Serbs are doing to the Bosnians is not state terrorism, I don't know what is,' a Palestinian businessman remarked to me in the mid-1990s). The common view in the Arab world was that the ritual humiliation of Iraq by the United States was a way of deflecting attention from Washington's unease at its failure to help the Bosnian Muslims. 'Put crudely,' one Western commentator in the Middle East wrote, '[President] Clinton needed to do something forceful to restore his foreign policy credentials; Islamic terrorism is a hot topic in the US at the moment; and Iraq is an unpopular and defenceless target. The fact that bombing Iraq to make up for Bosnia is about as logical as invading Grenada because of frustration with Cuba is neither here nor there.'[5]

The cautious response to the Baghdad raid of those Arab governments which did not condemn Washington stemmed from fear of the ultimate consequences of American military action. Arab regimes were uncomfortable at the way that popular reaction to the attack focused attention on the wider plight of Muslims – linking those in Bosnia with the

Palestinians and with other Arabs. The regimes also felt uncomfortable being linked (by association because of their friendship with the West) with such unpopular action. The reason for the discomfort, acknowledged throughout the region, is that the punitive action against Iraq inflamed still further Islamic fundamentalist and anti-Western sentiments in the region. And for the regimes that was ominous news.

It was with one eye on the growing popular support for Islamic fundamentalism that three Arab governments and the Palestinian leaders committed themselves to the peace process for the Middle East that began at the Madrid conference in 1991. The PLO, in particular, realized that if it could not win concessions from Israel to alleviate the suffering of the inhabitants of the occupied territories, and show that it could achieve progress towards the establishment of an independent state, then its influence would be eroded further by Hamas and other Islamic groups. The PLO also faced severe financial difficulties because the oil-producing Gulf states, angered by Yasser Arafat's support for President Saddam Hussein after the Iraqi invasion of Kuwait, had cut funds to the organization in 1990. Under these pressures, Yasser Arafat realized that he would have to reach an accommodation with Israel if he was to have any chance of remaining leader of the PLO and achieving his overriding ambition to be the first president of an independent Palestine. So he authorized his senior aides to begin secret contacts with Israel. These ended with the agreements of mutual recognition and limited autonomy in the occupied territories which were signed in Washington in September 1993. Egypt and the Gulf states were quick to applaud the development. Jordan was close behind, and a Jordanian–Israeli peace treaty was signed in October 1994.

In the West, the popular assumption was that comprehensive Middle East peace was a foregone conclusion and Western statesmen and the Western press turned their attention to other crises around the globe. The shock was all the greater, therefore, when a number of events shook the foundations on which the peace process was built and showed its structure to be considerably more fragile than had been assumed in the

West. The first blow came with a series of suicide bomb attacks
carried out by Hamas inside Israel which led to heavy loss of
life and injury among both civilians and military personnel.
Then came the assassination of Yitzhak Rabin by an Israeli
citizen in November 1995 followed by the election, in May
1996, of a right-wing Likud government in Israel led by
Benjamin Netanyahu, who made no secret of his dislike of
the peace process. But for all these blows to the peace
structure, the West was still shocked by the events during the
summer of 1996 when serious violence broke out across the
West Bank and Gaza Strip. With armed Palestinian police
exchanging fire with Israeli troops, the loss of life and injuries
on both sides were considerable. The spark for the violence
was the decision by the Israeli government to open up a tunnel
which passed under the Haram al-Sharif in East Jerusalem –
the 'Noble Sanctuary', on which sits the Dome of the Rock
and the Aqsa Mosque, sacred sites in Islam. The action was
interpreted by Arabs as a further move by Israel to tighten its
grip on East Jerusalem, the Arab part of the city captured in
1967. The Palestinians insist that East Jerusalem should be
the capital of a future state. The Israeli government, on the
other hand, insists that the city will never be divided again.
But if the tunnel controversy was a spark, the conflagration
that followed was a reflection of the depth of anger and
frustration felt among the Palestinian people at the failure of
the peace process to deliver the economic or political gains
they had expected.

The issue of Jerusalem is one of several that remained on
agenda to be tackled by Palestinian and Israeli negotiators at
the end of 1996. The prospects of it being resolved did not
look good. But just as worrying for Palestinians were the
shortcomings in many of the deals already signed with Israel
by their leaders. Among the Arab people – Palestinians and
others – the signing of peace deals with Israel had never been
a cause for celebration, even among those who supported the
policies of Yasser Arafat. As the details of the agreements
became known, the shortcomings of deals negotiated under
pressure by Palestinian leaders became obvious. For example,

while the West was expressing satisfaction that Israeli troops
were withdrawing from the Gaza Strip and from towns and
cities in the West Bank, the Palestinians living in these areas
knew that this was not the truth. Israeli troops had indeed
withdrawn from Gaza City, but they still controlled major
roads inside the Strip leading to Jewish settlements. Similar
settlements remained in the West Bank, and the Israeli army
still controlled the roads connecting one isolated Palestinian-
controlled town or city from another. The shortcomings of
this arrangement, from the Palestinians' point of view, became
clear when the whole population was effectively imprisoned
in these urban centres in the wake of the Hamas suicide
bombings.

Not for the first time this century, then, the Western
perception of what was happening in the Arab world was
flawed. For those who chose to look carefully, there were
plenty of ominous signs. Some Arabs tried to convey a message
to the West that cut across the perceived view there. A
handshake between Yasser Arafat and Yitzhak Rabin on the
lawn of the White House in September 1993, witnessed by
television viewers around the world, was not sufficient in itself
to transform decades of hatred and mistrust into lasting peace.
This was particularly the case, the argument went, because of
serious shortcomings in what Arab leaders had agreed upon.
In 1955 Edward Said wrote 'Peace and its Discontents' a
perceptive critique of the peace process. In his introduction to
he made a number of assessments of the search for a Middle
East settlements that bore little relation to the tone of most
other comments published in the English language at the time.
Edward Said argued that Western reporters were guilty of
concentrating on the positive trappings of the peace process
brokered by Washington and did not examine or publicize
the underlying worries expressed by the Arabs who were being
required to accept, without question, what had been negotiated on their behalf by the leadership of the PLO. The result
was that 'there has been a unanimity in public discourse in
the West that the peace process has been a good thing. When
reports appear of the torture and killings of Palestinians by

Israeli and Palestinian police they are neither connected with
the deeply flawed Oslo accords nor with an Israeli, and behind
it, an American policy which has maintained hundreds of
Israeli settlements on Palestinian lands, continues to deploy a
major army of occupation, intransigently confiscates and builds
on Arab land in East Jerusalem (as part of the city's forced
Judaization) and resolutely denies Palestinians true freedom
and national self-determination.'

Few Palestinians outside the immediate circles of Yasser
Arafat and few Arabs elsewhere would have taken exception
to Edward Said's assessment of the peace process. 'From the
secret negotiations in Oslo between the PLO and Israel to the
Israeli–Jordanian agreement proclaimed in Washington, and
after, there has run a clear and, to me, unnecessary line of
Arab capitulation by which Israel has achieved all of its tactical
and strategic objectives at the expense of nearly every
proclaimed principle of Arab and Palestinian nationalism and
struggle ... Always disunited and dithering, the Arabs have
simply lost the will to resist.'[67] This theme was echoed by the
Egyptian academic Galal Amin writing in *Al-Ahram* in 1996:
'No nation has been so utterly humiliated while showing so
little sign of resistance.' The Arabs, in short, were yet again
this century accepting much less than they wanted and much
less than they felt they deserved: Israel was not agreeing to
withdraw immediately and unconditionally from all occupied
Arab land, as it was required to do under the terms of UN
Security Council resolutions, and there were no guarantees
either about the establishment of a Palestinian state or the
future of Jerusalem. Also, the arrangements were sealed, like
so many other, under Western patronage. In September 1993,
as plans were being discussed to provide financial help for the
occupied territories, the American Secretary of State, Warren
Christopher, said, 'Just as the United States organized a
successful international coalition to wage war in the Gulf, we
now organize a successful coalition to breathe life into the
Israel–Palestinian declaration of principles.'

The challenge for Arab regimes will be to convince their
people that the era of formal peace with Israel will offer greater

opportunity than the preceding decades for regional coordination, the improvement of economic and social conditions, the acceptance of the principle of accountability by ruling elites and the elimination of corruption in high places. The overall mood of the Arab people in the new era of Middle East peace was captured in a commentary by the Cairo-based political scientist Jamil Matar. 'We got what we deserve,' he wrote. 'If what we got was little, that was because we deserve little. And if we deserve little, then there is no need to slap our faces, as some despairing people are doing. Nor is there reason to call people traitors, as some important people are doing. There's no cause either for celebrating, as some frivolous people are doing. What we got is the product of acts of Arab politics over the past half-century – a stubborn insistence on igniting and inflaming internal differences; a continuous disregard of the rights and wishes of the Arab people; the wasting of human resources; the absolute refusal to coordinate, consult and promote mutual trust; the mixing by leaders of personal moods with national policies, and the personal monopoly of leaders in decision-making or the failure to take decisions.'[8]

The expectation among Arabs that a Palestinian state would emerge eventually from the peace process raised hopes that the lessons of history might be applied as the new national institutions were established in Gaza and the West Bank. But to the grave disappointment of Arab people everywhere, the performance of Yasser Arafat and the Palestine National Authority turned out to be distressingly similar to that of other Arab regimes. The new Palestine was being built, like the states which emerged earlier in the century from European colonial rule, on nepotism, corruption and intimidation. The conclusion must be that these negative qualities have themselves become institutionalized. Rooting them out will require a fundamental change of attitude from the highest level of Arab society to the lowest. With every day that passes, the task gets harder. As Edward Said has written, 'Years of unsuccessful wars, empty bellicosity, unmobilized populations, and incompetence and corruption at every level bled the life out of our societies, already crippled by an almost total absence of participatory democracy and the hope that goes with it. We must take the blame for this colossal failure.'⁹

Western countries should be as aware as the regimes which they back in the Arab world of the resentment that simmers among ordinary people over the failure of successive genera-tions of Arab leaders to meet even the most basic of public expectations. Unless these grievances are addressed, support for Islamic fundamentalist groups is likely to continue – regardless of deals concluded by Arab governments with Israel or any other country. And the more flawed the deals are perceived to be by the Arab people, the more that fundament-alist groups will be able to rally support for their campaigns against the regimes and their Western patrons.

Looking to the future, conflict within the Arab world and between that region and the West can be avoided only if a rational view is taken of Islamic fundamentalism. For Arab leaders or Western statesmen to ignore or dismiss the roots of the movement on the basis of acts of terror perpetrated by small groups of extremists in Egypt or elsewhere would be as ill-judged as ignoring the claims of the Palestinians because of hijackings carried out by small groups in past years. Just as the Arabs must stop blaming the West for all the difficulties which beset them, so the West must learn to accept Islam as an integral part of life in the Arab world. Adhering to the fundamental tenets of the religion is a way of taking refuge from adversity and a means of protesting against leaders who have failed to provide clear political or moral vision.

The final word comes from an eminent university professor in Egypt, a country which is as much a platform for Western interests in the region at the end of the century as it was at the beginning. It is fitting too, in the climate of the contempor-ary Middle East, that the professor, who is closely connected with the ruling establishment, did not want his name men-tioned, for fear of losing his teaching job because of his recent identification with the Islamic movement. He warned that for the West to go on being antagonistic towards Islam 'would be the gravest mistake it could make. By doing this they would simply be driving more and more Muslims to go back and find out whether Islam can be an answer to their questions, particularly after the collapse of Marxism–Leninism. As an Arab, the so-called capitalist society ideology is giving me hell everywhere, draining my natural resources, backing Israel, and the like. So I am caught between accepting this ideology which is no good for me, or trying to find out if I have my own. And I do. It may not be complete; it may need updating. But it is definitely more likely to suit my life than any imported ideology. Islamic fundamentalism means exactly what it says: going back to the roots of Islam and finding out if it provides a foundation for an economic system based on social justice. Is Islam a good response to the increasing problems of life – economic, political, social, whatever? The West is trying to distort this by labelling a person like me a radical. Be that as it may. If I am a radical, they are making me more radical. All the time they are not gaining anything but my animosity.'

The response of both the West and Arab regimes to the challenges posed by Islam will determine the pace of change – if change there will be – in the region. The best guess at the moment is that change will be slow, given the West's dependence on Arab oil and its concurrent interest in maintaining good relations with a number of the key states in the Middle East. The Arab–Western relationship at one level is wedded by the mutual pursuit by leaders on both sides of short-term goals, and buttressed by millions of dollars-worth of sophisticated weaponry. The Arab people, despite the growth of the Islamic movement, look set to remain passive observers – in large part because the West and the Arab governments do not want a change in the status quo, no matter how far some of the governments fall short of the standards on human rights and other issues on which the industrialized powers purport to insist. A recent proof of this occurred when the suppression of democracy in Algeria once Islamic fundamentalists looked certain to win free elections caused not a stir in Europe and the United States. The Arab people, then, have no choice but to go on looking helplessly at the markers of history – Jebel Tariq and the Horns of Hittin – rocks which are symbols of past glories. For now, and for the foreseeable future, it will be their fate to remain caught between these rocks and the hard places of daily life – in the slums and shanty-towns of Tangiers, Algiers, Cairo, Gaza, Damascus and Baghdad – dreaming not of the future, but of the past.

Notes

INTRODUCTION

1 Nader Fergany. His views can be found at length in Chapter 5.
2 Fawzy Mansour, *The Arab World: Nation, State and Democracy* (Zed Books, London, 1992), p 33.
3 Interviewed by the author in Cairo, January 1992.
4 Majid Atiya in *Sourakia* (London), quoted by *Middle East International*, 23 November 1990.
5 Quoted in *Al-Ahram* (Cairo, 1 April 1992).
6 *Modern Poetry of the Arab World*, translated and edited by Abdullah al-Udhari (Penguin, London, 1986), p 35.

7 *Al Hayat* (London, 1 October 1991).
8 Interviewed in *Al Quds Al-Arabi* (London, 29 January 1992).
9 *Al Quds Al-Arabi* (28–29 March 1992).
10 Mahmoud el-Saadani in *Akbar el-Yom*, quoted in *Al-Ahram* (1 April 1992).
11 Tawfig Y. Hasou, *The Struggle for the Arab World* (KPI Ltd, London, 1985), p 35.
12 Hazem Zaki Nuseibeh, *The Ideals of Arab Nationalism* (Cornell University Press, Ithaca, 1956), p 56.

CHAPTER 1: SEEDS OF BETRAYAL

1 Elie Kedourie, *England and the Middle East: The Destruction of the Ottoman Empire 1914–1921* (Mansell Westview, Colorado, 1987), p 47.
2 L. Carl Brown, *International Politics and the Middle East: Old Rules, Dangerous Games* (I.B. Tauris & Co. Ltd, London, 1984), p 25.
3 ibid.
4 Peter Mansfield, *A History of the Middle East* (Viking, London, 1991), p 44.
5 Nuseibeh, p 35.

6 Mansfield, p 48.
7 Quoted by Mansfield, p 58.
8 Interviewed by the author in Amman, December 1991.
9 Albert Hourani, *Arabic Thought in the Liberal Age* (Oxford University Press, Oxford, 1962), p 67.
10 Mansfield, p 94.
11 ibid., p 95.
12 Hourani, p 110.
13 ibid., p 111.
14 ibid., p 157.
15 Nuseibeh, p 110.

16 ibid., p 121.
17 William L. Cleveland, *The Making of an Arab Nationalist: Ottomanism and Arabism in the Life and Thought of Sati' al-Husri* (Princeton University Press, Princeton, 1971), p 9.
18 ibid., p 27.
19 Quoted by Hourani, p 198.
20 Quoted by Nuseibeh, p 147.
21 Hourani, p 202.
22 Ronald Storrs, *Orientations* (Ivor Nicholson & Watson Ltd, London, 1939), p 78.
23 Public Records Office (P.R.O.), Kew, F.O. 371 42080.
24 Storrs, p 116.
25 ibid., p 122–3.
26 Mansfield, p 109.
27 P.R.O., F.O. 371 1640.
28 P.R.O., F.O. 371 2667.
29 P.R.O., F.O. 371 42080.
30 Hourani, p 287.
31 Storrs, p 129.
32 ibid., p 156.
33 ibid., p 159.
34 Brown, p 114.
35 David Fromkin, *A Peace to End All Peace: Creating the Modern Middle East 1914–1922* (Andre Deutsch, London, 1989), p 98.
36 ibid., p 96.
37 *The Israel–Arab Reader: A Documentary History of the Middle-East Conflict* (Penguin Books, London, 1969), p 16.
38 Storrs, p 205.
39 Quoted in Elie Kedourie, pp 68 and 69.
40 ibid., p 67.
41 Roger Adelson, *Mark Sykes: Portrait of an Amateur*, Jonathan Cape, London, 1975), pp 122 and 123.
42 Nabil al-Sharif, in *Al-Dustur*, quoted by *Middle East International* (London, 1 May 1992).
43 Interviewed by the author in Amman, December 1991.
44 Interviewed by the author in Nicosia, October 1992.
45 Interviewed by the author in Amman, December 1991.
46 Muhammad Abd el-Wahab Sayed-Ahmed, *Nasser and American Foreign Policy 1952–1956* (The American University in Cairo Press, Cairo, 1991), p 148.
47 ibid., p 149.
48 ibid., p123.
49 Interviewed by the author for 'File On Four', BBC Radio 4, 1991.
50 ibid.
51 Interviewed by the author in Cairo, January 1992.
52 Elizabeth Monroe, *Britain's Moment in the Middle East, 1914–56* (Chatto & Windus, London, 1963), p 31.
53 Fromkin, p 219.
54 Mansfield, p 158.

CHAPTER 2: A FESTERING GRIEVANCE

1 Interviewed by the author in Jordan, December 1991.
2 *The Arab Image in Western Mass Media* (Outline Books, New York, 1980), p 177.
3 Monroe, p 43.
4 *The Arab Image...*, p 227.
5 Monroe, p 43.
6 *The Israel–Arab Reader*, p 13.
7 Fromkin, p 196.
8 Mansfield, p 160.
9 ibid., p 161.
10 Kedourie, p 69.
11 Kedourie, p 85.
12 Fromkin, p 286.
13 Ritchie Ovendale, *The Origins of the Arab–Israeli Wars* (Longman Group, London, 1984), p 32.
14 Mansfield, p 162.
15 Quoted by Mansfield, p 162.
16 Ovendale, p 29.
17 ibid., p 30.
18 ibid., p 32.
19 ibid., p 33.

20 ibid.
21 Storrs, p 373.
22 Hourani, p 302.
23 A.W. Kayyali, *Palestine: A Modern History* (Third World Centre for Research and Publishing, London, 1981), p 37.
24 Mansfield, p 163.
25 P.R.O., F.O. 395 (13 December 1917).
26 Kayyali, p 64.
27 Storrs, p 366.
28 P.R.O., C.A.B. 23 (24 January 1918).
29 P.R.O., F.O. 371 3412.
30 Mansour, p 35.
31 P.R.O., F.O. 371 4153.
32 Paul C. Helmreich, *From Paris to Sèvres: The Partition of the Ottoman Empire at the Peace Conference of 1919–1920* (Ohio State University Press, Columbus, 1974), pp 8 and 9.
33 *The Israel–Arab Reader*, pp 28 and 29.
34 Storrs, p 352.
35 ibid., p 378.
36 Peter Mansfield, *The Arabs*,

(Penguin, London, 1980), p 222.
37 Documents on British Foreign Policy, Series I, Vol IV, 1952, p 345.
38 Ovendale, p 63.
39 ibid., pp 64 and 65.
40 *The Israel–Arab Reader*, p 57.
41 ibid., p 61.
42 Mansour, p 25.
43 *Israel–Arab Reader*, p 73.
44 ibid., p 77.
45 Derek Hopwood, *Tales of Empire: The British in the Middle East, 1880–1952* (I.B. Tauris & Co. Ltd, London, 1989), pp 156 and 158.
46 ibid., pp 167–168.
47 Interviewed by the author in Amman, December 1991.
48 Mohamed Heikal, *Illusions of Triumph: An Arab View of the Gulf War* (HarperCollins, London, 1992), p 29.
49 *The Arab Image . . .*, p 177.
50 Interviewed by the author for 'File on Four', BBC Radio 4, June 1991.
51 Abdel-Wahad Bourdechan in *Al-Hayat* (27 October 1991).

CHAPTER 3: DISINTEGRATION AND DIVISION

1 Quoted by Hourani, p 313.
2 Interviewed by the author in Cairo, January 1992.
3 Quoted in Cleveland, p 57.
4 Fromkin, p 400.
5 Quoted by Helmreich, p 52.
6 Hourani, p 291.
7 Fromkin, p 409.
8 Cleveland, p 55.
9 Brown, p 119.
10 Quoted by Brown, p 121.
11 Quoted by Mansfield, *History of the Middle East*, p 182.
12 P.R.O. C.A.B. 23, War Cabinet (12 March 1917).
13 Fromkin, p 503.
14 Storrs, p 449.
15 Malcolm Brown (ed.), *The Letters of T.E. Lawrence* (J.M. Dent & Sons Ltd, London, 1988), p 189.

16 Mansfield, *History of the Middle East*, p 184.
17 Fromkin, p 562.
18 Mansfield, *History of the Middle East*, p 96.
19 Quoted by Mansfield, ibid., p 176.
20 Muhammed Hussein Heikal, *Mudhakkirat fii 'l-siyasa 'l-masriya* (Recollections of Egyptian Politics), Part 1 (Cairo, 1951), p 89.
21 Hopwood, pp 106 and 107.
22 Mansfield, *History of the Middle East*, p 179.
23 Cleveland, pp 58 and 59.
24 Quoted by Hasou, p 2.
25 Interview with the author in Cairo, January 1992.
26 Hourani, p 294.

27 Interviewed by the author in Cairo, January 1992.
28 Hourani, pp 294 and 295.
29 ibid.
30 Quoted by Cleveland, p 130.
31 *Al-Zamaan al-Baghdadiya* (Baghdad, April 1950).
32 Sati' al-Husri, *Difa'a 'an il-uruba* (Defence of Arabism), (Dar al-Ilm, Beirut, 1956), p 17.
33 Quoted by Hasou, p 3.
34 Interviewed by the author in Amman, December 1991.
35 Hasou, p 5.
36 Quoted by Hasou, p 5.
37 Interviewed by the author in Amman, December 1991.
38 Quoted by Hasou, p 12.
39 Mansfield, *History of the Middle East,* p 231.
40 Hasou, p 5.
41 Hourani, p 345.
42 Interviewed by the author in Cairo, January 1992.
43 ibid., pp 85 and 86.
44 Hourani, p 362.
45 ibid., p 370.
46 Helmreich, pp 48 and 49.
47 Mansfield, *History of the Middle East,* p 171.

CHAPTER 4: DEFEAT AND DESPAIR

1 Abd al-Wahhab Badrakhan in *Al-Hayat* (27 October 1991).
2 *Sunday Times* (7 June 1992).
3 Mansour, p 38.
4 Interviewed by the author in Amman, December 1991.
5 Mansfield, p 235.
6 Ovendale, p 112.
7 Ovendale, p 121.
8 ibid., p 120.
9 ibid., p 112.
10 ibid., p 106.
11 Mansfield, *History of the Middle East,* p 236.
12 Ovendale, p 122.
13 Quoted by Ovendale, p 124.
14 Mansfield, *History of the Middle East,* p 239.
15 See Chapter 3, page 105.
16 Mansfield, *History of the Middle East,* p 236.
17 Ovendale, p 122.
18 Mansfield, *History of the Middle East,* p 239.
19 ibid., p 240.
20 Hourani, p 354.
21 Qustantin Zurayq *Ma'ana al-Nakba* (Beirut, 1948), p 41.
22 Mansour, p 37.
23 *Al-Hayat,* quoted by *Financial Times* (7 June 1992).
24 Fouad Ajami, *The Arab Predicament:* *Arab Political Thought and Practice since 1967* (Cambridge University Press, Cambridge, 1981), p 4.
25 Abdullah al-Udhari, p 23.
26 From 'Footnotes to the Book of the Setback', a twenty-verse poem, in Abdullah al-Udhari, p 96.
27 ibid., p 97.
28 Anwar el-Sadat, *Those I Have Known* (Jonathan Cape, London, 1985), pp 134, 135, 137 and 138.
29 *Sunday Times* (7 June 1992).
30 Mansfield, *History of the Middle East,* p 274.
31 ibid., p 273.
32 Abdullah al-Udhari, p 98.
33 Robert Stephens, *Nasser: A Political Biography* (Simon & Schuster, New York, 1971), p 506.
34 *The Israel–Arab Reader,* pp 190 and 192.
35 ibid., pp 203 and 204.
36 Ajami, pp 31 and 32.
37 General Saad al-Shazly, *The Crossing of Suez: The October War (1973)* (Third World Centre for Research and Publishing, London, 1980), p 67.
38 Stephens, p 514.
39 Abdullah al-Udhari, p 101.
40 Interviewed by the author in Cairo, January 1992.

41 Mansfield, *History of the Middle East*, p 294.
42 ibid., pp 295 and 296.
43 *The Israel–Arab Reader*, p 464.
44 Interviewed by the author in Amman, December 1991.
45 Quoted by Ajami, p 36.
46 Dr Al-Mahdi Al-Manjara, *Al-Quds Al-Arabi* (30 January 1992).
47 Interviewed by the author in Amman, December 1991.
48 Salama Ahmed Salama, *Al-Ahram*, quoted by *Middle East Mirror* (London, 11 February 1992).
49 Quoted by Sayed-Ahmed, p 111.
50 *Guardian* (26 February 1991).
51 *Al-Quds al-Arabi*, quoted by *Middle East Mirror* (20 January 1992).
52 Heikal, p 333.
53 Interviewed by the author in Amman, December 1991.
54 Heikal, pp 333 and 334.
55 Interviewed by the author in Nicosia, October 1992.
56 Interviewed on Jordan Radio, 6 December 1991.
57 Amin Maalouf, *The Crusades Through Arab Eyes* (Al Saqi Books, London, 1984), p 265.
58 ibid., p 39.
59 Beiram el-Tounsi, extract from *The Egyptian Worker*, published in *Al-Ahram* (9 January 1992).
60 Naguib Mahfouz, *Autumn Quail* (The American University in Cairo Press, Cairo, 1985), p 33.
61 Quoted by Ajami, p 24.

CHAPTER 5: ABSOLUTE POWER

1 Stephens, p 557.
2 Interviewed by the author in Cairo, 1986.
3 Heikal, p 75.
4 Interviewed by the author in Beirut, November 1992.
5 Albert Hourani, *A History of the Arab Peoples* (Faber & Faber, London, 1991) pp 26 and 31.
6 Mansour, pp 55 and 56.
7 Hourani, *Arabic Thought in the Liberal Age*, pp 73, 76 and 117.
8 Paraphrased and quoted by Hourani, *Arabic Thought in the Liberal Age*, p 175.
9 Anis Mansour, *Abdel Nasser*, (Al-Maktab al-Masri al-Hadith, Cairo, 1988), p 6.
10 Majid Khadduri, *Arab Personalities in Politics* (The Washington Middle East Institute, Washington DC, 1981), pp 2 and 3.
11 ibid., p 5.
12 Abdallah Laroui, *The Crisis of the Arab Intellectual: Traditionalism or Historicism* (University of California Press, Berkeley, 1976) p 171.
13 Interviewed by the author in Cairo, January 1992.
14 Khadduri, p 6.
15 ibid., p ix.
16 *Middle East International* (28 June 1991).
17 Khadduri, pp 309 and 310.
18 David Holden and Richard Johns, *The House of Saud* (Pan Books, London, 1982), p 199.
19 Khadduri, p 38.
20 Holden and Johns, p 240.
21 Francis Ghiles, *Financial Times* (13 January 1992).
22 *Al-Ahram* (5 March 1992)
23 Interviewed by the author in Cairo, January 1992.
24 *Financial Times* (10 June 1992).
25 Mansour, p 102.
26 General Saad al-Shazly, pp 81 and 83.
27 Mansfield, *History of the Middle East*, p 288.
28 *Guardian* (2 May 1992).
29 *Washington Post* (8 June 1992).
30 *Guardian* (8 June 1992).
31 Interviewed by the author in Damascus, December 1991.

32 Hussein Ahmed Amin, *Al-Ahram* (25 March 1992).

33 *Empty Reforms: Saudi Arabia's New Basic Laws* (Middle East Watch, New York, 17 May 1992).

34 Arab Organization for Human Rights, Reports for 1990 and 1991 (Cairo).

35 Laroui, p 176.

36 Mansour, p 46.

37 Interviewed by the author in Cairo, November 1992.

38 Ajami, p 33.

39 *New York Times* (18 December 1991).

40 Interviewed by the author in Cairo, October 1992.

41 Interviewed by the author in Cairo, January 1992.

42 Interviewed by the author in Cairo, January 1992.

CHAPTER 6: OIL WEALTH AND POVERTY

1 Interviewed by the author in Cairo, January 1992.

2 Mansour, p 86.

3 Hourani, *History of the Arab Peoples*, p 322.

4 Yusif A. Sayigh, *Arab Oil Policies in the 1970s* (Croom Helm, London, 1983), pp 34–35.

5 ibid., p 21.

6 ibid., pp 41–44.

7 ibid., p 1.

8 ibid., p ix.

9 Hossein Askari, 'Saudi Arabia's Oil Policy', from *After the Oil Price Collapse: OPEC, the United States, and the World Oil Market*, edited by Wilfrid L. Kohl (The John Hopkins University Press, Baltimore, 1991). pp 31–32.

10 Anwar el-Sadat, *Those I Have Known* (Jonathan Cape, London, 1985). pp 70–71.

11 Holden and Johns, p 334.

12 Ajami, p 10.

13 Sayigh, p 240.

14 Hourani, *History of the Arab Peoples*, p 427.

15 Saad Eddin Ibrahim, *The New Arab Social Order: A Study of the Social Impact of Oil Wealth* (Westview/ Croom Helm, Colorado, 1982). p 168.

16 Interviewed by the author in Cairo, January 1992.

17 Mansour, p 103.

18 Interviewed by the author in Cairo, January 1992.

19 Interviewed by the author in Cairo, January 1992.

20 Mansour, p 4.

21 Interviewed by the author in Cairo, January 1992.

22 Mohamed Heikal, p 40.

23 Saad Eddin Ibrahim, p 30.

24 Mansour, pp 84 and 85.

25 Heikal, p 22.

26 *Wall Street Journal* (29 May 1992).

27 Interviewed by the author in Cairo, April 1992.

28 Saad Eddin Ibrahim, p 29.

29 ibid., pp 32–33.

30 Interviewed by the author in Cairo, June 1987.

31 Interviewed by the author in Cairo, January 1992.

32 Mansour, pp 117–18.

33 Fadhil J. Al-Chalabi, 'The World Oil Price Collapse of 1986: Causes and Implications for the Future of OPEC', from *After the Oil Price Collapse*, p 1.

34 Mansour, p 88.

35 *Wall Street Journal* (9 June 1992).

36 *Jordan Times* (8 December 1992).

37 *Huqquq al-Insan fii-lwatan il-Arabi* (Human Rights in the Arab World), *Report of the Arab Organization for Human Rights*, Cairo, 1992, p 66.

38 Abdullah Al-Udhari, p 98.

39 Hussein Ahmed Hussein, *Al-Ahram* (25 March 1992).

40 Interviewed by the author in Damascus, December 1991.

41 Quoted by William and Fidelity Lancaster, *Middle East International* (12 October 1990).

42 *Middle East International* (7 December 1990).

43 *Middle East International* (11 January 1991).

44 Quoted by the *Guardian* (10 December 1991).

45 Interviewed by the author in Amman, December 1991.

46 Interviewed by the author in Cairo, January 1992.

47 *Washington Post* (1 June 1992).

48 Interviewed by the author in Cairo, January 1992.

49 *Middle East International* (28 June 1991).

50 *New York Times* (2 March 1991).

CHAPTER 7: FAMILIES AT WAR

1 Interviewed by the author in Beirut, November 1992.

2 Kamal Salibi, *A House of Many Mansions: The History of Lebanon Reconsidered* (University of California Press, Berkeley, 1988). pp 55–6.

3 Ajami, p 44.

4 Halim Barakat, *Women and the Family in the Middle East: New Voice of Change* (University of Texas Press, Austin, 1985). pp 27–46. Summarised by *Al-Raida*, magazine of the Institute for Women's Studies in the Arab World (1 February 1987), pp 6–7.

5 Interviewed by the author in Cairo, October 1992.

6 Interviewed by the author in Amman, December 1991.

7 Interviewed by the author in Damascus, December 1991.

8 Lois Beck and Nikki Keddie (ed.) *Women in the Muslim World* (Harvard University Press, Cambridge MA, 1978), p 25.

9 ibid. Noel Coulson and Doreen Hinchcliffe, 'Women and Law Reform', pp 37–8.

10 Evelyne Accad, *Al-Raida* (1 August 1985), p 2.

11 Sukaina Bu'Aoui, *Al-Raida* (Spring 1992), p 16.

12 Homa Hoodfar, *Al-Raida* (Spring 1992), p 11.

13 Rena Mus'aad, *Perspectives: Magazine of the Middle East Council of Churches*, Issue 9–10 (1991), p 43.

14 From *The Hills of Sidon: Journal of an American Doctor in Lebanon* (Adama Books, New York, 1988). Quoted by *Perspectives*, ibid., p 38.

15 ibid., p 39.

16 Nizar Qabbani, *Al-Mara' fii Mashra'a fii Hayati* (Manshurat Nizar Qabbani, Beirut, 1982), p 24.

17 *Al-Raida* (Summer 1992), p15.

18 Nuha Samara, *Perspectives*, Issue 9–10 (1991), pp 49–55.

19 Soha Abdel Kader, *The Image of Women in Drama and Women's Programmes* (The Population Council, Cairo. 1985). Quoted by *Al-Raida* (Summer 1992), p 17.

20 Nadia H. Youssef, 'The Status and Fertility Patterns of Muslim Women' from *Women in the Muslim World*, pp 78–9.

21 Interviewed by the author in Beirut, November 1992.

22 Naguib Mahfouz, *The Beginning and the End*, translated by Ramses Awad (Doubleday, New York, 1989), pp 72–3.

23 Nawal el-Sadawi, *My Travels Round*

320 THE ARABS

the World (Minerva, London, 1991), p 21.

24 Mahfouz, p 79.

25 Nawal el-Sadawi, *Searching* (Zed Books, London, 1991), p 7.

26 Abd al-Salam al-Ujayli, *Al-Khail wa 'l-Nisaa'* (Dar al-Sharq, Beirut, 1989), p 124.

27 Juliette Minces, 'Women in Algeria' in *Women in the Muslim World*, p 168.

28 ibid., p 16.

29 *Al-Raida* (Spring 1992), p 25.

30 Interviewed by the author in London, November 1992.

31 Kamal Boullata, (ed.) *Women of the Fertile Crescent: Modern Poetry by Arab Women* (Three Continents Press, Washington, 1978). p 15.

CHAPTER 8: TO WAR WITH WORDS

1 Michel al-Hayek, quoted in Ajami, p 26.

2 Sylvia G. Haim, *Arab Nationalism: An Anthology* (University of California Press, Berkeley, 1964), p 83.

3 BBC Summary of World Broadcasts, ME/1214 A/15 (28 October 1991).

4 *Al-Ahram* (10 November 1991).

5 BBC Summary of World Broadcasts, ME/1216 A/11 (30 October 1991).

6 Zaki Neguib Mahmoud, quoted by Ajami, p 28.

7 Interviewed by the author in Cairo, January 1992.

8 Jihad al-Khazin, quoted by Ajami, p 3.

9 *Index on Censorship*, Vol. 21, No. 2 (February 1992), p 21.

10 Majid Atiya in *Sourakia*, quoted by *Middle East International* (23 November 1990).

11 Abdullah al-Udhari, p 102.

12 Heikal, pp 156–7.

13 Interviewed by the author in Cairo, January 1992.

14 Paraphrased by Cleveland, p 152.

15 *Perspectives*, Issue 9–10, p 34.

16 Interviewed by the author in Cairo, January 1992.

17 Reported by Associated Press, Cairo (19 January 1992).

18 *Index on Censorship*, Volume 21, No. 2 (February 1992), p 21.

19 *Al-Ahram* (23 January 1992).

20 *The Arab Image in Western Mass Media*, p 75.

21 ibid., p 76.

22 Cleveland, p 143.

23 Edward W. Said, *Orientalism* (Routledge & Kegan Paul, London, 1978) p 204.

24 Interviewed by the author in Amman, December 1991.

25 *The Arab Image in Western Mass Media*, p 22.

26 Pat Booth, *Miami* (Arrow Books, London, 1993), pp 204 and 206.

27 Mansour, p viii.

28 Interviewed by the author in Cairo, January 1992.

29 Said, p 204.

30 Interviewed by the author in London, November 1992.

31 Interviewed by the author in Cairo, October 1992.

CHAPTER 9: REVOLUTION AND REFUGE

1 Interviewed by the author in Cairo, November 1992.

2 Mansfield, *History of the Middle East*, p 134.

3 Hourani, *Arabic Thought in the Liberal Age*, p 228.

4 ibid., p 360.

5 Interviewed by the author in Cairo, November 1992.

6 Interviewed by the author in Amman, December 1991.

7 Interviewed by the author in Nicosia, October 1992.
8 Interviewed by the author in Cairo, November 1992.
9 ibid.
10 Interviewed by the author in Cairo, November 1992.
11 Dr Isa Darwish, *Al-Ahram* (10 November 1991).
12 Interviewed by the author in Cairo, January 1992.
13 Interviewed by the author in Cairo, October 1992.
14 Interviewed by the author in Amman, December 1991.
15 Dilip Hiro, *Islamic Fundamentalism* (Paladin, London, 1988). p 66.
16 Interviewed by the author in Cairo, November 1992.
17 Hourani, *History of the Arab Peoples*, p 452.
18 Interviewed by the author in Cairo, November 1992.
19 Interviewed by the author in Cairo, January 1992.
20 Interviewed by the author in Cairo, November 1992.

21 Interviewed by the author in Cairo, November 1992.
22 Interviewed by the author in Cairo, January 1992.
23 *Al-Ahram* (9 January 1992).
24 Interviewed by the author in Amman, December 1991.
25 Hourani, p 360.
26 Interviewed by the author in Cairo, November 1992.
27 George Melloan, *Wall Street Journal* (7 January 1992).
28 William S. Lind, *Foreign Policy*, No. 84 (Fall 1991), p 45.
29 Interviewed by the author in Byblos, November 1992.
30 Interviewed by the author in Limassol, November 1992.
31 Interviewed by the author in Nicosia, October 1992.
32 Interviewed by the author in Cairo, October 1992.
33 Interviewed by the author in Jerusalem, October 1992.

CHAPTER 10: PERCEPTIONS OF PEACE

1 Hugh Seymour Davis, *Philips Travel Guides: Andalusia*, (George Philip, London 1990), p 11.
2 'Al-Andalus', *The Art of Islamic Spain*, (The Metropolitan Museum of Art, New York, 1992), p 4.
3 Edward W. Said, *Peace and its Discontents – Gaza-Jericho 1993–1995* (Vintage, London, 1995), p xxvii.
4 Abdel-Razzaq Faris al-Faris. *Al-Mustaqbal Al-Arabi*, (May 1993).
5 Charles Snow, *Middle East Economic Survey* (Nicosia, 5 July 1993).
6 Said, p xxi.
7 Jamil Matar, *Al-Hayat* (10 September 1993)
8 Said, p xxii.

Index

Uqair 98
'Ujayli, Abd es-Salem al- 236

Valentino, Rudolph 262
veiling 225, 237–8
Voice of America 168, 251
Voice of the Arabs radio 109

Wafd party, Egypt 100, 102
Wahhabi sect 97–8, 211, 286
Wall Street Journal 286
Weizmann, Dr Chaim 59–60, 67, 74
West Bank 61, 76, 81, 119–21, 132, 143, 194
Wilson, Pres. Woodrow 69–71, 90, 100
Wingate, Sir Reginald 67, 100–1
women 221–41, 255, 287
   Western 235–7
words *see* rhetoric
World War I 38–9, 54, 56, 60, 90, 97
   peace conference 70, 89, 100, 103, 113–14

World War II 107, 122
writers 240–1, 253–7
   see also books, journalism

Yacoub, Dr Megdi 5
Yamani, Sheikh Ahmed Zaki 162
Yared, Prof. Nazak 213–14
Yemen 33, 109, 135, 171, 183, 206, 209
   border disputes 98
   terrorism 78
Yom Kippur War 136–7, 185, 188–91
Young Turks 33
Yugoslavia 15

Zaghloul, Sa'ad 35, 100–2, 103
Zayid, Sheikh 163
Zionism 55–60, 62–71, 73–4, 76–7, 90, 123–4, 128, 146
Zionist Congress 75
Zubi, Mahmoud al- 161
Zurayq, Qustantin 128